ANTHONY COGAN, 1826–1872

Monument to Anthony Cogan in Slane Catholic Church. It was commissioned from public subscriptions raised in Navan by the Dean Cogan Memorial Society in the weeks following his death and erected a year later. The work was carried out by Neill and Pearse of Brunswick St, Dublin. The Pearse of that partnership was the father of Patrick H. Pearse, the executed leader of the Easter Rising in Dublin in 1916.

Faith, Famine and Fatherland in the Irish Midlands

PERCEPTIONS OF A PRIEST AND HISTORIAN
ANTHONY COGAN
1826–1872

Alfred P. Smyth

FOUR COURTS PRESS

This book was typeset
in 11 on 13 Ehrhardt by
Koinonia Ltd, Manchester for
FOUR COURTS PRESS,
Kill Lane, Blackrock, Co. Dublin, Ireland.

A catalogue record for this title
is available from the British Library.

ISBN 1-85182-109-0

Printed in Ireland by
Colour Books Ltd, Dublin

ACKNOWLEDGEMENT

The publication of this book
and of the re-issue of *The Diocese of Meath*
have been made possible by generous grants in
aid from Mr Séan Galvin and Maynooth College.

IN MEMORY OF MY FATHER

There are few instances even in Catholic Ireland, in which the 'Soggath Aroon' acquired a stronger hold on the affections of the people among whom he laboured.

Freeman's Journal on the death of Anthony Cogan

CONTENTS

ACKNOWLEDGEMENT   5
LIST OF ILLUSTRATIONS   10
PREFACE   13
ABBREVIATIONS   15
INTRODUCTION   17

I   A BIRTHPLACE RICH IN HISTORY   31
II   THE HIDDEN IRELAND OF THE BOYNE VALLEY   40
III   THE AGONY OF POST-FAMINE POLITICS   52
IV   LEGACY OF RELIGIOUS STRIFE   85
V   THE MAKING OF A LOCAL HISTORIAN   100
VI   OUTSPOKEN CRITIC AND CONSCIENCE OF A DIOCESE   117
VII   FRIENDS AND ENEMIES   126
VIII   AN ARCHIVE RESCUED AND DESTROYED   133
IX   HARVESTING THE COLLECTIVE MEMORY OF HIS PEOPLE   140

APPENDICES

1   TESTIMONIAL PRESENTED TO ANTHONY COGAN (1861)   161
2   LETTER FROM ARCHBISHOP JOHN MACHALE (1863)   161
3   YOUNG MEN'S EXCURSION TO LAYTOWN (1863)   163
4   ANTHONY COGAN IN LIVERPOOL (1863)   163
5   PROTEST AGAINST NAVAN EVICTIONS (1864)   167
6   LETTERS FROM VARIOUS BISHOPS (1867)   170
7   PROTEST AGAINST THREATENED EVICTIONS AT MULLAGH (1871)   172
8   THE FAMILY OF ANTHONY COGAN   175
9   ANTHONY COGAN'S LAST ILLNESS AND DEATH   177
10   THE DEAN COGAN MEMORIAL   178
11   EXTRACT FROM HALLS' IRELAND   180
12   THE CONYNGHAMS OF SLANE   183
SELECT BIBLIOGRAPHY   199

INDEX   211

LIST OF ILLUSTRATIONS

MONUMENT TO ANTHONY COGAN IN SLANE CATHOLIC CHURCH, CO. MEATH *frontispiece*

		page
1	PORTRAIT OF ANTHONY COGAN IN CATHOLIC YOUNG MEN'S HALL IN NAVAN	16
2	SECTION OF MEDIEVAL FONT, KILCARNE, CO. MEATH	17
3	ST MARY'S ABBEY, DROGHEDA, CO. LOUTH	18
4	MAGDALEN STEEPLE, DROGHEDA, CO. LOUTH	18
5	ST LAURENCE'S GATE (INTERIOR), DROGHEDA, CO. LOUTH	18
6	ST LAURENCE'S GATE (EXTERIOR), DROGHEDA, CO. LOUTH	18
7	HIGH CROSS AT MONASTERBOICE, CO. LOUTH	20
8	ROUND TOWER AND GRAVEYARD AT DONAGHMORE, CO. MEATH	22
9	RUINS IN DULANE GRAVEYARD, CO. MEATH	23
10	BECTIVE ABBEY, CO. MEATH	25
11	ATHLUMNEY CASTLE, NEAR NAVAN, CO. MEATH	26
12–13	RUINS OF FRANCISCAN FRIARY, HILL OF SLANE	29
14	ST ERC'S HERMITAGE, SLANE, CO. MEATH	31
15	ENTRANCE TO NEWGRANGE, CO. MEATH	32
16	THOMAS FLEMING, ARCHBISHOP OF DUBLIN (1623-51)	34
17	SLANE CASTLE, CO. MEATH	37
18	WILLIAM BURTON CONYNGHAM (1733-96)	38
19	NEOLITHIC TUMULUS AT DOWTH, CO. MEATH	40
20	ROMANESQUE ARCHWAY, CANNISTOWN, CO. MEATH	43
21	MEDIEVAL FONT FROM KILCARNE, CO. MEATH	45
22	RUINS OF AUGUSTINIAN FRIARY ON HILL OF SKRYNE, CO. MEATH	47
23	ST KIERAN'S WELL, NEAR KELLS, CO. MEATH	49
24	VIEW OF NINETEENTH-CENTURY DROGHEDA	50

25 JOHN BOYLE O'REILLY (1844-1890)   53

26 CHURCH OF IRELAND, HILL OF TARA, CO. MEATH   56

27 THE CROPPIES' GRAVE, HILL OF TARA, CO. MEATH   56

28 DANIEL O'CONNELL ADDRESSING MONSTER MEETING ON TARA, 1843   58

29 JOHN CANTWELL, BISHOP OF MEATH (1830-66)   61

30 FORGING PIKES IN IRELAND, 1848   66

31 EVICTION IN IRELAND, 1848   67

32 MARKET CROSS, KELLS, CO. MEATH   70

33 OLD GATEWAY AT FORE, CO. WESTMEATH   72

34 STARVING MOTHER AND CHILDREN, GREAT FAMINE 1849   76

35 DESERTED VILLAGE AT MOVEEN, 1849   77

36 PORTLOMAN CHURCH AND GRAVEYARD, CO. WESTMEATH   79

37 KILCOLMAN, CO. OFFALY   83

38 KING JOHN'S CASTLE, TRIM, CO. MEATH   86

39 YELLOW STEEPLE, TRIM, CO. MEATH   87

40 BRIDGE AT NEWTOWN, TRIM, CO. MEATH   87

41 MONUMENT AT OLDBRIDGE, CO. MEATH   91

42 DANGAN CASTLE, NEAR SUMMERHILL, CO. MEATH   93

43 LYNALLY CHURCH, CO. OFFALY   95

44 COLLÈGE DES LOMBARDS, PARIS   97

45 HIGH CROSS AT DURROW, CO. OFFALY   99

46 MASTERS AT ST FINIAN'S COLLEGE, NAVAN, c. 1867   101

47 ANTHONY COGAN c. 1867   102

48 ROMANESQUE WINDOW, RAHAN, CO. OFFALY   105

49 CLONMACNOISE, CO. OFFALY   107

50 INCHCLERAUN, LOUGH REE, CO. LONGFORD   108

51 INIS AINGIN (HARE ISLAND), LOUGH REE, CO. WESTMEATH   110

52 FENNOR, NEAR SLANE, CO. MEATH   113

53 ST COLUMKILLE'S HOUSE, KELLS, CO. MEATH   115

54 ARDBRACCAN, CO. MEATH   122

55 MEDIEVAL FONT FROM CLONARD, CO. MEATH   123

56 MULTYFARNHAM ABBEY, CO. WESTMEATH   143

57 DONORE CASTLE, CO. MEATH   146

58 MEDIEVAL DOORWAY AT ARDMULCHAN, CO. MEATH   147

59 THE SORBONNE, PARIS, c. 1650   151

60 ENGRAVING ON WALKING-STICK PRESENTED TO ANTHONY COGAN, 1862   159

61 AUTOGRAPH OF ANTHONY COGAN PRESENTED TO HIS MOTHER, 1867   159

62 SECTION OF MEDIEVAL FONT FROM KILCARNE, CO. MEATH   160

63 CHARLES COGAN OF SHALVANSTOWN, SLANE (1830–1907)   176
64 HOVEL ERECTED BY DISPOSSESSED FAMILY AFTER EVICTION,
        1848   181

MAPS
  1 THE DIOCESE OF MEATH   185
  2 THE PARISHES OF THE DIOCESE OF MEATH   186
  3 DETAIL OF SLANE AREA FROM BEAUFORT (1816)   187
  4 BEAUFORT'S MAP OF THE DIOCESE OF MEATH, 1816
        NORTH–WEST SECTION   188–9
        SOUTH–WEST SECTION   190–1
        NORTH–EAST SECTION   192–3
        SOUTH–EAST SECTION   194–5
  5 TAYLOR AND SKINNER'S MAP OF ROADS IN SLANE AREA, 1777   196
  6 THE TOWN OF NAVAN, c.1840   197

PREFACE

The decision to re-issue Anthony Cogan's *Diocese of Meath: Ancient and Modern* was in part inspired by Cogan's own wish that the story of his diocese should not be forgotten and that the contribution of the men and women at the centre of that story should be properly acknowledged. The decision to write a book on the subject of Cogan himself was prompted in turn by the desire to rescue the memory of a local historian from oblivion, and to examine the man's own perceptions on the history of his native diocese and on his country. This project would never have been carried through to completion without the crucial financial support of three people, of whose vision and idealism, Anthony Cogan would have been proud. Monsignor Michael Ledwith, President, St Patrick's College, Maynooth, willingly and generously first offered to subsidise this work. He thus initiated a project that not only honours the memory of a Maynooth student of the nineteenth-century, but one which also strives to underline the importance of studies devoted to Irish regional history and to the people who gave their lives in the service of their own regions. Mr Séan Galvin's generous sponsorship honours the Irish county of his adoption, and when others were indifferent, he has been prepared to offer crucial support for a work devoted to the study of those people and places which Cogan held so dear. Mr Michael Adams of Four Courts Press belongs to a vanishing species of publisher who support projects for their intrinsic value and whose services to historical, cultural and religious studies in Ireland are more in keeping with the dedicated and philanthropic tradition appropriate to Cogan's century, rather than to this cash-driven age. As readers, we too easily ignore the fact that without the vision and generosity which inspires financial sponsorship in the first instance, books of a specialised interest and appeal would never come into being.

A small number of friends and scholars have shown extraordinary patience in dealing with an endless series of queries and requests, whose prompt attention was essential for the completion of this book. Mrs M. T. O'Connell has helped as my research assistant in the National Library of Ireland, diligently tracking down newspaper articles on Dean Cogan. Fr Conor McGreevy has been especially helpful in matters relating to the history St Finian's and of Navan. Fr Michael Sheerin's work on St Finian's has also been a valuable aid. Fr Gerard Rice generously placed his encyclopaedic knowledge of matters relating to newspaper archives and to the Meath diocese generally, at my disposal. I am grateful to Fr Rice for his help with locating the reporting on Navan evictions of 1864, and for providing the photograph of Dean Cogan (ill. 47). Fr Rice also placed at my disposal an interleaved copy of Cogan's *Diocese of Meath* with the annotations of Fr John Brady, the Meath diocesan historian (c.1937). I have not made use of that material because of its unedited nature. Some of Fr Brady's notes were later published by him elsewhere. Others need a considerable amount of effort spent in checking and editing, and other parts still—especially those relating to the Middle Ages—have been overtaken by more recent scholarship. Professor Pádraig Ó Fiannachta, provided information on Maynooth staff in the time of Anthony Cogan, and—with characteristic warmth and generosity—supplied me with the works of Séamus Dall Mac Cuarta. Monsignor Patrick Corish provided invaluable information from Maynooth student archives on the details of Cogan's matriculation and progress as a student. Dr Michael Smith, the bishop of Meath, generously and frankly provided information on his nineteenth-century predecessors. Dr James Maguire gave up his time in a busy university term to read the typescript and, by bringing his wide knowledge of Irish history to bear on this work, has saved me from numerous errors. He may well dissent from many views expressed in this book, and its remaining errors are my own.

I wish to record my gratitude to Mr Ray Cogan and his family of Shalvanstown House, Slane, who supplied me with an extraordinary amount of family history and anecdote relating to their collateral ancestor, and who made me feel part of the family of Dean Cogan. Their help and hospitality extended to a conducted tour of the Hill of Slane as well as the supplying of several photographs and memorabilia. My wife, Margaret, has as ever, brought her invaluable skills as a librarian to helping with bibliography and proofreading. I am grateful to the librarians on the staff of the Inter-Library Loans Department at the University of Kent; of the British Newspaper Library at Colindale; and of the National Library of Ireland. Fr Fergal Grannell OFM, Librarian of the Franciscan Library at Dún Mhuire, Killiney, Co. Dublin, was especially kind and helpful in assisting with my enquiries regarding Franciscan convents and friars within the diocese of Meath. Mr Cecil Humphery-Smith, Principal, Institute of Heraldic and Genealogical Studies, Canterbury, generously supplied me with most helpful information on the pedigree of the Conynghams of Slane. Mr Martin Healy has kindly helped with an index to *The Diocese of Meath* left unfinished by an ailing Anthony Cogan in 1870.

My greatest debt is to Anthony Cogan who first introduced me as a schoolboy to the study of the past, and who, because of his own great love of Meath, brought the local past to life in an enduring way. My father first began reading extracts to me from Cogan's *Diocese of Meath* on summer nights at Tara in July 1956. This book is dedicated to the memory of that kindest of readers.

A.P.S.

Canterbury,
St Patrick's Day, 1992

ABBREVIATIONS

References in brackets refer to the volume and page number of Anthony Cogan's *The Diocese of Meath: Ancient and Modern.* Thus (ii, 597) refers to page 597 of volume ii of Cogan's work, and (iii, ix) refers to page ix (of the Preface) in Volume III.

RnM = *Ríocht na Midhe: Records of Meath Archaeological and Historical Society* (1955–). See *Bibliography.*

For the expansion of bibliographical references for illustrations, consult Select Bibliography at the end of this volume.

1 Detail of a portrait of Anthony Cogan as a young priest. The picture shows him holding a book, perhaps the first volume of his *Diocese of Meath* which appeared in 1862. In that same year Cogan supervised the building of the Catholic Young Men's Hall in Navan, which still houses this portrait.

2 (*Opposite page*) Section of the late fifteenth-century font from Kilcarne, Co. Meath. The panels show the Coronation of the Blessed Virgin by Christ (left), St Paul with sword (second left), St James of Compostela with pilgrim's satchel (third from right), St John (second from right) and St Peter with keys (right). Anthony Cogan, when he was a young curate in Johnstown organised the dispatch of this font to the Dublin Exhibition in 1853.

INTRODUCTION

Anthony Cogan was an Irish country priest who rarely strayed beyond his own county of Meath during his short life. Apart from his time as a student in Maynooth; a brief summer in which he visited Westmeath and Offaly; and annual preaching forays to Irish congregations in Liverpool, he was a man who spent all his life ministering in country parishes in and around Navan, as well as teaching boys in a school in that town. He himself admired priests who rarely left their parishes apart from attending obligatory diocesan retreats, and although he was born and lived within thirty miles of Dublin, few references to the capital, intrude in his extensive writings on Meath. Cogan began his scholarly life writing articles for the *Tablet* in 1856, and he went on to write the first complete post-Reformation history of an Irish Catholic diocese in three great volumes between 1862 and 1870. He also gave himself tirelessly in the service of the youth of Navan, and in his later years he threw his energies into defending the rights of slum-dwellers in that town. He addressed rallies in defence of the rights of tenant farmers threatened with eviction by grazier landlords who, in his own words, strove to turn Meath into a grass-walk for cattle at the expense of people whose ancestors had lived on the soil for centuries. Cogan was not a great historian. He was largely self-taught, and although extraordinarily well read, he was too deeply and emotionally involved in the trials of eighteenth-century Ireland to achieve an objective analysis. He was at his best as an abstracter and a recorder of information, both medieval and modern, and he accomplished valuable if somewhat patchy work as an antiquary. The fact that he published the greater part of an archive which was

3–6 Medieval ruins surviving in nineteenth-century Drogheda included St Mary's Abbey (3) and the Magdalen Steeple, belonging to the Dominican friary (4). The interior (5) and exterior (6) of St Laurence's Gate show views of this well-preserved late fourteenth-century gate of the fortified town which fell before Cromwell's brutal assault in 1649.

subsequently destroyed, has lent the posthumous quality of a primary source to much of his *Diocese of Meath*. Anthony Cogan was not an important political figure—indeed he was not a political figure in the accepted sense. He was a priest of the people who, from an abiding love of Ireland and especially of his native place, attended and addressed local meetings which he felt would further the cause of those whom he considered to be down-trodden and disadvantaged in every respect. Although considered by his contemporaries to be a patriotic Irish nationalist, he was happy to leave the political limelight to others, and being a born respecter of authority, he admired the political leadership offered by his bishop, John Cantwell, and by Frederick Lucas, his Member of Parliament for Meath.

Cogan was a small player on a provincial stage who has left us an extraordinary body of written records detailing not only his views on Ireland's past, but also on major contemporary events of Irish history as he observed them happen. His primary interest for the historian must be that he was an observer of Irish political life at the grass-roots, among the people to whom he ministered and who regarded him as an archetypical *sagart aroon*. Cogan was not interested in analyzing economic theories which might explain British government attitudes and reactions to the Irish Famine. Nor did he confuse statistics with real people, or adopt a so-called objectivity in his assessment of conditions among the starving poor which obscured the reality of their suffering through a clinical detachment. If Cogan was a biased witness in defence of the 'down-trodden serfs of Ireland' that was because of the human misery resulting from malnutrition, over-crowding, and homelessness which he encountered in his lifelong ministry in rural Meath. Cogan observed the evils of the Navan workhouse, the poverty of its slums and the seething resentment of the rural peasant population of Offaly, Westmeath and Meath as he encountered his people from his pulpit and in his confessional, and as he observed their daily struggles to survive. His observations are important, not necessarily because they are any more objective than those of other witnesses to the events of his time, but because they represent a point of view which today's generation of historians has too frequently ignored.

Cogan's writings demonstrate the survival of what were essentially medieval mental attitudes into modern Irish life. These writings remind us that he came from a cultural background which had remained virtually untouched by Renaissance, Reformation,

7 High cross at Monasterboice. This and the adjacent Cross of Muiredach, together with the round tower, all date from the tenth century and were regarded by Cogan as symbols of Ireland's early Christian past. Monasterboice, although in Co. Louth and in the diocese of Armagh, lay but a few miles from Cogan's home.

Enlightenment and Industrial Revolution. Many historians might rush to contradict such a sweeping statement and protest that Ireland was deeply affected by all of those great events. Others might protest that rural Ireland was no different from other peasant societies in southern Europe which were also largely by-passed by the great intellectual movements of the developing urban civilisations round about them. But Ireland's unique position rests on the fact that her medieval Celtic past on the Atlantic fringes of Europe was different from that of her European neighbours, and that very powerful and conservative pre-Christian elements in that past proved impervious to forces of change coming from outside. Furthermore, all those major movements which formed modern European civilization were operative in Ireland—even in Dublin—only in a peripheral sense. And because of the two-nation syndrome whereby the Anglo-Irish élite was separated from the native Irish by deeply-rooted cultural divisions, the Reformation and Enlightenment were prevented from filtering down and across into other social enclaves of indigenous Irish life. The Catholicism to which the native Irish adhered, acted as a shield against the great cultural and intellectual novelties from without. Ireland at large, in so far as it was affected by major ideological developments on the Continent, was influenced by the conservative forces of the Counter Reformation. So, when we read Anthony Cogan's discussions on the seventeenth and eighteenth centuries, we find ourselves in a world of medieval hagiography, and a world where the ancient Irish ability to combine folklore with historical narrative is still alive and well. We find a priest narrating stories—replete with circumstantial details—of how villainous priest-hunters of the early seventeenth century were struck dead for daring to plot against their priestly victims. And we find that Cogan the conscientious priest, supported the notion of local pilgrimage to holy wells in spite of official opposition to such ancient piety on the part of his own hierarchy. Gatherings at wells and other ancient cult centres combined genuine primitive Christian penitential spirituality with equally strong elements of pre-Christian carnival and licence. In matters of historical investigation, we find in Cogan's accounts of the Great Rebellion of 1798, for instance, little mention of the intellectual driving forces behind that movement from Republican France. When external influences on the Rebellion are obliquely hinted at, Cogan cites from the contemporary diaries of Bishop Plunket who knew the French scene well, but who saw the Irish unrest as an essentially local phenomenon. Cogan viewed the '98 Rebellion in Ireland as a heroic stand made by Meathmen and Wexfordmen against hated local masters. Ideologies of the United Irishmen, Wolfe Tone and other leaders, are never discussed. '98 was rather, in Cogan's mind, a heroic struggle involving a patriotic peasantry which had been goaded into taking up arms against a local yeomanry. In this respect, Cogan, in spite of his learning, acts as a mirror allowing us to see how such events were perceived by the ordinary people of Meath in his own time. Although he might have been reluctant to admit as much, he recorded tales of the Rebellion of '98 very much in the light of struggles going on in his own day in Meath and Westmeath between Ribbonmen and those landlords who were perceived as tyrants by the evicted tenantry.

A close study of Anthony Cogan's attitudes raises the question of Irish identity in the nineteenth century. Much has been made in recent times of the notion of the rediscovery of Ireland's past in the late eighteenth and throughout the nineteenth century. The notion of a discovery or rediscovery of Ireland's Celtic identity was indeed real in antiquarian and intellectual circles, especially among the Anglo-Irish of Dublin. Antiquarian studies into the art, archaeology, architecture, music and folklore of ancient Ireland had unleashed a

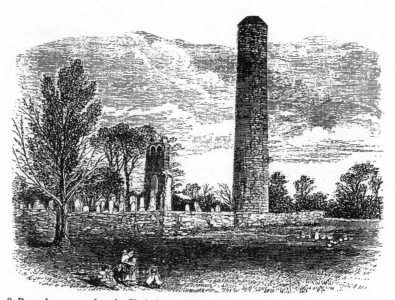

8 Round tower and early Christian ruins at Donaghmore on the road from Slane to Navan. This ancient Patrician site, along with nearby Ardmulchan (ill. 58) provided one of the cemeteries for the people of nineteenth-century Navan. The place is almost unchanged since Cogan's time, when he trekked past here regularly as a boy on his way to school in Navan.

huge interest in things Celtic, and which had found their counter-part in related antiquarian pursuits in mainland Britain. Cogan, was not of course unaffected by Celtic antiquarianism which had already evolved for over a century by the time he had begun to write. His good schooling in Navan, his Maynooth training, and his personal reading of the works of William Wilde and translations from early Irish by John O'Donovan and Eugene O'Curry, meant he was a man profoundly influenced by book learning. Cogan was no north Meath *seanchaidhe*, untouched by nineteenth-century intellectual thought. He did, however, grow up among such people—Gaelic speakers immersed in the folk tradition of the Boyne valley, and surrounded by monuments such those at Newgrange and on Tara from the cradle land of ancient Irish civilization. So, Cogan's starting point was altogether different from that of Dublin intellectuals who were driven to recreate a Celtic fantasy world with which they could identify. Men such as William Wilde, and later John Millington Synge and Patrick Pearse, would for their different reasons travel west of the Shannon in search of the 'real' Ireland. Some were driven by antiquarian curiosity, others by a desire to portray the thought-world of the Celtic mind in Anglo-Irish poetry and drama, while others still, were driven in search of an elusive Celtic political order from an epic past, calculated to restore Ireland's national self-respect. Cogan had no need to tramp the roads of the West in order to expose himself to genuine Irish life. The son of the Slane baker and a Protestant farmer's daughter had sufficient confidence in his Meath background not to feel the need to search for any other.

It might be argued that his own mixed religious background combined with the traumatic demographic and cultural changes in Meath—induced by famine, land clearance and the decline of the Irish language—all combined to challenge established social and cultural attitudes in Cogan's environment. But in rural Ireland, the conversion of Anne Sillary to Catholicism, on her marriage to Thomas Cogan, meant that she had left her father's kindred and joined that of her husband's in true medieval fashion. Anthony Cogan's decision to become a priest served to reinforce him in the faith of his father, although he remained generous in his praise of those Protestants who stood out against bigotry and persecution:

> For the honour of human nature be it recorded, that there were found men of high and lofty principles, who soared above the low prejudices of the hour, and neutralized by their philanthropy the intolerant spirit of the times (i, 268).

As for the decline of the Irish language, although Cogan lamented that phenomenon, it was clearly not a major issue in his mind. Irish had not yet quite declined to a vanishing state in Meath of Cogan's

9 Ruins in Dulane graveyard, Co. Meath.

day, and besides, the people of Meath had a greater cultural resilience in regard to language, than others in remoter parts of Ireland, in that rural Meath and Westmeath must have had a large bilingual population from the seventeenth century onwards if not before. The demographic crisis, on the other hand, was indeed catastrophic, with large-scale population movements occurring throughout the central and eastern midlands, and with the total population falling after the famine on a scale consonant with that of reduced population levels in post plague-ridden Europe of the late fourteenth century. This was indeed a crisis which struck at the heart of Cogan's love for his own region and its people. But Cogan belonged to a family with substantial means, by the standards of that time, which was capable of weathering the economic storms which brought ruin to thousands of less fortunate souls. And Cogan, at a personal level, had enough resilience to fight back in the way he knew best—by immersing himself in the study of Meath's troubled past.

Anthony Cogan came from an aspiring lower middle class background of nineteenth-century rural Ireland which was quintessentially Irish. Men like Cogan entertained few complexes about their cultural or national identity. Individually they may not have been of great political or economic account, but they were central to Irish life in every respect and formed the backbone of nationalist sentiment in every county. Cogan exhibited what was virtually a tribal sense of pride and loyalty in his county and in his native place. He was obsessed above all, with the concept of association with place— a concept not resurrected from antiquarian book learning, but one deeply ingrained in the Irish rural psyche, and one which survives in Ireland to this day. This in turn meant that for Cogan - like so many other Irishmen of his time—the political struggle hinged not on the urgency of setting up a national parliament, or wider issues associated with national emancipation from Britain, but with more immediate matters relating to the land. That is not to say that men like Cogan were not interested in achieving national goals. But the potency of the struggle for the land, and for the rights of tenant farmers, was that this struggle was both national and local—and being local, it exercised a peculiar power on Irish minds.

Cogan was a devout priest, and although outspokenly critical of his clerical colleagues, he had a conservative's respect for ecclesiastical authority and a love for his diocese which equalled that for his native place. He saw bishops, priests and people of his diocese of

10 Bective Abbey on the Boyne between Navan and Trim. The well-preserved Cistercian abbey here became a private mansion after the dissolution of the monasteries within the Pale in 1539 when a sixteenth-century tower house (left) was built on part of the site.

Meath as part of an eternal family moving forward relentlessly to join those who had gone before them in faith. For Cogan, the dead of the local community were ever present to the living. The dead were those from whom the living had received their faith and culture, and with whom the living would be reunited for all eternity. Keeping faith, therefore with the dead, was an essential feature in Cogan's spiritual outlook. And keeping faith meant much more than adhering to a set of spiritual or doctrinal beliefs. It did of course primarily mean that, but it also included a whole set of political and social values as well. For just as Orthodox clergy forged powerful links with their enslaved Christian peoples under Ottoman domination, so too, persecution and discrimination against Catholics in eighteenth-century Ireland brought the priesthood into a special place of prominence in Irish life. And just as the priesthood under the patriarchate of Constantinople appropriated to itself the role of political leadership in the absence of a Greek aristocracy, so too, Irish Catholic clergy filled the vacuum left by the exiled and dispossessed Gaelic and Old English lords of the seventeenth century. Comparisons with other societies are only helpful up to a point. It could be argued that Orthodoxy under the millet system as administered by the Turks, enjoyed a greater degree of toleration than Catholicism under Protestant rule in eighteenth-century Ire-

11 Athlumney
Castle near Navan
in 1849.

land. But the irony remains, that discrimination and draconian legislation against Catholics served to elevate the priesthood into a position of overall leadership among their people. We find in Meath that to a significant extent the old ruling families of the sixteenth-century Pale survived, albeit in very modest form, as clerical dynasties of Cusacks, Chevers, and Plunkets who provided the diocese with its bishops and leading priests, and who alone stood between their people and a legal system calculated to maintain them in a state little better than slavery. While the Irish clergy may not have exercised their political power until the nineteenth century in Ireland, there is no doubt that the circumstances which made that power possible were created in the century of persecution before. And for those historians who would claim that penal legislation against Catholics was not enforced for long or with universal rigour, Cogan would reply with some justification that the popery code of Queen Anne's reign had placed a legal instrument in the hands of a conquering élite capable of maintaining the great mass of the population in servitude, and capable of being upheld before the courts wherever and whenever a need presented itself.

It is no coincidence that in spite of his extensive medieval researches, Cogan's attention, throughout his three-volume history centred largely on the eighteenth century. As we read this priest's account of his own diocese, and as we share his involvement with every parish and half-forgotten graveyard, we realise we are close to the very heart of the Irish nation as it grew to confidence and emerged into the modern world of the nineteenth century. For Irish nationalism, like that of Greece, in spite of whatever foreign ideologies it might press into the service of its cause, had an undeniably powerful religious basis. That religious basis was in turn organised within diocesan boundaries which coincided with ancient tribal and territorial loyalties which were already old even before Strongbow had set foot on Irish soil. The people of the diocese of Meath, for instance, were not just a collection of souls who inhabited a random number of midland counties. Their lives had been linked together within Hugo de Lacy's Lordship of Meath from the late twelfth century. But that medieval English lordship - from the Shannon to the Irish Sea—had been based in turn on the old Irish kingdom of the Southern Uí Néill, with its two internal divisions of Mide and Brega which formed the counties of Westmeath and Meath respectively. These internal divisions—going back into prehistory—were sustained culturally and politically into the seventeenth century. For Meath, lying largely within the Pale, represented the tamed and Anglicised part of the old lordship, while Westmeath remained Gaelicised and more defiant in the face of English rule. The nature of the landscape also played a major rôle in defining the personality of the region. Co. Meath, with its richer farmland lying closer to the centre of English power in Dublin Castle, was inevitably brought under tighter control, while Westmeath being further away from the centre of power and containing less profitable and more inaccessible terrain, remained less anglicised. Such considerations help to interpret the distribution of centres of agrarian violence in Meath in the early nineteenth century. The parishes of Meath most effected by violence were those of the north and north-west—Drumconrath, Nobber, Kilmainhamwood, Moynalty, Kilskyre, Sydden, Kilbeg, and Loughan (Mooney, *RnM*, VIII, i (1987), 51)—or those remote areas bordering on the poorer lands of Cavan and Westmeath. Among the mass of farm labourers and small tenant farmers in the nineteenth century, Westmeath seems to have provided a focal point for agrarian unrest which had reached crisis proportions by 1870 and which overflowed into north-west Meath. In Celtic times, the kingdom of Meath had traditionally looked north for its political and cultural alliances. Hence the Meath diocese in modern times, owed nothing to its close and powerful neighbour in Dublin, and looked instead to Armagh as the head of its province. A powerful ingredient in Irish nationalism, therefore, had strong tribal roots which owed little to contemporary nationalist movements in nineteenth-century Europe, and almost everything to time-honoured regional loyalties within Ireland, which were preserved and fostered by diocesan territorial organisation.

A noticeable feature of Cogan's writings on the eighteenth century was his interest in the graves of the Meath clergy. Cogan's obsession with discovering and honouring the resting places of Penal Day and later eighteenth-century priests, and especially bishops, was partly motivated by his vivid grasp of the concept of the Communion of Saints. Great spiritual leaders from Penal times ought never to be forgotten because the living Christian community who had benefited from their spiritual heroism was still united with them in Christ. Cogan's interest in the graves of such men was partly inspired, too, by the medieval cult of relics and the sense that a trace of the spiritual power of saintly individuals somehow resided in their earthly remains. The interest of the Irish Church in the graves of saints owed something too, to the Celtic past. Cogan was far more concerned, for instance, with the location of priests' graves than he was in identifying houses which they had lived in, or the mud-walled chapels in which they had celebrated Mass. Witness his joy at visiting the tomb of Michael Plunket (died 1727), one-time vicar-general of the diocese of Meath, a cousin of, and secretary to, the saintly Oliver, archbishop of Armagh. Cogan found Michael Plunket's grave in the east end of the ruined church of Killegland near Ashbourne 'sheltered by the arms of a large palm tree':

> One hundred and thirty five-years have rolled over his grave since the great priest went to rest after his labours, and his memory is as fresh to-day amongst the parishioners as if they—not their forefathers—had left him in his tomb. Verily, 'the memory of the just man shall live forever'. (i, 270)

This spiritual potency of the grave of a priest who had given his life in the service of his people was extended in Cogan's mind to the graves of patriot laymen who had served Ireland well or who had given their lives for their country. The bodies of the fallen Croppies on Tara and of Daniel O'Connell from his tomb in Glasnevin were all capable of inspiring the Irish people in maintaining their struggle for liberty. It is easy to see from Anthony Cogan's writings how such an unlikely development as the cult of Wolfe Tone was to emerge by the end of the century. Republican gatherings at Wolfe Tone's grave at Bodenstown owe much to the tradition of pilgrimage to the tomb of a medieval saint.

Anthony Cogan was writing in the middle of the nineteenth century, at a time when Irish nationalism was inching its way

HANLON.

12 Ruins of the Franciscan friary on the Hill of Slane in Wilde's *Boyne and Blackwater* (1849). Anthony Cogan's parents and three of his brothers are buried within the friary church (right). The Franciscan College lies to the left of the church tower. The surviving ruins, erected by Christopher Fleming, date from the early sixteenth century. An early Christian monastery once stood here, whose buildings included a tenth-century round tower.

13 Ruins of the Franciscan friary on the Hill of Slane in O'Hanlon's *Lives* (c.1870). O'Hanlon had been a friend of Anthony Cogan and was a leading subscriber to the Cogan Memorial Society in 1873.

forward after the death of O'Connell and the collapse of the Repeal movement. The Repealers had endeavoured to reverse the Act of Union whereby the government of Ireland had been subsumed into the Westminster parliament in 1801. Cogan in his short life reflected through his great outpourings on local history, the sense of political uncertainty regarding the future of Irish nationalism. His attitudes changed over his relatively short life from that of a man content to follow a constitutional path blocked out by O'Connell and supported by his bishop in the 1840s and '50s, to one of impatience and despair over what he saw as British intransigence in the early 1870s. In the year before Cogan died, he was pessimistic for the future, and he laid the blame squarely on British government policy which he perceived in an entirely negative light. He claimed that Britain had only two real policies towards Ireland. One was to play the loyalist establishment and the nationalist majority off against each other, and the other was to resort to coercion when unacceptable compromise had failed. Cogan was convinced, above all, that Westminster had little knowledge of, or interest in, the social and economic problems facing the poorer elements in Irish life, and that it showed even less capability of solving them. The future, in Cogan's view, promised little alternative to revolution and the forcible ending of the Union with Great Britain. Yet he was too conservative a man to succumb to extremism, and his deeply held faith tempered all his political ideas and acted as a brake on his emotional view of the recent past. As for the extremists, he included among them the landlords and their agents who pursued a policy of coercion with wilful disregard for the social and political consequences. Cogan as a devout priest found it easy to take a longer view. And in that longer view, he saw, beyond the sufferings of his people, a happier vision. Reading all the historical outpourings of this Meath historian leaves one keenly aware that he somehow transcended the catalogue of wrongs and miseries that one day—*i ndeireadh na dála*—Ireland and its people would be free to manage their own affairs.

I

A BIRTHPLACE RICH IN HISTORY

The village of Slane in Co. Meath, where Anthony Cogan was born in 1826 or '27, is remarkable in many respects. It lies on the side of a steep hill in the heart of the Boyne Valley with ancient monastic ruins on the hilltop above, and the waters of the Boyne in the valley below. Beside this village, and almost a part of it, are the fields and woods of Slane Castle, whose grounds have been part of a lordly demesne since at least as early as the twelfth century. The natural beauty of Slane is enhanced by the extraordinary historical associations with the countryside round about. On the crown of the hill, hagiographical tradition from the seventh century proclaimed it was there that Patrick first lit his paschal fire in his campaign to evangelize the pagan Irish. That was a fire which had attracted the attention of the high king, Lóegaire, as he scanned the night sky of Meath with his druids from the heights of Tara, some twelve miles

14 St Erc's Hermitage; situated in the grounds of Slane Castle. The Hermitage ruins date to *c*.1500 and have associations with the later medieval Franciscan community in Slane. But the church site forms part of an earlier Christian complex which includes Lady Well (*Tobar Muire*), the centre of an annual pilgrimage on 15 August (Feast of the Assumption) since the Middle Ages. Cogan would have most certainly attended that pilgrimage throughout his childhood and indeed during the rest of his life.

15 Entrance to the neolithic Passage Grave at Newgrange as it appeared in 1849. It was possible to gain access to the great central chamber under the tumulus in Cogan's time, and view the wealth of prehistoric art on the megaliths by candle-light. Cogan tells us in his *Diocese of Meath* of the profound impact this monument from Ireland's pagan past exerted on his historical imagination.

to the south. Patrick's first convert from the high king's court was Erc, who became the first bishop of Slane. Erc's Hermitage in the grounds of Slane Castle survived to be the focus of one of the few places of continuous pilgrimage in Ireland from Early Christian times to the present day. Lady Well (the traditional name of this pattern) in Slane is an annual pilgrimage on the Feast of the Assumption (15 August) and, whatever its precise association with Erc, it has unquestionable later medieval credentials. Slane's assoc-iation with the origins of early Irish Christianity is matched by its equally powerful associations in the *Dind Shenchas* or ancient topographical lore, with the monuments and traditions of Ireland's pagan past. The village is within three miles of Brugh na Bóinne, the megalithic cemetery of Newgrange, Knowth and Dowth, whose giant tumuli exercised such a fascination on the pagan Celtic mind. Celtic traditions centring on the mystical nature of the river Boyne provided a synthesis of mythological lore which incorporated neolithic tumuli at Newgrange and nearby Rosnaree into tales of the pagan kings of Tara. Best known among those shadowy kings was Cormac mac Airt, the exemplary lawgiver who was supposedly slain by his druids for having embraced Christianity, at the palace of Cleitech, or Cletty, near the bridge of either Slane or Stackallen on the Boyne. And so it happened, that neolithic passage-graves which had been built to house the long-forgotten dead of the third and fourth millenium B.C. were remembered by the early Irish as the burial places of the pagan kings of Tara in the Celtic Iron Age. The waters of the Boyne flowing below Slane provided a sinewy thread of continuity between the ruined hill-forts on Tara and the passage graves at Brugh na Bóinne and other places of ancient association in the landscape of Meath. None of this was lost on Cogan who viewed these monuments as enduring symbols of nationhood:

> The meanderings of the historic Boyne, the great pagan cemetery of Brugh-na-Boinne, the round tower and crosses of Monasterboice, the once great Cistercian abbey of Mellifont, the old bell-tower of Skryne beautifying and hallowing the distance; the memorable Hill of Tara, once the seat of royalty and of national aspirations; the ivy-clad ruins of Slane—all shall impress the beholder with solemnity, and shall teach him that we have a history. (ii, 306–7)

That history was all changed irrevocably with the invasion of Strongbow at the end of the twelfth century, when eastern Ireland was overrun by Anglo-Norman Lords and their camp followers, and the old Celtic kingdom of Brega was shired off into the County of Meath. Hugo de Lacy had charge of the greater lordship of Meath which included not only the present county but also Westmeath and parts of Offaly, and formed the territory which was later to define the extent of Anthony Cogan's diocese. From the thirteenth century onwards, there were to be two nations in Ireland—the native Irish kingdoms ruled by their own Gaelic aristocracies, and the English, or subsequently Old English, who ruled the conquered territories. There was forever the suspicion on the part of the Gaelic lords that the invader was bent on their ultimate extermination. This notion was well understood as late as the second half of the sixteenth century by a prominent Meathman, Sir Thomas Cusack (1490–1571), one time Lord Chancellor of Ireland and one of the Lord Justices. Cusack, who lived at Lismullen near Tara, travelled

16 Thomas Fleming archbishop of Dublin (1623–51) and former professor of theology at Louvain. He was the son of the sixteenth baron of Slane. He and his kinsman, Patrick Fleming (1599-1631) were both Franciscans and prominent in the Counter-Reformation on the Continent and in Ireland. From a wall-painting by Fra Emanule da Como (died 1701) in the Aula of St Isidore's College, Rome.

tirelessly in the service of the English administration in an effort to reconcile the most far-flung Gaelic lords to English rule. Even when old antagonisms had been overtaken by the religious wars of the seventeenth century, past differences could not be put aside. So, in spite of the fact that many of the Old English—such as the Cusacks and Plunkets—held on to the Catholic faith, and although they had most to lose in the face of Puritan and Williamite opposition, it proved impossible to forge an effective and lasting political alliance between old enemies—native Irish and Old English—hardened by centuries of tribal conflict.

With the coming of the Anglo-Norman invaders, Slane was chosen as the head or *caput* of a barony extending from the Boyne along Meath's north-eastern border with Louth. Slane's Anglo-Norman roots went deep, and its barons, the Flemings, made a lasting contribution to Ireland's political and religious life into the seventeenth century. As powerful lords of the Pale, the Flemings helped to consolidate the English administration in eastern Ireland, but the onset of religious wars found them on the losing Catholic side. This family, which for centuries had ruled unchallenged on its great estates in north-east Meath, produced its most noble sons in its hour of crisis and defeat. Patrick Fleming (1599–1631), a close relative of the Nugents and Cusacks, was educated at Douai and at St Anthony's, Louvain, where in 1617 he became a Franciscan friar. Fleming was an enthusiastic member of that team of scholars who set out to rescue the scattered records of Ireland's early ecclesiastical history, and to publish those records on the Continent. The fruits of Patrick Fleming's labours included not only the eventual publication of the *Life* of St Columbanus of Bobbio but of countless other manuscripts later published under the corporate efforts of John Colgan and others. This son of Meath and Louth eventually ended his days as superior and professor of divinity in the College of the Immaculate Conception in Prague, and he was martyred in Bohemia by sectarian fanatics in 1631. Later in the seventeenth century, yet another of the Flemings—Thomas, son of the sixteenth Baron of Slane, also a Franciscan friar and professor of theology at Louvain, became Catholic archbishop of Dublin. He returned to Ireland to lead his church through the days of the Confederation of Kilkenny. Archbishop Fleming ruled his diocese from 1623 to 1651. But the Flemings, along with the Plunkets and other magnates of the Pale had found themselves in uneasy alliance with their old Gaelic enemies in Westmeath and elsewhere and, in spite of their shared loyalty to a common Catholic cause, it was too late to patch up old tribal differences between the two nations which were now about to be destroyed by the wars of Protestantism. Cromwell landed in Ireland on 14 August 1649. In the following December, Catholic bishops met in synod at Clonmacnoise—an Early Christian monastery and later a bishopric with one of the most splendid records for scholarship and cultural achievement of any centre in Western Christendom. The bishop of Clonmacnoise who attended in 1649 was Anthony Mageoghegan, a Gaelic aristocrat whose dynasty had been lords of Moycashel and large portions of Cenél Fhiachach for over a thousand years. During that millenium they had provided Ireland with a succession of kings, bishops, chroniclers and writers. Even on the eve of the extinction of their house in the seventeenth century, one of their number, Conal Mageoghegan (*fl.* 1635) translated the *Annals of Clonmacnoise* into English, and later the Abbé Mageoghegan (died 1750) became chaplain to the Irish Brigade, and wrote his splendid *Histoire de l'Irelande* in France. Compared with such a family record, the Flemings, Barnewalls, and Plunkets were mere newcomers—interlopers with little more than four centuries of history to back their claim for a stake in Ireland! Even with Cromwell at the very gates, the bishops meeting in Clonmacnoise in 1649 had to outlaw 'all such distinctions as Old Irish and Irish of English descent, or any divisions between provinces or families, as most detrimental to the common cause' (ii, 64).

Distinctions between Gaelic Irish and Old English were put aside too late to avert the destruction of their society in the Cromwellian massacre at Drogheda and the later Williamite victories at the Boyne and Aughrim. The Catholic aristocracies were scattered in exile across the Continent, and of the few who remained, many abandoned the old faith in an attempt to salvage their estates. The Williamite victory on the Boyne in 1690 ensured the downfall of the Flemings, who had adhered to the Jacobite cause. Their estates at Slane were confiscated, and the last of their line, Christopher, twenty-second Baron of Slane, who had fought and lost on the Catholic side in the battle of Aughrim, died in 1726. Their replacement in Slane by the Conynghams ushered in the era which came to be known as that of Protestant ascendancy in the eighteenth century. The earlier polarisation between the Gaelic Irish and the Old English was now replaced by that of two even more irreconcilable nations—a conquering but insecure Protestant élite, and a demoralised and resentful Irish people stripped of their property and of their civil and religious liberties. For even if the great Catholic estates had been forfeited because of the adherence of their owners to a lost Jacobite cause, the 'popery code' of the early eighteenth century revealed the discrimination on the part of the Irish parliament to be as essentially anti-Catholic as it was economic and political.

Slane, in the heart of anglicised Ireland, now had a ruling family which was to form the closest ties with the Hanoverian monarchy in England and which under the first marquis of Slane was to enjoy the personal friendship and attentions of George IV. Slane was the village whose Protestant rector in the late eighteenth century was Mervyn Archdall, author of *Monasticon Hibernicum: or an History of the Abbies, Priories, and other Religious Houses in Ireland* and of the *Peerage of Ireland*. Archdall was a Dublin antiquary who enjoyed the patronage of Richard Pococke during that prelate's time as Protestant bishop of Ossory and later, very briefly (1765), as bishop of Meath. On becoming chaplain to the second Lord Conyngham

17 Slane Castle, Co. Meath. The medieval Fleming castle is incorporated in the present building which dates from the time of William Burton Conyngham (ill. 18) who had the place enlarged and redesigned by James Wyatt and Francis Johnston in 1785.

(Francis Pierpoint Burton), Archdall resigned his preferments in Leix and Kilkenny to become rector of Slane. His *Monasticon Hibernicum* appeared in 1786 and his edition of Lodge's *Peerage of Ireland* in 1789. Archdall died as rector of Slane on 6 August 1791, and he was buried there in the Protestant churchyard. The owner of Slane Castle in Archdall's time was Francis Pierpoint Burton's brother, William Burton Conyngham (Trench, *Ríocht na Midhe*, viii (1987), 113–28). This enlightened man was a founder member of the Royal Irish Academy, a philanthropist and patron of the arts. He was not only a friend of Charles Vallency and other Anglo–Irish antiquaries who acquired a new-found and passionate interest in early Irish antiquities, but he also included in his scholarly circle the old Gaelic aristocrat, Charles O'Conor of Belanagare in Roscommon. In the case of the Conynghams, we have an example of an Anglo–Irish family which profited from Williamite confiscation, and which as Protestant landlords proved in their philanthropy (both in Donegal and Meath) to have the interests of their tenants and the

18 William Burton Conyngham (1733–96), traveller and antiquary, founding member of the Royal Irish Academy and a leading patron of the arts in Georgian Ireland and in Portugal. William, who was the younger brother of Francis Pierpoint Burton, second Lord Conyngham, inherited Slane Castle (ill. 17) in 1781. His Dublin home was in Harcourt Place. William Conyngham consulted leading architects of the day in the renovation of Slane Castle in the 1780s and he was the friend and patron of Mervyn Archdall, Church of Ireland rector of Slane. Archdall who was chaplain to Francis Pierpoint Burton, dedicated his *Monasticon Hibernicum* to William in 1786. Conyngham Road, leading from the Phoenix Park into Dublin was named after William Burton.

country at heart. William Burton died unmarried in 1796. His brother, Lord Conyngham (Francis Pierpoint), was succeeded by his son, Henry, in 1787, and this Henry eventually added the Conyngham inheritance of his uncle, William, in Slane and Donegal, to his own holdings in Clare, Limerick and England. This Henry, third baron Conyngham was, in gratitude for services rendered in the promotion of the Act of Union in 1800, and later because of the friendship between his wife, Elizabeth, and the Prince Regent, created first Marquis Conyngham in 1816. With the succession of the Regent as George IV, the first Marquis Conyngham and his wife spent most of their time with the royal household at Windsor and Brighton, and Conyngham was created Baron Minster of Minster Abbey in Kent in the peerage of the United Kingdom. A study of the Flemings and their successors, the Conynghams, highlights the fundamental change in the make-up of the Irish aristocracy in the aftermath of the Battle of the Boyne. The Flemings were a quintessentially Catholic and Old English baronial family of the Pale, descended from a feudal aristocracy which was hibernicised but not Irish, and while anglicised was not English. They had been replaced by a Protestant élite which had bought up great estates confiscated by a government bent on creating a new order in Ireland. And so, while Flemings of the seventeenth century wandered about Europe in their commitment to the Counter-Reformation, Conynghams of the eighteenth century toured that same continent in search of the Enlightenment. Both Henry Conyngham (created first Lord Conyngham in 1753) and his nephew, William Burton (died 1796), travelled in Europe. When George IV visited a later generation of his Conyngham friends— Henry the third baron and his wife, Elizabeth—at Slane Castle in 1821, the last of the Flemings had died in exile almost a century before. The King's visit to the Irish estate of the lord steward of his household and Constable of Windsor Castle, epitomised the thoroughness and seemingly irrevocable nature of the Act of Union and the total integration of Ireland with Great Britain and the British Empire.

II

THE HIDDEN IRELAND OF THE
BOYNE VALLEY

S lane, lying as it did, in the heartland of anglicised Ireland, continued to maintain a duality in its cultural traditions in more senses than one. The majority of the disaffected and largely poverty-stricken Catholic population drew on an ambiguous heritage made up of medieval or 'Old English' traditions from the Pale towns of Drogheda, Navan, Kells and Trim, combined with surprisingly strong links with an even older Gaelic past. Writing to Cogan in 1863 (Appendix 2), John MacHale, archbishop of Tuam, testified to the survival of spoken Irish in Meath up to that time, and paid tribute to the resilience of its people in clinging to Gaelic ways:

> To the credit of Meath, be it recorded that though amongst the earliest districts to be brought within the dominion of the Pale, it was one of the last to adopt its foreign dialect.
> The ancient language still survives in some of the remote parishes [of Meath] but though the language of the country has at length decayed, its spirit is there in full vigour, for the soil of Meath was too well saturated with the native seed ever to yield to the growth of exotic and anti-national influences.

Little detailed research has been done on the survival of the Irish language in eastern Ireland. Thanks to the labours of Anthony Cogan, we have the record of a will drawn up by Fr Andrew Barnewall, parish priest of Clonmellon, in 1753, in which he established a bursary for the education of a Meath priest 'in one of the seminaries depending on St Sulpice, in the city of Paris, and nowhere else' (ii, 290). Among the conditions attached to this award was the following: 'He is to read and write (if possible) tolerably the Irish language and carry with him abroad some Irish books or manuscripts to practice said Tongue.'

40

19 The neolithic tumulus at Dowth, east of Slane. Wilde, in 1849, described the
tiny structure on the top as a tea house built by Viscount Netterville (*Boyne and
Blackwater* p. 204). Cogan censured Wilde for this facetious comment and
explained the structure as a vantage point erected by John, sixth Viscount
Netterville (1744-1826) to enable him follow key stages in the Mass being
celebrated in the nearby penal-day chapel. According to Cogan (ii, 306) the
Catholic viscount followed the progress of the Eucharist by means of a flag
signalling system operated by his servant down at the chapel.

Irish then, was assumed to be an essential part of the training of
a priest for his ministry in mid eighteenth-century Meath. The
donor, Andrew Barnewall, was believed by Anthony Cogan to have
been a relative of the Trimlestons, who, like the Plunkets, were
among the few surviving aristocratic families of the Pale. That
assumption must be correct, given that Andrew Barnewall was rich
enough to endow his bursary to the value of £400 sterling. Since the
donor insisted that a relative of his should be preferred to all other
competitors for this award, we may equally conclude that families
like the Trimlestons were able to converse in Irish into the 1750s
and beyond. In Cogan's own time, he tells us of one James Martin
of Millbrook, Oldcastle, who died in 1860, and was celebrated
locally as a poet and scholar in Irish and Hebrew (ii, 336). Among
Cogan's vast store of local memories was the tradition at nearby
Dowth on the Boyne, of how Patrick Dunan, an old blind parish
priest (died May 1761) was led on his nephew's arm to the mud-
walled thatched chapel at Dowth to celebrate Sunday Mass (ii, 309).
That nephew was Chistopher Chevers, later parish priest of Kilbeg.

Fr Chevers was known to his flock as 'Thar Chevers Mor' (*An t-Athair Chevers Mór*, 'Great or the Older Fr Chevers'). He died in 1785 and was buried without a gravestone in Staholmock. He was a poet who wrote in both Irish and English (ii, 278–9).

Cogan himself was later to record (iii, 654) that Fr Paul O'Brien who was born in Moynalty in north Meath in the middle of the eighteenth century and who died as professor of Irish in Maynooth as late as 1820, was the great-grandnephew of Turlough O'Carolan the Gaelic musician, harper and poet (1670–1738), a native of Nobber. Fr O'Brien, the author of a *Practical Grammar of the Irish Language*, was remembered by his contemporaries as 'a living magazine of the poetry and language of his country'. He could personally draw on memories of a unique Gaelic enclave of poets, musicians and scribes which survived in south Cavan and north Meath from the seventeenth to the early nineteenth century, and he had access to their manuscripts and oral renderings. O'Carolan had been the leading light of that school, but he was by no means alone. O'Carolan's contemporary Cathaoir Mac Cabe, who died in 1740, and who was a native of Mullagh in Cavan (but within Meath diocese), was also an accomplished Irish poet and harper, while Fiachna Mac Bráduigh (MacBrady) a schoolmaster from Stradone in Cavan (*fl.*1712) was yet another accomplished poet. These last exponents of the Gaelic tradition had lived in a remote corner of Meath and Cavan which lay some ten to fourteen miles to the north and west of Slane. There were others also who lived in Cogan's own area. Séamus Dall Mac Cuarta (*fl.*1712), although probably born in Omeath in Louth, spent most of his life in Slane, where as Cogan tells us (iii, 648) 'he composed innumerable songs and poems in the Irish language', among which, incidentally, was a work in 88 verses on a mammoth football match played in Boyne Meadow near Slane between men from Louth and Meath. Mac Cuarta spent most of his life among the peasants of the Boyne Valley, but he was well schooled in ancient Irish traditional lore (the *seanchas*), Classics and the Bible. This eighteenth-century Gaelic poet, who was a contemporary of Mac Bráduigh and who has left us a lament on the battle of Aughrim, was buried in Monknewtown cemetery, near Slane. Close by at Stackallen, also in the early eighteenth century, an Irish scribe, John McSolly, was busy transcribing Irish poems from older manuscript collections, thereby preserving a fragile inheritance to await the interest of some future generation. Cogan tells us (iii, 654) of one William O'Brian from Rosnaree near Slane who 'composed

20 Romanesque archway of Cannistown Church near Navan in 1849.

many songs in Irish' *c.*1760. That these poets and scribes of the Boyne were in close contact with their colleagues in the south Cavan and Moynalty area is proved by the fact that Fr Paul O'Brien could repeat the first lines of seventeen lost poems of Séamus Dall Mac Cuarta which he passed on to Edward O'Reilly, the author (in 1817) of *An Irish-English Dictionary* and (in 1820) of a work on Irish writers.

Scholarly families in the Gaelic tradition, and indeed lesser folk who spoke Irish, and who survived on into the early nineteenth century, must have formed an enclave of opinion and inhabited a world which was unintelligible to the Protestant gentry. There could have been no starker contrast between the two nations than this fundamental divide of language, culture and religion. It might seem safe to argue that the distance between the Williamite aristocracy and the native Meath peasantry was no greater than that which had formerly existed between the Old English lords and that same peasantry before the Williamite conquest. While that may have been true in the narrowest social terms, such a viewpoint overlooks the fact that pre-Williamite Irish society was united by common cultural bonds which had been violently severed after 1690. Séamus Dall Mac Cuarta—that rough poet who lost his sight as a youth when he caught an infection tending horses at Kellystown near Slane on a cold winter's night—does not strike us as suitable company for Baron Fleming. Yet Fleming was indeed his patron and was

43

probably the main reason why Séamus Dall resided in the Slane area for most of his life. Not only did Séamus Dall write on the defeat of the Irish at Aughrim where Christopher Fleming was wounded, but he has also left us a poem on that last of the Slane Barons—*Barún Bhaile Shláine* in which the poet awaits the return of his lord from exile. This poem was probably written in 1713 or soon after, when Fleming was hoping for the restoration of his lands and titles under Queen Anne. Fleming (*Fléimeannach*), addressed in this poem as *Chriostóir óg mac Raghnaill* (Young Christopher, son of Randall) is hailed as a *bráthair ceart Uí Néill* (true brother of O'Neill).

So, in spite of their Anglo-Norman (or Flemish) origins, the barons of Slane, like the Geraldines and others, had finally won acceptance from the Gaelic bards. Séamus Dall addresses Christopher Fleming in this poem in a timeless idiom befitting a medieval Irish king, associating his lord on his hoped-for return with fertility and times of plenty. Christopher Fleming, like the Barnewalls, understood and promoted the use of Irish—which is what we should expect from a family which had included the scholar, Patrick Fleming, who had worked in the tradition of the Four Masters to save the manuscript heritage of his land. But the contrast with the post-Williamite victory on the Boyne remains. The gap of religion and language which separated the new ruling class from the mass of the people was not in itself insurmountable. Nor was the fate of the Flemings any more unfortunate than that of countless other great landowners who found themselves on the losing side in the religious conflicts which plagued Europe elsewhere in the sixteenth and seventeenth centuries. But Ireland's case was special in so far as the defeated aristocracy was replaced or dominated by an essentially alien élite who enforced their rule, in the first generation at least, through coercion and penal legislation. So, however philanthropic the Conynghams might have been as landlords, and however truly interested they might become in Celtic antiquities, none of these things could be properly appreciated by a people deprived by a new governing class, of their self-respect. Séamus Dall might celebrate the hoped-for homecoming of Christopher Fleming in the early eighteenth century. By the middle of that century, there was no Gaelic poet on the Boyne who could summon the muse to celebrate the homecoming of William Burton from his Grand Tour.

If the eighteenth century was characterised in Ireland by the consolidation of the hold which the new Ascendancy class had acquired over government and all aspects of Irish life, the nineteenth was dominated by a relentless struggle on the part of the suppressed Catholic majority to regain civil and religious liberties and to manipulate the new Reformists' goals within Britain to their own advantage. This mobilisation of the Catholic masses was organised against a background of endemic poverty, disease and famine, and accompanied by violent struggle at local level for possession of tenant rights. Anthony Cogan had entered Maynooth in 1844, some three years before the Great Famine. That was a disaster which Cogan personally believed had been artificially brought about by the Government of the day 'as there was then food enough in the country to satisfy the wants of all' (iii, 513). The devastation caused by the Famine, although less in eastern Ireland than in poorer parts, was compounded by land clearances in the eastern counties. And while the Great Famine may have wreaked less havoc in Meath than elsewhere, its accompanying diseases— especially cholera—had become a regular feature of life in the overcrowded urban slums of Meath long before and after the catastrophe of 1847–48. Bishop Nulty estimated that he had lost over 200,000 people from his diocese in the period from 1843 to 1871 (Flynn, *RnM* VIII, iii (1984), 21). It was estimated that 95,000 people had been evicted in Co. Meath between 1843 and 1866. Cogan believed the number of homes which had been destroyed within a few years by land clearance and eviction to have totalled

21 Late fifteenth-century font from Kilcarne, Co. Meath, now in Johnstown Catholic Church. Once used by locals in a game involving the throwing of horseshoes into the bowl, it was rescued early in the nineteenth century and Cogan helped organise its dispatch to the Dublin Exhibition of 1853.

300,000 in Ireland as a whole (iii, 513). However these figures may be debated, and allowing for rhetoric and exaggeration, there can be no denying the major demographic upheavals in Irish society between 1820 and 1870.

Emigration, changes in the local population, and the death of the Irish language went hand in hand in Meath. When John O'Donovan visited Slane and Rathkenny—Cogan's native parishes—during his topographical studies with the Ordnance Survey in July 1836, he reported for Slane: 'As to family names, I could not get any of the ancient stock of this Parish pointed out to me; they say the inhabitants are not of the ancient families of this place' (*Letters . . . County of Meath ... of the Ordnance Survey, 1836*, ed. M. O'Flanagan (Bray, 1928 [typescript]) p. 45). We need to treat such statements with an element of caution. O'Donovan and his topographers moved with some speed through the countryside, and the accuracy of their information depended on the calibre of their informants. The Ordnance Survey Letters for Meath are not among the most useful or reliable in the series. But we do have independent evidence to suggest not only mass emigration out of the county in the middle of the nineteenth century, but also large-scale dislocation of population within the county and its towns at this time. Connell's excellent study of nineteenth-century Navan emphasises the insecurity of pre-Famine society, and shows that some two-thirds of all families in the town in 1821 had migrated elsewhere or died out by 1854 (Connell, *RnM*, VI, iii (1977), 51).

While the Halls in their tour of Ireland in 1840 remarked on the opulent landscape of Meath, they also concluded that 'much of this apparently prosperous character is . . . hollow and unsubstantial', for while the larger farmers were indeed wealthy, there were few or no small farmers (*Hall's Ireland*, ii, p. 373).* The tenant farmers were either being forcibly evicted or offered inducements to emigrate to the United States, to Liverpool and London. Those whose houses had been levelled and who could not afford or undertake a voyage overseas crowded into Navan and elsewhere as unskilled manual labourers, doomed to remain, for the most part, jobless.

While Irish words and placenames were clearly plentiful in the local Anglo-Irish dialect, spoken Irish was already in retreat in east Meath before the Famine. Cogan in the *preface* to his first volume specifically tells us that he felt impelled to write his *Diocese of Meath* because 'the change of language, the wholesale emigration of the people, the disruption of old ties consequent on the famine years,

*See Appendix 11.

46

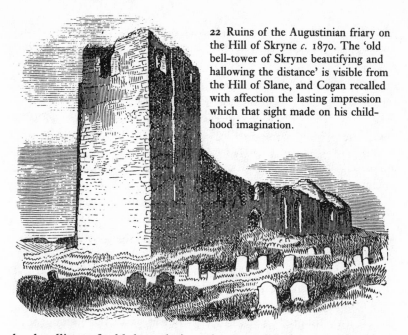

22 Ruins of the Augustinian friary on the Hill of Skryne *c.* 1870. The 'old bell-tower of Skryne beautifying and hallowing the distance' is visible from the Hill of Slane, and Cogan recalled with affection the lasting impression which that sight made on his childhood imagination.

the levelling of old boundaries, the consolidation of farms, the inhuman clearances of the land to make room for "flocks and herds" ' (i, xi) had made it imperative to rescue past records from 'oblivion and neglect'. He returned to this theme in his *preface* to the second volume (in 1867) when he wrote of 'the barbarous and suicidal expulsion of the people to make way for cattle—the exodus to the land of the free, under whose stripes and stars the Irish exiles have invariably found a home' (ii, viii).

For Cogan, 'the generous flag of America' (iii, 512) offered shelter and new life to a starving people driven from their own land in the notorious emigrant ships. Occasionally he gave vent, without any warning, to his strong feelings on the subject of evictions and clearances, in the course of his historical narrative. He records that he visited the churchyard of Clonfad, some five and a half miles south-east of Mullingar in the Barony of Farbill, Co. Westmeath in August 1863. While citing references to this ancient place in the *Annals of the Four Masters*, the *Acta Sanctorum* and the *Martyrology of Tallaght*, and correcting Archdall's record, he goes on: 'The country round about is now deserted; the people are gone, whether willingly or unwillingly; cattle abound; silence and desolation reign around. God help poor Ireland' (iii, 554).

The towns and the countryside of Meath cannot be described as happy places during Anthony Cogan's lifetime. Nineteenth-century illustrations of landscapes and romantic ruins peopled by Irish peasants in shawls and frock coats conceal the misery of poverty and insecurity of tenure which the tenant farmers and labourers had on their mud-walled hovels. Navan and other towns of Meath offered even worse social conditions for the poor than the open countryside. Food could be grown, bought or stolen in rural areas, while in towns the prospects for survival were harsher. William Wilde in his *Beauties of the Boyne and Blackwater* (p. 262), while copiously illustrating the medieval ruins of Drogheda, was scathing on the appalingly squalid condition of that town as he encountered it in Famine times. Writing of the Magdalen Steeple, he wrote:

> It is now surrounded by the most miserable hovels, inhabited by the most wretched portion of the population, and not only is the adjoining locality a disgrace to the town, but the very site itself stands more in need of the efforts of a Sanitary Commission than any other place that we know of in the British dominions. As soon as the Corporation of Drogheda cleanse their city, we hope to conduct the Boyne tourists round some of its other memorable ruins.

Wilde was a distinguished physician, thoroughly familiar with slum conditions in Dublin, and his horror and indignation at the insanitary conditions in Drogheda are all the more significant. Drogheda at that time must have become a major clearing centre for emigrants on their way to Liverpool.

Navan, where Anthony Cogan ministered as a priest for fourteen years, harboured the same type of urban squalor as that encountered by Wilde in Drogheda. Connell (op. cit, pp 39, 44) shows how the population of this town rose from 2500 in 1760 to 3500 in 1821, and climbed to over 6000 in 1842. While the proportion of agricultural labourers almost doubled from 28 per cent to 48.5 per cent in the decade between 1821 and 1831, there was a marked fall in the proportion of those engaged in manufacturing. In other words, Navan was experiencing a Third World type immigration accompanied by the growth of shanty town enclaves of one-roomed mud-walled hovels in Brews Hill, Barrack Lane, Sandymount and Infirmary Hill. However prosperous the town's manufacturing or retail base might be, it could not absorb such an influx of unskilled immigrants. Overcrowding reached catastrophic proportions in the slums of Brews Hill at the height of the famine in 1848, when seven families were recorded as living in one room. Although famine, emigration and disease reduced Navan's population by about 2000 or one-third, thereby easing the pressure on housing and the unskilled labour market, the place continued to present immense social and economic problems throughout Anthony Cogan's time there, in the late Fifties and all through the Sixties. In spite of slum clearances—carried out by ruthless landlords in the face of local and clerical opposition—the *Meath People* continued to report on the presence of dung heaps outside every door in the back streets and 'the accumulated filth of all the higher parts of the town' being added to local refuse and squalor in the back alleys on the periphery (Connell, op. cit., p. 52). The ongoing crisis was compounded by famine and by eviction of tenant farmers in rural Meath and Westmeath. As tenants were evicted, their hovels were levelled and the more destitute headed for the Union workhouses. The number of inmates in the Navan workhouse rose from 295 in 1844 to 900 in 1848–49. As many as 30 per cent of these paupers were discharged into the community every month to make way for further influxes from the countryside. Those who were released from the workhouse on the southern edge of Navan in the famine years ended up as recipients of outdoor relief and lodged as sub-tenants in the disease-ridden slums of nearby Brews Hill. It is little wonder that cholera in Navan was not confined to the black years of 1847–9. Cogan reports on cholera raging in Navan in the 1830s, and Bishop John Cantwell in his Lenten Pastoral in Meath for 1855 (*Tablet*, 17 February 1855, p. 101) relaxed the rigours of the Lenten fast because of 'the

23 St Kieran's Well, north of Kells, Co. Meath.

24 View of Drogheda in the nineteenth century as Cogan and John Boyle O'Reilly
would have known it. The paddle steamers and sailing ships on the waterfront on
the Boyne had specially strong contacts with the port of Liverpool, and it was along
this route that O'Reilly sailed in his uncle's ship, *Caledonian*, to join his aunt in
Preston in 1859. The *Drogheda Argus* where O'Reilly worked as a boy, ran a weekly
column with Liverpool news throughout Anthony Cogan's lifetime, and Cogan was
a regular visiting preacher at St Mary's and St Patrick's Catholic Churches in
Liverpool. In August 1863, a contingent of the Young Mens' Society from
Liverpool sailed to Drogheda to join Dean Cogan's excursion for the Navan CYMS
at Laytown.

prevailing fear of a return of cholera which has lately afflicted some
districts'.

Cogan personally admired those of his clerical friends and
colleagues who ministered to cholera victims, and he himself cared
throughout his life for the young men from those deprived areas of
Navan. A letter written from Navan by *A Correspondent* (who was
clearly Anthony Cogan) to the editor of the *Tablet* (14 February
1857, p. 108) pays tribute to the charitable work done by the Sisters
of Mercy in that town at a time when Cogan was curate there, and
when he was writing historical pieces for the *Tablet*:

Silently and unostentatiously, the little community, is, day after day, pursuing its work of charity among the poor of Christ. In the Union Workhouse, in the county hospital, on the cold, damp floor of the wretched hut in some lane or alley of the town, those angels of peace may be seen by the side of the sick bed, alleviating the pains of this life, and cheering the dying sinner with the hopes of a better. The haunts of sickness and homes of misery unknown to most of us are the familiar resorts of the sisters of Mercy.

It is not possible to understand Cogan's emotional outbursts on the social and political conditions of the Irish poor in his *Diocese of Meath* unless we understand that in addition to his scholarly pursuits, this priest was a man of the people who lived through times of immense hardship. As he read his weekly copy of the *Meath People* or the *Drogheda Argus* Anthony Cogan was faced with endless reports on the struggle between tenant farmers and their landlords or agents, and the front pages of those weeklies carried prominent advertisements giving details for the cost of a passage on the White Star or Eagle Lines to the United States, Australia, New Zealand and Tasmania.

III

THE AGONY OF POST-FAMINE
POLITICS

It was into this confused cultural milieu of Protestant ascendancy, dispossessed Norman lords whose Catholic ghosts stalked the Irish Colleges of France and Spain, a down-trodden Catholic peasantry, and a lingering but stubbornly ailing Gaelic cultural tradition, that Anthony Cogan was born in 1826 or 1827. In a land where deep-seated and competing cultural traditions claimed the loyalties of adherents, and whose objectives appeared to be in constant conflict, no one easy or final panacea was in sight. Ireland had lost its own parliament under the Act of Union in 1800, and nationalist hopes, under O'Connell's leadership, for the Repeal of the Union and the restoration of an Irish legislature had been dashed by the death of O'Connell in 1847 and by the onset of the Great Famine. Yet the winning of Catholic Emancipation in 1829 had heightened expectations for greater political freedoms within Ireland. Expectations had been fanned by O'Connell's orchestration of monster meetings for the Repeal of the Union and later by other more radical alternative proposals for a complete break with the British parliament by violent means if all else failed. For while Cogan's Catholic superiors still clung to the hope that a limited element of autonomy (later to be labelled as Home Rule) was attainable from Britain by continuing to work along the guidelines set out by O'Connell, a body of revolutionary Fenians looked back to the tradition of the United Irishmen and the abortive but heroic struggle of the Men of '98, whose defeat in the Great Rebellion was followed by the abolition of the Irish parliament two years later, in 1800. The Protestant ruling élite had profited from the politics of those troubled days. Henry Conyngham, the first Marquis of Slane was created Viscount Mount Charles and Earl Conyngham in the peerage of Ireland in November 1797. Conyngham had personally raised the Londonderry regiment in 1794—one of the many militias raised within Ireland at this time to defend the realm if need be, from French invasion or from internal revolt. Defence of the Protestant nation and support of the Act of Union went hand in hand, and for his support for the Union in 1800, Conyngham was rewarded with £15,000 in cash for his close borough of Killybegs in the old Irish House of Commons. As it happened, his was an exceptional family which gave back much to Irish life by way of investment in the economy, in public works, and in the arts. Anthony Cogan was to chronicle the favourable light in which the new lords of Slane were viewed by the Catholic community.

The country at large, however, was in financial chaos. It was devastated by poverty and by land clearances, and misruled from a distant parliament in Westminster. Some, like Anthony Cogan, were to find fulfilment in pursuit of the spiritual and by losing themselves in the study of Ireland's past. But as Cogan's short life progressed, he became increasingly involved in championing the cause of the poor and in joining the fight against arbitrary eviction of tenants in town and country. Others like Cogan's younger contemporary, John Boyle O'Reilly, who was born only three miles away on the Boyne at Dowth, would seek more dramatic solutions. O'Reilly, the son of a Dowth schoolmaster, was born in 1844. His father taught at the national school founded by the sixth Viscount Neterville of Dowth Castle (1744–1826). Cogan revered the memory of 'the once lordly house of Neterville' (ii, 306) which had provided

25 John Boyle O'Reilly (1844–90), Fenian, poet and writer, who achieved fame and political respectability in Boston, was the son of a schoolmaster in Viscount Netterville's charitable foundation at Dowth. This neighbour of Cogan's shows in his writings that the two men shared the same patriotic imagery in expressing, in their different ways, their great love of Ireland. They drew inspiration from the same mixture of folklore, ancient history, Catholic piety and the Celtic antiquarian revival of the early nineteenth century.

so many champions to his Catholic cause. Young John Boyle O'Reilly, meanwhile, was compelled by family circumstances to begin his working life at the age of eleven as an apprentice compositor with the *Drogheda Argus*. After emigrating to Preston in Lancashire, he became a reporter for the *Guardian*. Even this brief English phase in John Boyle O'Reilly's career was matched in the life of Anthony Cogan. For at that very time when O'Reilly lived with his aunt in Preston, Cogan regularly visited Liverpool as a popular preacher for special occasions in Liverpool churches. In 1863, a year after Cogan's first volume of the *Diocese of Meath* was published, O'Reilly had returned to Ireland, enlisting as a trooper in the 10th Hussars then stationed at Drogheda, and set to work as a secret agent for the Fenians. This subversive activity led to his court martial and eventual deportation to Western Australia in 1867. By the time of Anthony Cogan's death in 1872, John Boyle O'Reilly had escaped to the United States. Cogan's old neighbour on the Boyne had by now established himself as a successful writer and journalist in Boston. While he had lost little of his revolutionary ideals, he had learnt to temper his patriotism with a caution born of experience. He was involved as a very critical press reporter only, in the Fenian invasion of Canada under General John O'Neill in 1870, but four years after Anthony Cogan's death, in 1876, O'Reilly contributed to the dramatic rescue of the political prisoners from the convict settlements of Western Australia. John Boyle O'Reilly's daring adventures and dazzling career in exile, not to mention his talents as a writer, must have impressed on Anthony Cogan that the life of the revolutionary from Dowth exhibited many of the hallmarks of the Wild Geese in centuries before. For like those Irishmen who had joined the service of France, O'Reilly proved himself to be not only an Irish patriot, but also a good American. Cogan may not have known O'Reilly personally, but he would certainly have been well informed on his career. Yet the times were too dangerous for a priest—even of Cogan's outspoken nature—to reveal his thoughts on such matters. By 1864, the Catholic bishops were leading their clergy in denouncing this new secret revolutionary organisation—the Fenian Brotherhood—and besides, Cogan had at least one brother (Francis: see genealogy p. 176) who served as a surgeon-major in the British army. The Fenians staged their Rising in 1867, in what was a gesture of defiance rather than a practical attempt to seize power. In that same year Cogan published 560 pages by way of a second volume to his *Diocese of Meath*. Cogan demonstrated his passion for the people of Ireland and for their past in his own way, and in this he was no less dedicated and intense than those who showed their patriotism through armed struggle or political agitation.

If Anthony Cogan's prose sometimes reads like that of a 'gentle antiquary' that should not be allowed to obscure the deep-seated cultural and political conflicts that exercised his mind and which were evident all around him from a childhood spent in Meath. Cogan, like other Catholic Irishmen of his generation, was forced to grapple with the competing recipes for solving the perceived woes of Irish political life in the mid nineteenth century, and as in Ireland over a century later, the argument was complicated by a legacy of patriotic heroism, rhetoric and myth from an earlier age. Cogan himself appears to have supported Bishop Plunket's denounciation of Carders and Ribbonmen in the period 1816–19 by describing those secret and local terror groups who fought back against equally ruthless landlords as 'nefarious' societies, and he adds: 'Gangs of robbers at this time infested the country, and many of them paid the penalty of their wickedness by being hanged and gibbeted' (iii, 425).

As for Cogan's own romantic view of a past blameless age of down-trodden Catholic innocence, that, too, is elsewhere in his work flatly contradicted by his own comments on Bishop Plunket's visitations of *c.*1820:

> Drunkenness, cursing and swearing, rioting, detraction, immorality, bad example of parents, absenteeism from the Sacraments, and dangerous amusements on Sunday evenings, were all denounced [by Bishop Plunket] with a vigour worthy of his younger and more active episcopal career. (ibid.)

Plunket's episcopacy had survived the Great Rebellion of 1798 which left an enduring scar on the folk memory of Meath. Some four or five hundred Croppies fell in the Battle of Tara on 26 May 1798, and the Catholic bishop lined up firmly on the side of law and order as enforced by the yeomanry of his kinsman, Lord Fingal. For ironically, it was Fingal's Catholic yeomen who played a decisive role in the suppression of the rebellion in Meath. Patrick Plunket was an aristocrat whose Catholic kin had held on grimly to their position in the Pale, and whose own personal contacts in France had taught him what the horrors of the Terror had achieved in Republi-

26 Church of Ireland on the Hill of Tara, *c.*1870. The rebels of Meath made a desperate stand here behind the graveyard wall on 26 May 1798.

27 The Croppies' Grave with the Stone of Destiny (*Lia Fáil*) on top, marks a mass grave of some of the 400 fallen rebels in the battle of Tara, 26 May, 1798. These Men of '98 were buried in a platform ring fort of the Celtic Iron Age, known as Cormac's House (*Teach Chormaic*) on Tara. The neolithic Mound of the Hostages is to the right. Cogan, who came here as a youth to hear Daniel O'Connell address his monster meeting in 1843, recalled the powerful effect which the Croppies' Grave had on the emotions of the vast crowd.

can Paris. Such a man, who was also a devout Christian and committed to his pastoral role as bishop, would indeed be expected to fulminate against peasant rebellion and 'dangerous amusements on Sunday evenings' alike. Thanks to Anthony Cogan we now know what Bishop Plunket's personal reaction to the '98 Rebellion was. He ascribed it to: 'the credulity of the lower classes, the decay of Christian piety, and the prevalance of the impious principles that are disturbing a great part of the Continent.' (iii,298). Plunket railed against 'the spirit of insurrection that disgraced some parts of the kingdom' and on his progress through Duleek, Stamullen and Ardcath in 1798, preached against the 'folly and guilt' of rebellion.

But not all of Plunket's priests shared their bishop's loyalty to the English crown. His diary for late May and June 1798 shows Meath to have been in a state of turmoil so that no children had been prepared for Confirmation at Ratoath for 3 June 'on account of the confusion produced by the Insurrection' (iii, 298) and such a state of anarchy prevailed in Fr Pat Keonan's parish of Curraha, that the bishop was advised by the magistrate not to proceed with his visitation on 2 June. Pat Ferrall, parish priest of Donnymore and Kilbride 'did not appear' before his bishop 'nor give notice to the flock of the visitation' for 5 June. 'Seeing the flock deserted by the pastor, I appointed Rev. Mr Halligan administrator in the *interim*' (iii, 298–9). On the following day, Bishop Plunket found the village of Dunboyne reduced to ruins 'burnt in punishment it is supposed of the treasonable practices of the people. Mr [James] Connell [the parish priest] did not appear to me and I withdrew with grief' (iii, 299). In this time of violence and tension, pastor was set against pastor, and priest against bishop. And while in other societies, such traumas might have been forgotten by Anthony Cogan's day, not so in Ireland, where memories—especially tragic memories—were long. Cogan's transcription of Bishop Plunket's thoughts on the '98 Rebellion in Meath, form a priceless vignette in his lengthy work. In one sense, the loyalist bishop's attitude reflects however dimly, the last glimmer of tension between the 'Old English' mentality—of loyalty to the status quo imposed by Britain—as against native Irish rejection of the British presence altogether. The great difference in 1798, of course, was that the mass of the Irish people had already lost their traditional leaders as well as their liberties, and in fairness to Plunket, his family like the Barnewalls and others, were the last of the few Old English lords who had held on to their Catholicism when all others had fled the land or gone over to the Protestant side.

28 Daniel O'Connell addressing the monster meeting on Tara, 15 August 1843. Anthony Cogan was present as a youth of 17 in the great crowd of 200,000. (*Illustrated London News* 26 August 1843). Cogan's account confirms that at these extraordinary gatherings, people on the fringes of the crowd and out of earshot of the speaker paid their own 'respects' and resorted to their own disciplined amusements.

Cogan himself harboured confusing thoughts about 1798. As a dutiful Catholic priest and curate he recorded the terse record of his revered but pro-British Bishop Plunket, without comment. Yet elsewhere he gives his own version of the battle of Tara, when as a boy he recalled being present at O'Connell's monster meeting on the Hill of Tara on 15 August 1843. That day would also have been memorable for Cogan and his people who had travelled from Slane, for it was coincidentally, Lady Well, the annual pilgrimage to St Erc's Hermitage in the grounds of Slane Castle. While all Ireland and a crowd estimated at over one million (more likely 200,000) listened to hear O'Connell speak on the repeal of the Act of Union and the restoration of an Irish Parliament, the young Cogan was looking characteristically backwards, to the tragedy of Ireland's past and to the ghosts of the Croppies who lay entombed in the sacred ground of Cormac's House on Tara—that same Cormac mac Airt who was reputedly slain by his druids by the Boyne in the House of Cletty near Slane in the prehistoric Celtic past:

The writer of this, then a little boy, sat for hours on that day, at the foot of the "Lia Fail" [the Stone of Destiny—a Neolithic standing stone which marks the mass grave of the fallen Rebels on Tara] listening to the music, and watching the sobs and lamentations of the old men and women from Wexford. (iii, 508)

Bishop Plunket would definitely not have approved of Cogan's version of events on Tara as he viewed them on that day in 1843:

While O'Connell was addressing the masses from the platform, thousands, who were unable to get within hearing of him, turned to another object of attraction, and that was 'the Croppies' grave', the tomb of the Wexfordmen who were shot and sabred on the hill of Tara, in the year 1798, and whose bodies were shovelled into this grave. Many of the trades planted their banners round this lonely tomb, and each band in succession, formed a circle and played 'The Harp that once through Tara's Halls', and 'Rousseau's Dream'.

It would take a tear from a stone to witness the grief of the old men and women, who, availing themselves of the great Repeal Meeting, came all the way from Wexford to take a last look at the grave that sheltered all that was mortal of their fathers, brothers, or children. They well remembered how numbers of the poor victims were literally driven to defend their wives, their sisters, their daughters, their altars, and their homes, by the lawless and brutal yeomanry and soldiery, who, with more relentless wickedness than savages, plundered, burned, and destroyed everything that came in their way. Free quarters and unbridled military licence drove numbers of the defenceless peasantry to congregate for self-defence, many of whom never returned to tell their sad tale of suffering and disaster. The head-stone that marks the 'Croppies' grave' was another object of great attention, as it is popularly believed to be a portion of the 'Lia Fail', or Stone of Destiny, so celebrated by the bards of ancient Erin, and so ominously and significantly placed here. The whole scene at the grave of the Wexfordmen was truly impressive and grand, and many were moved to tears thinking of the past history of Ireland, and then looking around at the imposing demonstration of the day. Few of the spectators turned away from the Croppies' grave without uttering a fervent prayer to Almighty God for the eternal

59

repose of the souls of the unfortunate men who, 'in dark and evil days', were goaded by remorseless tryanny into resistance, and then shot down without pity, far away from home and kindred, far away from their village churches and the graves of their fathers, and flung into a deep pit, in one of the ancient mounds, on Tara of the Kings, where they are taking their long, lonely sleep, awaiting the sound of the Archangel's trumpet. (iii, 508–9)

Cogan's neighbour, John Boyle O'Reilly, would have found little to fault in this uncritical outburst, which owes nothing to Bishop Plunket's views on a misguided drunken peasantry duped by the rhetoric of purveyors of the French Revolution. For Cogan, the fallen on Tara had become blameless heroes 'goaded by remorseless tyranny into resistance'. Nor need we worry unduly about the striking inaccuracies of Cogan's account of the Great Rebellion of 1798. He himself could scarcely have been 'a little boy' in August 1843 when he was, rather, sixteen or even seventeen—which accounts for his vivid memories of that great gathering which 'was perhaps the greatest political meeting which ever assembled in Ireland or in any other country' (iii, 507). Cogan's insistence that the fallen rebels were Wexford men, who were mourned at the 1843 meeting by the Wexford contingent is also a curious comment from an historian who was himself present at O'Connell's meeting only 45 years after the Battle of Tara took place. The majority of the fallen on the field of Tara must have been Meathmen, especially from the Dunshaughlin and Curraha areas, as well as from East Meath generally and north Kildare.

What is far more important than accuracy of detail is how the conflict was perceived by a man of Cogan's education and standing when he wrote in 1870. He must have been aware of Presbyterian participation on the Rebel side in Ulster, and even more so of the loyalist role of Fingal's Catholic yeomanry on Tara. Elsewhere and in a less emotive context (ii, 546–7), he tells us of Constantine Molloy, a prominent Catholic in Tullamore who served in the yeomanry during '98 and who was exonerated by Cogan on grounds that 'he did good service in protecting the people from the oppression and persecution of the Orange troopers' (ii, 547). He was aware, too, that large numbers of Catholics had served in the loyalist militia at Slane during the summer of '98. Cogan must have known of the atrocities committed on all sides in the Rebellion, even if

29 John Cantwell, bishop of Meath
(1830–66) ruled the diocese during most
of Cogan's life. A friend of O'Connell
and a staunch supporter of Repeal of the
Union, he encouraged his clergy to
participate in nationalist politics.
Cantwell supported Cogan's historical
labours by giving him leave of absence
to visit Westmeath and Offaly in the
summer of 1863.

Meath had escaped the worst horrors of sectarian violence. Yet only
forty-five years on, the Men of '98 had achieved in Cogan's mind a
heroic stature, and as he looked back as a young middle-aged man in
1870, on that day on Tara in his youth, his memories were not of
the details of O'Connell's speech, or of that charismatic and
powerful orator, but rather of the ghosts of those fearless men of
'98. Cogan, characteristically, pitied their interment far from home
and from their family graves. But more prophetically, and as an
indication of the mirror which his work holds up to us on mid
nineteenth-century Ireland, he saw that Destiny, exemplified by the
Lia Fail, was on the side, not of O'Connell and his constitutional
formula, but on the side of Revolution. John Boyle O'Reilly would
have been pleased.

Cogan's personal view of the Irish political situation is clearly set
out in his account of the life of Bishop John Cantwell, under whose
episcopate he had spent almost all his days as a priest. Cogan's
account of Cantwell's rule in Meath (1830–66) and his observations
on the political scene should be treated quite separately from the
remainder of his lengthy history of the diocese, for in this section
Cogan suspended his activities as a church historian and allowed
himself the licence of a political commentator. His account of John
Cantwell, has the added advantage, therefore, of allowing us access
to Cogan's own political thoughts. As always, there was an element
of 'double think' and contradiction in his approach. On the one
hand, he dutifully recorded Bishop Cantwell's hopes for an Irish
domestic legislature constitutionally attained. Reporting Cantwell's

reply to O'Connell's toast at a banquet held after a monster meeting in Mullingar on 14 May 1843, the bishop is made to say: 'We will leave England to the English and we desire no separation from her. We abhor the very idea of the dismemberment of the Empire; our only object and that of the Liberator of the Irish people is to procure the advantage of a domestic legislature' (iii, 505). The hope for an Irish parliament was a goal officially pursued by the Irish Catholic establishment and it was one which would develop from the Seventies onwards and come to ambiguous fruition in the early twentieth century under the banner of Home Rule. Its roots lay in the Repeal movement of O'Connell, which clearly enjoyed the support of Bishop Cantwell. Cogan emphasises the close personal friendship which he believed existed between John Cantwell and O'Connell. Cantwell had been especially active in promoting the Repeal movement and had lent his moral support at banquets and meetings not only within the Meath diocese, but outside in Longford and as far afield as Galway (P. Connell, *RnM* vii (1984), 44–60). He had been one of the first Irish Catholic bishops to declare openly his support for Repeal and he encouraged his diocesan clergy to do likewise. But at the time when Cogan wrote his account of John Cantwell's episcopate in the late Sixties, Irish politics had moved on. O'Connell's Repeal movement had collapsed even before the Great Famine had reduced Ireland to beggary and political exhaustion. Men with alternative ideas had taken over from O'Connell—Thomas Davis and the Young Irelanders who attempted an abortive rising in 1848, and Charles Gavan Duffy who formed the Tenant Right League in 1850.

Anthony Cogan may be excused if his nationalist objectives or those of his new bishop, Thomas Nulty, as expressed in the third volume of his *Diocese of Meath*, seem to lack focus or cohesion. He wrote at a time of confusion and division in the ranks of those who sincerely sought a restoration of the Irish parliament on the one hand, alongside an improvement in the condition of the post-Famine tenant farmers of Ireland on the other.

Cogan, in the midst of all the turmoil and confusion was, characteristically, looking back. He was insistent that O'Connell's failure to achieve Repeal of the Union had not exhausted the possibilty of realising that political objective: 'No—a thousand times, no. The dread famines ... the death of O'Connell ... these and other causes have tended merely to interrupt the Repeal movement, but certainly not to extinguish it. The spirit of the mighty dead still lives; his principles have become national traditions' (iii, 501).

Bishop Cantwell's speeches on Repeal reveal, as we might expect, that his primary preoccupation was with the elimination of discrimatory laws and practices which continued to operate to the disadvantage of the Catholic Church and to what he perceived as the spiritual wellbeing of his flock. More than ten years on, in his Lenten pastoral (*Tablet*, 17 February 1855, p.101) this deeply Nationalist Meath bishop had lost nothing of his fire. Having quickly disposed of regulations regarding the rigorous Lenten fast in his diocese, the sixty-three year old patriarch fulminated against the 'unchristian cruelties practised under the oppressive and iniquitous laws which enforce the rights without compelling the duties of landlords—an evil which has banished millions of our countrymen.' He spoke out, as he did back in the days of O'Connell, against residual anti-Catholic bigotry and discrimination in the army, military schools, and indeed all public institutions in the country. Most significantly, Cantwell urged in that same Lenten pastoral, that all his flock must press their political representatives for the redress of Catholic grievances. It is against the background of the rule of John Cantwell in Meath—who was one of the most politically minded of mid nineteenth-century Irish bishops—that we must view Anthony Cogan's own increasing political awareness.

Anthony Cogan displayed a great ambiguity in his romantic view of Ireland's future which had been shaped by his perception of its tragic and heroic past. He goes on to hope for an Ireland reborn which 'shall take that elevated and dignified position amongst the kingdoms of the earth, which God and nature have manifestly intended for her' (iii, 501–2).

This was a somewhat different and more ripe vision than that of Bishop Cantwell's rather tamer view of a domestic legislature, loyal to the queen and lost within a greater British Empire. The fellow priests whom Cogan admired within his own diocese were all political activists such as Peter O'Reilly, parish priest of Kingscourt, 'conspicuous in every struggle for civil and religious liberty' (ii, 302), and a champion of the tenant farmers; or Patrick Kelly from Kilbeggan in Westmeath, who was then parish priest of Kilskyre. Fr Kelly who was born back in 1797, had championed most of the great patriotic causes of the nineteenth century—Emancipation, Repeal and Tenant Right (ii, 326). He had also exhorted 'the youthful priesthood of the diocese to glory in love of country, and to regard devotion to her cause as a sacred duty'. It was Cogan's prayer that this veteran would live to see 'the independence and prosperity of the land which he loves.' He died not long after Anthony Cogan in 1874.

While Cogan dreamt of a free Ireland taking her place among the 'kingdoms' of the world (ii, 501–2), so too, he viewed Ireland's more immediate past from a different perspective from his bishops—or different, at least, from the perspective revealed in his bishops' public utterances. So, however much Cogan might have agreed with Bishop Plunket's view that Ribbonmen of the eighteenth century had acted beyond the law, and therefore suffered their just deserts under the law, Cogan was much more sympathetic to those activists of his own time who fought back against eviction and land clearance:

> The frequent and cruel exercise of such arbitrary, irresponsible power [on the part of evicting landlords]; the wholesale evictions of the people in the most inclement time of the year; and the hard hearted insensibility of their cries for mercy naturally provoked, on some occasions, terrible retaliation; but on the whole, considering what retribution would have swiftly followed the exterminator had such iniquities been perpetrated against life and property in any other country in the world, we have reason to be grateful to the good God, ... that the cases of 'the wild justice of revenge' have been so few amongst us. (iii, 515)

Cogan's softer line on the local politics of terror contrasts with more forthright statements of his bishop and of some of his fellow priests. John Cantwell took an uncompromising line in his Lenten pastoral for 1858: 'We have learned with the deepest sorrow that in a few districts symptoms have appeared of revival of the abominable system of Ribbonism, which we had hoped to be extinct within the diocese.' The bishop exhorted his clergy 'to denounce the criminal folly of those who become members of that or any other secret society' (*Tablet*, 27 February 1858, p. 137). In the previous year, Fr R. Mullen had held a political meeting in his chapel yard at Sonna in Westmeath, carrying out the mandate of his bishop to advise his parishioners on voting strategy in the forthcoming election. After fulminating against drunken behaviour at the polls, the priest went on: 'You will also be careful to avoid uniting or identifying yourselves with Secret Societies. From the experience of the last election

I have just grounds to apprehend that the same parties will have recourse to the same disgraceful means—namely to employ all the Ribbonmen, drunkards, and profligate characters of the county to secure a seat in parliament' (ibid., 21 March 1857, p. 188). Cogan was too much a man of the people to come down so heavily on the side of law and order—a side which he perceived also to be badly flawed.

Cogan's hatred of what he described as 'the crowbar brigade'—thugs employed by some landlords to bring about evictions—was so deep-seated that he may have had painful family memories of injustice suffered at their hands. During Anthony Cogan's early childhood, Slane along with Kells and some other areas in north Meath were the scene of sustained and serious agrarian and sectarian violence from 1828 to 1835 (D. Mooney, *RnM* viii (1988–89), 102–28). Public order had deteriorated to such a level that extra police and troops were drafted into the area. The reasons for the unrest were many. The transition from tillage to cattle grazing combined with the consolidation of small farms to depress the status of many tenant farmers to that of farm labourers, while the excess of labourers was in turn exacerbated by the arrival of outside labourers driven into Meath from other regions in search of work. Eviction, which continued to be a fact of life in Meath from the 1820s until twenty years after the Famine, went along with consolidation and drove homeless families onto neighbouring estates and into nearby towns. The whole process of ejection of tenants who failed to pay their rising rents inflamed public opinion and added a political dimension to what was initially an economic crisis. A final and fatal sectarian element in the conflict was added by the re-emergence of the forcible collection of tithes on an already impoverished peasantry. And so, landlord was seen to be pitted against tenant and farm labourer, while inevitably, the tithes question was perceived as a conflict between Protestant and Catholic. A war was also being waged within peasant society itself against those tenant farmers who paid tithes or who co-operated with the establishment in taking over land from evicted tenants, or against labourers who continued to work for blacklisted proprietors. To crown all of these woes—which put Meath at the top of the league in Leinster for agrarian and community violence—poor potato harvests brought cholera and the first dreadful premonition of famine. Slane was a violent place when Anthony Cogan grew up there. Blacksmiths were reported to be making pikes to arm the local peasantry, and calls went out for police and military protection. Seven thousand people assembled in

Rushwee near Slane to protest against tithes in 1832—the second largest rally in the county—and those who collaborated with the authorities in the recovery of tithes were threatened with boycott and violence. Protestants in Slane were attacked and beaten, and even those who associated with Protestants had their houses attacked. At nearby Rathkenny in the same year, another crowd of 7000 who had assembled for the pattern or local pilgrimage, were sworn in by the dreaded Ribbonmen. In the following year, the resident gentry in the Barony of Lower Slane had been so intimidated that not one of them was willing to become a Commissioner of the Peace. Lower Slane and Morgallion even produced a whole new secret society in 1833—the Whitefeet—which joined the ranks of the Ribbonmen, Carders and Captain Rock.

We must interpret Anthony Cogan's impassioned outbursts against eviction and other injustices, against the background of his personal experience of the violent unrest in Meath all through his life. Endless reports of assassination, attempted assassination and violent assaults and outrages against property, often conceal the root causes of such outrages—social injustice, indifference to changing

30 'Forging pikes - a recent scene in Ireland' from *Illustrated London News* 5 Aug. 1848. Many of the pike-heads surviving among north Meath families to this day may date from the unrest of the early and middle nineteenth century, as much as from 1798. Pikes were being made in Slane (when Anthony Cogan was a child there) to arm local peasants in 1830. The fact that London readers were treated to this somewhat embroidered image of contemporary Irish sedition sharply contradicts the view that social unrest in Ireland was no greater than in parts of provincial England.

31 Eviction scene from the *Illustrated London News* 16 December 1848. According to Bishop Nulty, close on 30,000 homes were levelled in the diocese of Meath in the period 1843-71. The scene shown here is full of Victorian melodrama, but Nulty's testimony bears out the injustice and horror of evictions which were still taking place in the 1860s: 'The speechless agony of men, the piteous wailings of women, the terror and consternation of children, as their houses are pulled down, their homes demolished, and themselves set adrift on the world – all contribute to make up a horrible scene that ... can never be forgotten throughout the length and breadth of the locality in which it occurred.' (Flynn, *Ríocht na Midhe*, vii (1984), 21). From 1864 onwards, Anthony Cogan was championing the cause of oppressed peasants and the dispossessed.

conditions, poverty and destitution, and a high-handed treatment of a hard-pressed and starving peasantry on the part of many Meath landlords. Most serious of all was the invariable resort of the authorities to coercion and sometimes brutality by way of remedy for all social unrest, and the damning evidence of police chiefs to the effect that magistrates failed to 'act without any party feeling and with even-handed justice' (Mooney, ibid., p.105). Significantly, Cogan justified his sympathy for those who resorted to violence and who took the law into their own hands, on the grounds that the laws which they fought back against were themselves iniquitous. Against the ruling landlord class, he railed:

These sapient legislators made laws, for their own amusement, to protect the birds of the air, the beasts of the field, the fish that swarmed up our rivers, but there was no law to protect the homes of the Irish farmer or the Irish peasant from the crowbar brigade—the tenants of Ireland were to live by sufferance, at the whim or caprice of the taskmaster, on that land which God gave their forefathers, and which he manifestly intended for themselves. Where then were the laws while a few men were depopulating the island? (iii, 514)

Cogan was writing only a few years after that time in 1848 when a contemporary correspondent in the *Illustrated London News* (22 December 1849, p. 404) was claiming that 71,130 holdings and nearly as many houses had been cleared away in Ireland during that year. He cited 16,000 people who had been dispossessed in the Union of Kilrush in the first five months of 1848 alone. That same correspondent put the total number of holdings (of between 1 and 5 acres in extent) which had been destroyed in Ireland as a whole at 254,000 between 1841 and 1848. Cogan set the figure at 300,000 (iii, 513). Bishop Thomas Nulty of Meath was claiming (in 1871) that during the period 1843 to 1871 a total of 200,054 people had 'disappeared' from his diocese and 29,461 houses in Meath, Westmeath and Offaly had 'disappeared from the face of the earth' (G. Flynn, *RnM* vii (1984), 14–28). Cogan was also writing at a time when agrarian violence, involving tenant farmers and farm labourers was again raging within the Meath diocese in the aftermath of the Famine. His notion of smallholders and tenant farmers having a God-given right to occupy the soil echoed that of Bishop Nulty, who was himself the son of a tenant farmer from Oldcastle. Nulty was a champion of the peasant cause in the face of land clearance and eviction in his diocese, and he placed the blame squarely on the landlords whom he accused of 'restoring nothing to the soil; they consume its whole produce, minus the potatoes strictly necessary to keep the inhabitants from dying of famine' (Flynn, op. cit.). Land clearance had been achieved by landlords, in the wake of famine and cholera, by offering tenants financial inducements to emigrate to North America. Assistance was usually only granted on condition that entire households abandoned their cottages and that such dwellings were levelled to the ground once they had been vacated. The precise statistics relating to evictions and the numbers of dispossessed tenantry will remain open for debate, not to say manipulation, on the part of historians anxious to wring a novel

68

interpretation from the sources for nineteeth-century Irish history. But even if we were to accept that the figures offered here were greatly exaggerated, it would still be difficult to assess the personal misery and want on the part of hundreds and thousands of victims of an iniquitous system. Their problems did not simply relate to accommodation. They were a people rooted in a Gaelic peasant tradition with ancestral ties in their localities and whose rural culture laid a major emphasis on precise association with place. To be forced off their holdings and separated from community was a kind of cultural death for the victims of eviction, and their material problems were invariably exacerbated by malnutrition and its accompanying diseases. The problems of famine, disease and eviction were inextricably linked, and the immense loss of population through starvation, land clearance and emigration combined to engender a holocaust mentality in the psyche of rural Ireland in the second half of the nineteenth century. From then on, and for many, no retaliation would seem too great against those who were perceived as the exterminator and destroyer. Anthony Cogan's prose smoulders with the resentment of a generation numbed by atrocities effected through mass social deprivation.

It could be argued that Anthony Cogan had a personal interest in furthering the downfall of the great landlords, since his own family benefited from judicious land purchases in the Slane area. His father, Thomas, built up such a successful business in his Slane bakery that his widow was able to buy a substantial house and farm at Shalvanstown for her son Charles, and to marry her daughters off to strong farmers such as the Mullens or the Blakes of Ladyrath. In addition to their priestly son, Anthony, Thomas and Anne Cogan produced Thomas, an architect, and Francis, who died as a surgeon-major in the British army. This was precisely the type of rapidly aspiring Catholic middle-class family which had all to gain from land purchase at the expense of the greater landlords in Meath. It was in the interest of such families to espouse the cause of moderate nationalism and to weaken the status quo sufficiently to benefit from it, without endangering its survival altogether. While these things need pointing out, it also has to be said that Cogan's political utterances can scarcely have been inspired by self interest. Prior to 1863 or '64, Anthony Cogan's name is not found among the formidable lists of Meath priests who appeared on tenant right and related platforms throughout the diocese. Cogan was then fully occupied in the late Fifties and early Sixties organising the Young

32 The tenth-century Cross of Kells, or Market Cross, said to have been re-restored by Dean Swift and later to have been used as a gallows for the hanging of insurgents after the Great Rebellion of 1798. Kells witnessed much political and sectarian unrest during Anthony Cogan's lifetime.

Men's Society in Navan and writing the first volume of his *Diocese of Meath*. The first volume was published in 1862, and although the Second did not appear until 1867, Cogan announced (*Drogheda Argus*, 12 September 1863, p. 3) that it was expected in 1864. So, by 1864 he had found a breathing space from historical writing, and it was in that year that we find him joining the political battle on the side of the dispossessed for the first time.

Irish politics in the post-Repeal years had centred on the notion of an independent party of opposition in which major constitutional issues—such as an independent legislature for Ireland—combined with more grass-roots and more pressing matters relating to land tenure, and religious and educational issues. As far as people living in rural areas were concerned, the Irish Tenant League (founded in 1850) must have provided the basic forum for discussion of pressing local issues—apart from more clandestine meetings of Ribbonmen and later of Fenians. The complicated sequence of splits within the independent party may fairly be summarised as a divide between those who sought to influence British government policy from within, and other more 'patriotic' or more nationalist elements who pursued a tougher line especially on tenant rights. This divide in the ranks of the independents, which went back to 1852, was reflected among the Catholic hierarchy in the friction between

Archbishop Paul Cullen of Dublin and his opposite number, John MacHale of Tuam. While Cullen and a majority of bishops backed the pro-government liberal administration, and represented what might be described as the Catholic middle class and commercial establishment in Ireland, MacHale was firmly in the camp of committed Tenant League priests who followed Frederick Lucas (died 1855) and G.H. Moore in the campaign for Tenant Right. In clerical circles, the MacHale camp preferred political agitation through Tenant Right platforms and political rallies, to Cullen's more subtle diplomacy. Cogan had sent MacHale copies of the first and second volumes of his *Diocese of Meath*, and that 'great archbishop of the West' had written the most fulsome praise of Cogan's works in published letters in 1863 and 1867 (Appendices 2 and 6). Further splits in the independent opposition in 1859 led on to Cullen's participation in the founding of the National Association of Ireland in Dublin in December 1864. This movement was an attempt to revitalise a party of independent opposition once more, and the fact that MacHale and G.H. Moore held aloof from it seems to have had more to do with personalities and approach than with any inherent dispute over ideology. The Association was committed to a programme of agrarian reform, church disestablishment and Catholic education. But although it continued into the 1870s, the National Association failed to sustain enthusiastic or widespread support. Bishop Thomas Nulty of Meath withdrew his clergy from the Association as early as November 1865 and formed the Meath Tenant Right Society at that time. By the mid Sixties, therefore, Anthony Cogan found himself in a political *milieu* of bishop and priests who were lined up on the side of John MacHale and that enthusiastic clerical faction which must have merged imperceptibly with former Young Irelanders and also—on the fringes at least— with Fenian sympathizers. Allegiances altered, too, as circumstances changed. So, while Fenianism had initially been attacked especially by Cullen's party, when it was perceived as a real threat to social stability, after its failure Fenianism took on the glamour which invariably accrues to victims of oppression in Irish political life. By 1864, Anthony Cogan's public stand against evictions in Meath coincided with Bishop Nulty's increasingly strong line against injustices in landlord-tenant relationships. Thomas Nulty, too, had his own personal memories of the miseries attributable to Irish landlordism. As a recently ordained priest back in 1848, he had witnessed the eviction of 700 people in south Cavan, a quarter of

33 Old Gateway at Fore, Co. Westmeath *c*.1870. Cogan was especially taken by the beauty of this monastic complex, set beside the Ben of Fore and the islands of Lough Lene.

whom, he claimed, had died within three years, and many others of whom had ended their days in the workhouse (Flynn, *RnM* VII (1984), p. 26, n. 6)

The issue which first brought Anthony Cogan onto the political stage did not involve tenant farmers or farm labourers, with whom, because of his rural origins, he had a natural sympathy. It was instead a pastoral matter, relating to the Navan slums—and one whose roots went back to before the Famine. In the height of the Famine crisis, in 1848, the Duke of Bedford, who was one of the four major landowners in Navan, ordered the clearance of slum properties on his land at Brews Hill, Chapel Lane and Bakery Lane (Connell, *RnM*, VI, iii (1977), 45–6). Compensation was offered to the dispossessed to facilitate emigration or rehousing, but since most of the families were existing on Poor Law rates, destitution or emigration was their inevitable lot. From the point of view of town planning and social control, the forcible evictions had much to recommend them. Slum areas were to be provided with a new and improved housing stock, and troublesome areas in the town would be cleared of what was percieved by the authorities as a crime-ridden population. The cost in personal suffering was another matter. The cause of the dispossessed was taken up back in 1848 by the then parish priest of Navan, Eugene O'Reilly, who argued that

the victims of forcible slum-clearance had obeyed the gospel pre-
cepts by taking in the dispossessed, and he blamed the consequent
overcrowding—not on the slum-dwellers, but on the landlord
guardians. Sixteen years later, there was virtually a re-run of the
same crisis in Brews Hill, and it was Anthony Cogan who now took
up the struggle on the part of the poor. Yet another sector of Brews
Hill was owned by Lord de Ros 'a gentleman' according to Cogan
'who seems to take little interest in the welfare of his tenantry, and
who has as agent, a worthy exponent in this respect, of his master's
neglected duties—a Mr Graham Johnston' (*Drogheda Argus*, 7 May
1864, p. 5). De Ros's agent had effected a slum clearance in Brews
Hill on 15 April 1864 'in the presence of the sheriff and a large body
of the police, by the unroofing of fourteen houses, the eviction of
fourteen families, and the consequent flinging on the roadside, and
scattering houseless and homeless, sixty-four of Her Majesty's
subjects.' While rural evictions might have fewer observers, this
high-profile spectacle of the forcible demolition of a sizeable part of
a street in Navan as late as 1864, points to the audacious and
ruthless lengths to which landlords were prepared to push the
confrontation in the battle over rents and tenancies.

The Brews Hill evictions made up a classic land war scenario,
with 'the crow-bar brigade' presided over by sheriff and constabu-
lary, lined up against the defiant masses, and with the church bells
of Navan rung to summon the populace to stand out against
tyranny. It was the stuff of which the mythology of the oppressor at
his most barbarous was made—only in this case the melodrama was
all too real. Anthony Cogan, fresh from his historical labours on his
second volume covering the eighteenth century in Meath, and
burning with all the indignation which those researches had
aroused, waded into the fray by publishing an open letter in the
Drogheda Argus (ibid.) addressed to Corbally and McEvoy, the two
Members of Parliament for Meath. Cogan's attack on the establishment was as carefully reasoned as it was inflammatory (Appendix 5).
He reminded the Members for Meath how he had been 'one of their
consistent supporters' and also reminded them of their obligations
to their constitutents. If the outrage perpetrated in Navan in April
1864 had taken place in the Papal States, it would have been used,
Cogan argued, as clear evidence for the discrediting of a Catholic
regime. He confronted the old argument that the demolished
dwellings had harboured the less virtuous element in the Navan
population with his characteristic logic and scorn:

The people were not good (how very virtuous some landlords and agents are!), and therefore their houses must be levelled! If these rules were applied to the lordly and rich, how many of their habitations would remain standing? Who constituted Lord de Ros or Mr Johnston judge or censor over the morals of the people? If family history or pedigree were pried into, would more virtues be discovered and less vices be conspicuous in the exterminators than in the evicted poor of Brewshill-street? If there have been evil-doers amongst us in '64, is the law not able to vindicate itself? Are the police unable or unwilling to discharge their duty? Are the magistrates leagued to connive at the violation of the law?

Cogan confronted the Members for Meath with what amounted to an ultimatum, declaring it

better that Ireland were disfranchised than be thus misrepresented. If these men were seriously anxious for the welfare of their country—if the public good and not personal favour, be the object of their ambition, then why not meet together, wait on the Premier, present their ultimatum for a Tenant compensation Bill—for employing the poor labourers in bringing to cultivation the waste lands of Ireland numbering upwards of six millions of acres, and for other remedial measures; and if such were refused, then separate from the so-called Liberal Party, wield the consitutional weapon placed in their hand by their confiding countrymen, and drive from office a government whose settled policy seems to be, the total disregard for Irish grievances, the extermination of the Irish people, and the conversion of our country into a grass-walk?

M. E. Corbally cannot have been pleased with Cogan's outburst, for although he was sympathetic to the views of those who believed Ireland was being treated badly, there were limits to both his liberalism and his patriotism. He had consistently held out against O'Connell's Repeal movement (Connell, *RnM*, VII, ii (1982–3), 103–4), and while locally, his family might behave as benign Catholic landlords helping to endow a church and school, he had much to lose from excessive Irish nationalism. Corbally was a great landowner who spent his days between his splendid home at Corbalton Hall in Skryne, and prolonged excursions to the south of

France. It was natural for such a man to maintain the status quo. A letter written by Fr Patrick Ferrall of Beauparc, appearing in the *Tablet* (11 April 1857, p. 233) insisted that Corbally was orthodox on Tenant League and that he was a supporter of George H. Moore. But the piece clearly reveals there was doubt about where precisely Corbally stood in relation to political struggles over land issues. Corbally's colleague, Edward McEvoy of Tobertinan, ran advertisments in the local and national press *to the Independent Electors of Meath* pledging his commitment to the Independent Irish Party in the General Election of 1857.

Cogan began to fight the cause of 'the defenceless poor' 'actuated by no feelings save those of humanity' in 1864 (*Drogheda Argus*, loc. cit.). He seems to have been active in that cause from then until his death—as well as completing the third volume of his *Diocese of Meath* and supervising the Young Men's Society. Cogan addressed a monster meeting held to express sympathy with the tenant farmers at Mullagh in south Meath on 29 June 1871. The landlord right of Mullagh had recently reverted to a Mr Keena, a Catholic gentleman, who had gone back on his assurances not to evict tenants (Appendix 7). Fifty cars, carrying leading Catholic and Protestant figures from town and country progessed from Navan via Kilmessan, Kiltale and Moynalvy and on to Mullagh to join the protest rally. Anthony Cogan headed his contingent of Navan Young Men's Society whose band played to the meeting. Cogan, by mobilising his Young Men's Society, had now combined his social programme with political protest. The priests who supported the farmers in their struggle against Keena were named as Fr Duncan, the vicar general of the diocese, Dr Nicholls, as well as Frs Tormey, Behan and Dean Cogan.

The crowd which Cogan harangued at Mullagh was estimated at 10,000—a great mass of humanity who had trudged from as far afield as Drogheda, Navan, Kells, Trim, Athboy and Summerhill. Many had walked as far as twenty miles, and the patriotic reporter made much of the empty aspect of the south Meath landscape denuded of people by the graziers of Meath: 'one passes for miles and miles through a once thickly populated district, now one vast stretch of pastureland, unbroken by ridge or furrow of cultivation— miles of solitude undisturbed by human voice, save the herdsman's shout. ... The landscape was beautiful; but something told him [the beholder] its richness and beauty were like the luxuriant verdure of a cemetery. The desolator had been there. ... The people who once

34 The face of Hunger: Ireland 1849. 'Bridget O'Donnell and her children' (*Illustrated London News*, 22 Dec. 1849, p. 404). The subjects of this drawing came from the Union of Kilrush, but similar scenes of starving and distressed humanity could be witnessed in and about the workhouses of Meath, during, and long after, the worst of the Famine. The *London News*, although sympathetic, devoted little space to Ireland's tragedy and did not let it detract from its preoccupation with parading the baubles of empire. Its Christmas Supplement accompanying this very issue carried a picture of well-fed London middle class children tucking into an outsize Christmas pudding around an opulent Christmas dinner-table.

dwelt upon these fertile fields were gone—gone forever' (*Drogheda Argus*, 15 July, 1871). The notion of a demographic cemetery brought about by a sinister 'desolator' was not peculiar to the heated rhetoric of the *Drogheda Argus*. Back in 1849, the correspondent for the *Illustrated London News* (22 December 1849, p. 404) wrote of walking through a famine landscape as in a land of the living dead, and that same source (16 December 1848, p. 380) quotes an extract from the *Tipperary Vindicator* referring to the eviction policy in that county which turned the landscape into a 'Great Desert'. London reporters then viewed famine and eviction as two sides of the same coin, and by citing statements which implied an establishment conspiracy to rid the land of its 'mere Irish' population (ibid.), they clearly gave credence to that view. 'We do not exaggerate; the state of things is absolutely fearful; a demon, with all the vindictive passions by which alone a demon could be influenced, is let loose and menaces destruction. ... The torpor and apathy which have seized on the masses are only surpassed by the atrocities perpetrated by those who set the dictates of humanity and the decrees of the Almighty at equal defiance.' The situation in 1871 had moved on from that of over twenty years before. The 'torpor and apathy' had given way to political agitation and violence that would soon lead to

land war and eventually to yet another cycle of revolution. But if the
worst of famine and disease were past, their memory was seared on
the souls of the people, and the struggle for tenant rights—also an
issue in famine times—was becoming ever more intense. The link
with past grievances was present at Mullagh as elsewhere:

> The sentiments so forcibly and courageously enunciated last
> week by ... the erudite and patriotic historian of Meath, Dean
> Cogan, were no opinions of yesterday. They were the creed of
> Meath—priests and people—in 1852 as they are in 1871.
> Whoever changed, whoever fell away, whoever has need to
> adjust their position now, Meath stands just where it always
> did, upon the great question of the land. And the other and
> the greater question still—the question that includes , and
> comprises all other political issues, great and small, for us
> Irishmen—the question of our National Emancipation—found

35 Deserted village in the wake of famine and eviction. The Drawing is that of
Moveen in the Union of Kilrush (*Illustrated London News*, 22 Dec. 1849, p. 405).
Meath, Westmeath and Offaly were no less effected by land clearances. Anthony
Cogan protested against the forcible demolition of 14 houses in Navan over the
heads of their tenants in April 1864, and he led a protest against threatened mass
evictions in Mullagh, only 15 miles from the centre of Dublin, as late as 1871. The
graziers' greed for pasture in the richer lands of Meath, produced conditions of
even greater hardship for the smaller tenant farmers and farm labourers of that
county than elsewhere.

noble advocacy also on the Mullagh platform' (*Drogheda Argus*, loc. cit.).

There can be little doubt that Cogan, the antiquary and historian, found an outlet for his anger over the political and social conditions prevailing in his own time, by indulging in violent anecdotes in his *Diocese of Meath*. These tales—mostly from the eighteenth century—tell us much about Cogan's own resentment over agrarian and social unrest generally, in mid nineteenth-century Meath. While many display folkloric characteristics, it is the element of heroic violence which Anthony Cogan narrates with such enthusiasm that reveals something of his own attitudes to contemporary issues. He describes how two Kells priest-hunters intent on the capture of Fr Myles O'Reilly in Kilskyre were dealt with by members of this priest's congregation:

> Two of the most active of the congregation left the chapel during Mass, observed the two Kells priest hunters approach, each armed. The peasants selected each his man, felled him, knocked out his brains, and then returned to Mass. After this Father O'Reilly was left unmolested. (ii, 324)

A similar tale is told concerning an incident in Dunshaughlin (ii, 354–5) in which 'a stout, athletic peasant' met a member of a bigoted family of 'landlords, magistrates, [and] priest-hunters' who proceeded to trash the lad with his riding whip because he was a 'damned papist'. The harassed peasant fought back:

> Maddened at the savage, unmerited treatment to which he was subjected, he let loose the formidable arm of the flail [he was on his way to thrash a neighbour's corn], and having wound it once or twice round his head, he brought it to bear with terrible velocity on the person of C—ke. In a moment he unhorsed him and laid him prostrate on the road. Again the flail was in motion, and again and again it descended on C—ke, until he was almost thrashed into a mummy.

Cogan's violent anecdote of the patriotic lad goaded into flailing the bigoted oppressor, echoes the imagery of a poem by John Boyle O'Reilly which he wrote on *The Priests of Ireland* on hearing that the clergy of Cloyne had declared in favour of Home Rule in September 1873:

36 Portloman old church and graveyard, Co. Westmeath c.1870.

Well they judged their time—they waited till the bar was
   glowing white,
Then they swung it on the anvil, striking down with earnest
   might.
And the burning sparks that scatter lose no luster on their
   way,
Till five million hearts in Ireland and ten millions far away
Feel the first good blow, and answer; and they will not rest
   with one:
Now the first is struck, the anvil shows the labor well begun;
Swing them in with lusty sinew and the work will soon be
   done!

(*Boyle O'Reilly*, ed. Roche, p. 474)

Cogan's yarn—for it is probably little more than that—had its
interesting sequel. The Dunshaughlin hero with his flail, who was
put on trial for his life, was let off through the good offices of a
Protestant gentleman in Dunshaughlin, named Webb, 'on the
ground of extreme provocation'. Cogan was always at pains to
distinguish between 'patriotic' and 'unpatriotic' Protestants, but
stories such as these coming from the pen of a Catholic priest,
underline the violence of the political and social climate in mid
nineteenth-century Meath. The local or tribal violence of the sort

which Cogan narrates in his anecdotes of the eighteenth century was alive and flourishing in Meath in his own day. At a second meeting on Tara in May 1845, Daniel O'Connell in an unusually direct reference to local issues launched into a tirade against an outbreak of Ribbonism in nearby Skryne (P. Connell, *RnM* vii (1982–83), 90–113). It was an indication that O'Connell felt his constitutional approach to Repeal was at risk if and when local terror groups were allowed to grow in the community at large. There was clearly a connection between local violence involving labourers or tenant farmers hitting out against oppressive landlords, and greater and wider issues involving revolutionary organisations bent on the violent separation of Ireland from the British crown. Although the connection between a violent approach to local issues and a resort to violence in national politics may not have been direct, nevertheless national movements depended on grass-roots activity for their support, and those who were capable of enforcing their will on local land politics through assassination, were clearly ideal candidates for recruitment for more ambitious enterprises. When attempted assassinations and attacks on landlords and their agents had reached crisis proportions in the midlands between 1869 and 1871, the authorities responded with the Peace Preservation Act in 1870 and the Westmeath Act in the following year. The latter allowed for the imprisonment of Ribbon suspects without trial. A magistrate testifying before the Westmeath Committee in 1871 claimed that 'Fenianism had become grafted on Ribbonism . . . and that had changed its character very much' (Flynn, op. cit., p. 16).

Anthony Cogan was probably typical of a whole generation of middle-class Irishmen in the middle of the century who longed for a free and better Ireland but who were confused as to how best this could be accomplished, and whose families were anxious to capitalise on the gains already made by Emancipation without rocking the political boat too violently. But Cogan's romantic views and his very personal type of fervent patriotism reveal ideas which were later to be taken up by more determined nationalists at the end of the century. Cogan's notion that the Croppies Grave on Tara provided a focus for people to contemplate the plight of Ireland, clearly implied that the grave of those Men of '98 challenged later generations to keep faith with the patriotic dead. O'Connell, too, had become for Cogan 'the mighty dead', and Cogan, as a young student, had journeyed to the Liberator's funeral as though he were on a pilgrimage. We shall see how Cogan declared it to be 'the ambition of my life to revive the memory of our saints and scholars—of our martyrs and confessors ... of those who laboured for us in the senate and those who shed their blood for us in the field.' This idea of the potency of dead patriots and in particular the potency of the graves of patriots, was shared in full by Cogan's neighbour, John Boyle O'Reilly. Some six years after Cogan's death (in 1878) O'Reilly wrote *The Patriot's Grave* to mark the Emmet Centennial in Boston. Here the notion of martyrdom and the sacrifice of the patriot's manhood to further Ireland's cause by inspiring future generations to strive for freedom, is clearly developed:

> But sweeter than all, for embracing all, is the young life's
> peerless price —
> The young heart laid on the altar, as a nation's sacrifice.
>
> . . .
>
> This was the heart he offered—the upright life he gave —
> This is the silent sermon of the patriot's nameless grave.
> Shrine of a nation's honour—stone left blank for a name
> Light on the dark horizon to guide us clear of shame.
>
> . . .
>
> Such is the will of the martyr—the burden we still must
> bear;
> But even from death he reaches the legacy to share.
> (*Boyle O'Reilly*, ed. Roche, p. 552)

Like Cogan, too, John Boyle O'Reilly viewed the struggle for civil and religious liberties in terms of cycles of latter-day heroes, rather like the catalogue of heroic cycles from early Irish literature:

> With one deep breath began the land's progression:
> On every field the seeds of freedom fell:
> Burke, Grattan, Flood, and Curran in the session —
> Fitzgerald, Sheares, and Emmet in the cell. (ibid., p. 551)

On 1 August 1915, Patrick Pearse delivered his oration at the graveside of the veteran Fenian, O'Donovan Rossa, in Glasnevin cemetery. O'Donovan Rossa had himself shouldered the coffin of John Boyle O'Reilly in Boston back in 1890. Pearse took up the imagery of Boyle O'Reilly's 'seeds of freedom': 'Our foes ... cannot undo the miracles of God who ripens in the hearts of young men the seeds sown by the young men of a former generation. And the seeds sown by the young men of '65 and '67 are coming to their miraculous ripening to-day.' Cogan would have recognised his own sentiments relating to the Croppies' Grave back in 1843 in Pearse's now legendary ending to his peroration:

> The fools, the fools, the fools!—they have left us our Fenian dead, and while Ireland holds these graves, Ireland unfree shall never be at peace. (Dudley Edwards, *Pearse*, pp 236–7)

All this, it can be argued, was a far cry from Anthony Cogan's indignant fulminating against rack-renting and evicting landlords half a century before. But men of Cogan's era are too easily catagorised into constitutionalists and revolutionaries, or—more crudely—Home Rulers and Fenians. The distinction between the two categories owes more to the hindsight of historians writing in the later twentieth century than to men of the 1860s. Fenians and nationalists of every hue shared the same hope of separating Ireland in some way from the British parliament. The degree of separation and extremes to which people were prepared to go to achieve that aim not only varied from person to person, but it must have varied throughout the lifetimes of individuals depending on how they perceived political issues at any given time. It is clear from an examination of Cogan's writings that his sense of despair in finding a political solution for Ireland's ills was increasing throughout the Sixties. Unlike the Dublin Anglo-Irish and middle-class Catholic intelligentsia, Cogan was a man who encountered squalor in his ministry as a priest and who cared for young men, who slept in overcrowded hovels without heat or light, and whose families were sometimes turned out on the streets to starve. Anthony Cogan, writing as the champion of the evicted in Navan in 1864 responded to what he percieved then as an arbitrary resort to violence and tyranny on the part of the establishment. He issued a prophetic warning to the Members of Parliament for Meath, and through them to distant Westminster:

> The state of Ireland at this moment is calculated to alarm the statesman and the philanthopist. Our artizans are idle, our labourers are unemployed, the cream of the population is flying abroad, and the remnant at home are awaiting remittances from their exiled friends to take them away from the land of their birth. All hope or confidence in parliamentary

37 Kilcolman, Co. Offaly.

legislation seems to have left the hearts of the people. They complain ... that parliament is occupied with foreign questions, such as the bombardment of Sonderborg, or again, in enacting new laws for the protection of game, and all this time her Majesty's subjects are allowed to perish, their homes are levelled and their petitions for justice disregarded. What wonder if in such a state of things, the masses of the population were disloyal and longing for a change? Loyalty has its correlative duties. No man however humble should be tempted beyond his strength... Let me suppose that the homes of the gentry were liable to be assaulted and demolished by the people, so that the law was so constituted that the police were obliged to look on as spectators (I will not say assistants) would the gentry be loyal? Let me suppose that they appealed repeatedly to parliament for legal protection, and that their claims were derided ... how long would the gentry remain loyal ? Ah, just so long as would suit their convenience. Let the landlords do to others as they would wish to be dealt with. Let them remember that many of themselves are high in this world inheriting abbey lands and Catholic church property because their forefathers bartered their faith for the flesh-pots of Egypt, and that many luxuriate in titles purchased by treason to Ireland in the unholy sale (at the Union) of the independence of our country. Let them bear in mind that there is instability in all human affairs; that revolutions are often followed by revolutions; that what was won with the sword can be lost by the sword. (*Drogheda Argus*, 7 May 1864, p. 5)

Cogan, in this address, drove home the point that what one party might claim as a constitutional right, another might see as being the exercise of violence, and he not only allowed for the strong possibility of revolution in Ireland, but by implication condoned it. Cogan the historian, was reminding the ascendancy that what was won by the sword at the Boyne in 1690, could all be lost in further revolution by the disaffected Irish masses. As he wrote, Ireland was at a crucial turning point in her development, and Cogan saw that the initiative lay with the British parliament as to whether the future for Ireland would lie in peace or war. He was carried even further by his vision into the future, from his experience as a regular visitor and preacher in Liverpool:

The people who, under just laws, would have been the bulwark of the empire, fly from Ireland with an intense burning hatred of England. The enemies of Great Britian are thus multiplied over the world. . . . Whoever reads the signs of the times, or is acquainted with the feelings of our emigrants, can easily conclude that the exiled Irish will form the vanguard of any assault on British supremacy. The retribution, the Nemesis, may be nearer hand than is anticipated; and it may be found when too late, that the right arm is withered, that the old nursery is uprooted, that the policy of extermination had overreached itself, that it was calamitous and suicidal (*Drogheda Argus*, 7 May, 1864, p. 5).

In the year before Cogan had written this, John Boyle O'Reilly had returned from Lancashire to infiltrate the British Army in Ireland with a view to subverting the Irish ranks within it.

IV

LEGACY OF RELIGIOUS STRIFE

You, whose hearts were sore with looking on your country's
  quick decay
You, whose chapel seats were empty and your people fled away
You, who marked amid the fields where once the peasant's cabin
  stood
You, who saw your kith and kindred swell the emigration flood
You, the *Soggath* in the famine, and the helper in the frost —
You, whose shadow was a sunshine when all other hope was lost.
  The Priests of Ireland (Boyle O'Reilly, ed. Roche, p. 473)

The iron had entered into the soul of a Catholic nation reduced
by poverty and disease and deprived of its dignity. Cogan's
great harvest of gossip and stories which reflect the preoccupations
of his clerical colleagues in the 1860s contains, as we might expect,
anecdotes about relentless priest-hunters and sectarian extortionists,
milking a people for tithes and for marriage fees and other church
dues. Cogan's tale that the bell for the Catholic chapel at Delvin
(once 'suspended from an old tree, on top of the moat of Delvin')
could only be rung to summon the flock to Mass, while the
Protestant bell announced Catholic deaths and funerals so that the
sexton might collect his fees (ii, 414) would seem too preposterous
to believe, were it not that he tells us that 'such humbug and fraud'
was only ended by Fr Birmingham who was a parish priest of Turin
(Co. Westmeath) when Cogan was writing. Whether the story as
reported is true or false is less important than the fact it was
accepted as true by Cogan, and certainly by his readers. Cogan's
wealth of tales such as this puts us in mind of Greek memories of
religious persecution under the Turks, with all the tribal animosities
such stories hold in the eastern Mediterranean to this day. Cogan's
work also contains stories of hated proselytisers operating all over

38 King John's Castle, Trim, *c.* 1849.

the diocese (ii, 382–3)—even a tale of 'shameless attempts made to proselytise the unfortunate prisoners in Trim gaol'. This pressure, put on Trim prisoners (*c.*1820), was resisted by the Catholic chaplain, Fr John Kearney, at some personal risk (ii, 528). Fr N. McEvoy, the administrator of Kells, writing in 1843, suggested that Catholic children 'separated as they are by the workhouse system from their parents' would fall a prey to proselytisers in the hated poorhouses (P. Connell *RnM* vii (1984), 47). Whatever evangelical motives may have lain behind this missionary zeal, proselytising was percieved by the Catholic community as an insult added to the injuries sustained throughout the eighteenth century. Rightly or wrongly, it was seen as an underhand and despicable attempt to rob people of a faith which they had held onto in the more brutally open and bloody conflicts for souls, in the seventeenth century. Catholic missionaries had of course established themselves in other corners of the world with a view to winning souls from the jaws of paganism, as reports on such organisations as *The Society of the Holy Childhood of Our Lord for the Redemption of Chinese Infants* in *The Tablet* in the 1850s testify (*Tablet* 10 March 1855, p. 149). In Ireland the religious question was inextricably linked with politics, and efforts to proselytise were seen as synonymous with attempts at political domination. So, proselytising in Ireland challenged established frontiers between the two religions and the two nations, and had a detrimental effect on long-established principles of co-existence. Peace and

39 The Yellow Steeple (part of St Mary's Abbey) in Trim with the Sheep Gate in the foreground.

40 View of the medieval ruins at Trim from the bridge over the Boyne at Newtown.

harmony had not, of course, always reigned before the proselytiser crossed established boundaries between Prostestant and Catholic communities of Meath. In Cogan's time and before, Orangemen were established in Meath, and held provocative and hostile processions in Castlepollard (ii, 402) and in other north Meath towns such as Kells. Rumours—most of them groundless—of Orange gangs assembling in Cavan with intent to march against Meath, inflamed sectarian unrest in north Meath towns. During Cogan's early childhood, Catholics and Protestants fought each other on the streets of Kells, although by then the tide of violence was flowing in favour of the Catholic peasantry (D. Mooney, *RnM* viii (1988–89), 102–28). While old-style religious persecution had become a thing of the past, the memory of those none-too-distant days had scarred the very soul of rural Ireland. Cogan, commenting on the priest-hunters and 'petty tyrants' of Meath noted with uncharacteristic but measured detestation: 'Like other such vermin, they have melted away, and the memory of their slime and wickedness has implanted in the hearts of the people a loathing and hatred of their very name' (ii, 341).

Although Protestants and Catholics faced each other across a formidable cultural divide in Meath as elsewhere, it would be wrong to suppose that the religious barrier was insurmountable. Apart from intermarriage between people of the two religions which was forbidden by law before 1792–3, there were Catholics who joined the Protestant faith and Protestants who embraced Catholicism. Anthony Cogan's mother, Anne Sillary, had as we shall see, married a Catholic and had become a Catholic herself. While such people may have been few, some were either socially prominent or exotic in other respects. Cogan mentions, for instance, the Rathkenny branch of the Hussey family—descendants of the baron of Galtrim—'a fine old Catholic family' who 'lost the [Catholic] faith within the last half century' (ii, 371). The Gaelic poets of Meath may seem unlikely material for proselytisers to work on, but they were potential translators of the Scriptures and prayer books which were essential for Protestant missionaries hoping to win souls among the Irish-speaking peasants and farm labourers and their children in the early nineteenth century. One such poet was Peadar Dubh Ó Dálaigh (Dark-haired Peter Daly) from Mountainpole near the Tower of Lloyd outside Kells. At first he wrote against the activities of the Bible Society, but it is thought he became a Protestant and he was certainly acknowledged for his help in translating a book of hymns and psalms for a Bible Society in 1835 (Ó Muirgheasa, *Amhráin na Midhe*, 174–5). The most flamboyant of all converts to Protestantism in Meath was Bishop Thomas Lewis O'Beirne (1748–1823). O'Beirne was the son of a Co. Longford 'humble farmer' (ii, 185) who was educated for the Catholic priesthood, along with his brother, John (or Denis ?), at the Collège des Lombards in Paris. Both boys seemed destined for a conventional career in the Catholic penal-day priesthood. That was true of John, but Thomas became a Protestant, and through a judicious mixture of opportunism and undoubted talent, he climbed high in the Whig establishment in England. He became chaplain and private secretary, first to the Irish viceroy, the Duke of Portland in 1782, and he later (1794) accompanied the Lord Lieutenant Fitzwilliam to Ireland in the same capacity. He was rewarded first with the Protestant bishopric of Ossory, and in December 1798 he was translated to Meath, where he ruled his flock for a quarter of a century. Cogan was understandably fascinated by this daring ecclesiastical turncoat whom he regarded with a mixture of admiration, awe and pity. Typically, Cogan supplies us with a mixture of fact, folklore and gossip on Bishop O'Beirne (ii, 185–7), stating that he received no orders in either the Catholic Church or in the Church of Ireland, and that hence he was known as 'the mitred layman'. It must be said that O'Beirne's early career was surrounded by some mystery. Cogan also tells us that at one point Thomas O'Beirne served as a parson in the same parish in his native diocese (Ardagh and Clonmacnoise) where his brother was parish priest. More plausible is the statement that Bishop O'Beirne was a good friend of his Catholic counterpart in Meath, Bishop Patrick Plunket, and that the friendship between the two men went back to a time in Paris when Plunket had taken pity on O'Beirne who was then a young consumptive clerical student. Cogan paid generous tribute to O'Beirne, who by the severe standards of Cogan's time, had become an apostate: 'Dr O'Beirne was an accomplished scholar, and, both as a speaker and writer, ranked amongst the foremost of his day (ii, 187).'

Because of Anthony Cogan's antiquarian interests, his generous view of the world as a clerical gossip, and his deeply held religious faith, it is often difficult to locate his own precise position in mid nineteenth-century Irish politics. Next to his faith, his abiding love for Ireland's past was paramount, and his interests in contemporary politics led him to use emotional, and at times inflammatory, language which needs to be interpreted with caution. It would be rash to argue that Anthony Cogan was a Fenian or a crypto-Fenian, even if by the time he was writing his third volume of *The Diocese of Meath*, the Fenian Rising of 1867 had already taken its place among the failed rebellions that punctuated the Irish march to nationhood. His writings reflect rather, a climate of disappointed political hopes, and a sense of grievance and loss upon which Fenianism and all later revolutionary activity were to feed. Anthony Cogan was no violent revolutionary—on the contrary his longstanding work as chaplain to the Catholic Young Men's Society would suggest otherwise. But his understanding of Ireland's past was such that he saw an irreconcilable struggle between the ruling landlord and Protestant élite on the one hand, and the great mass of the people on the other. Rightly or wrongly in Cogan's mind, he perceived that an element in the ruling class was bent on the extermination of the common people—'to rob tenants of the fruits of their industry, to level the homes of the people, and to banish the Irish race from their native country' (iii, 515). It is in reading the otherwise scholarly work of a man of Cogan's background, that we realise how much the Penal Laws, the coercion accompanying the Great Rebellion of 1798, the collapse of Repeal, and above all, what was percieved as the callous and self-righteous British approach to the appalling national tragedy accomplished by Famine, had embittered the Irish mind against the British parliament and against British attitudes to Ireland generally. For Cogan the historian, the Irish people were involved in a struggle for the very possession of Ireland, which had begun many centuries before, but whose battle lines had become more firmly drawn after King William's victory on the Boyne in 1690 and the final disasters at Aughrim and Limerick in the following year.

The result of that Protestant victory meant the ruin of those Irish aristocrats, both Anglo-Irish and Gaelic, who had backed the lost Stuart cause, and it spelt the end of all attempts on the part of the Catholic aristocracy in Ireland to organise resistance (constitutional or otherwise) to religious and political persecution. For a century to come, the great mass of the Irish people had been deprived of their traditional leaders and of their religious and civil liberties. The Williamite army had changed the course of Irish history at Old Bridge on the Boyne in 1690, only a few miles downstream from where Anthony Cogan was born. It was left to impovershed poets and writers in Meath, such as Séamus Dall Mac Cuarta to lament the passing of the old order. From then on, Ireland's heroic past was tinged with a tragic interpretation stretching from the field at Aughrim to the Great Rebellion of '98 and on to the Great Famine. But this tragic dimension was underestimated by a seemingly invincible opposition. It produced its own driving forces within society, and what were perceived as past grievances, fuelled the determination of many to keep faith with those generations of Irish dead who had laboured in the cause of religious and political liberties. So, Cogan spoke of those great priests who 'slept' in his Meath churchyards; in referring to O'Connell he proclaimed: 'the spirit of the mighty dead still lives' (iii, 501); and we have seen how the Croppies' Grave on the Hill of Tara fired his imagination with notions of the potency and destiny of the heroic dead of '98.

It was in this interpretation of Irish history that Anthony Cogan's devout religious life coalesced with his political views, and so he lost himself as a scholar in the pursuit of information on the forgotten

41 Monument at Oldbridge on the Boyne commemorating William III's victory over James II in 1690, and standing near the spot where William crossed the river. The foundation stone was laid in 1736. It was blown up by Republicans in 1923 and nothing of it survived. This giant symbol of Protestant ascendancy stood almost 100 feet high on a base over twenty feet square. Its inscription read: 'Sacred to the glorious memory of King William the Third, who, on the 1st of July, 1690, crossed the Boyne near this place to attack James the Second at the head of a Popish army advantageously posted on the south side of it, and did on that day, by a successful battle, secure to us and our posterity our liberty, laws, and religion. In consequence of this action James the Second left this kingdom and fled to France. This memorial of our deliverance was erected in the ninth year of the reign of King George the Second, the first stone being laid by Lionel Sackville, Duke of Dorset, Lord Lieutenant of the Kingdom of Ireland, MDCCXXXVI. This monument was erected by the grateful contributions of several Protestants of Great Britain and Ireland. Reinard duke of Schomberg, in passing the river, died bravely fighting in defence of liberty.'

priests of the Penal Days who had endured the worst rigours of religious persecution after the Williamite victory. Cogan's all-consuming interest in the Catholic past of his native diocese enabled him to square an ideological circle. For, devout priest that he undoubtedly was, Anthony Cogan's Catholicism took first place in his life. In that he was following the example of his bishop John Cantwell, and indeed of his veteran pope, Pius IX, who had endured the most traumatic political upheavals in nationalist Italy, but who protested that his policies struggled to put religious considerations regarding the Catholic Church ahead of mere political objectives. Cogan, by immersing himself in the history of his priestly forebears in Meath, was able to fulfil a spiritual goal as well as come to terms with an emotional need to help the cause of the people of Ireland. As he recalled that momentous day on Tara in his youth, when O'Connell rallied a great sea of humanity to the cause of Repeal, Anthony Cogan described those people whom he had seen on Tara Hill as 'The long-suffering serfs, the hereditary bondsmen, so long ground to the dust under foreign and domestic oppression' (iii, 507). And all that drama was played out before the tomb of the Men of '98 who were 'taking their long lonely sleep, awaiting the sound of the Archangel's trumpet' but who rested also, as Cogan tells us, beneath that Stone of Destiny, 'so ominously and significantly placed' above them. Irish history was punctuated by a sequence of heroic and tragic events, each one of which led on to the next, in a progession where the living kept faith with the dead, and whereby a whole nation of the living and dead moved forward to achieve the elusive goals of freedom. In his political views on the evolution of Irish society, Cogan's thinking reflected the spiritual concept of the Communion of Saints, where living believers share in a Christian fellowship with those who have already died in Christ. In Cogan's *Diocese of Meath* the reader is struck by the fact that there is scarcely no accommodation made for a division between the living and the dead. Cogan reminded his readers in 1862, that 'the old grave-yards where their fathers sleep, and where many of themselves expect to repose' also contain the remains of heroic priests whose records must 'be rescued from oblivion and neglect' (i, xi). And in all this, the writing of history played a key role in shaping the consciousness of the local community and the nation.

When Cogan entered into political debate he was quite capable of cutting corners when it came to summarising arguments that appealed to history. So, he accused the Ascendancy (in his open letter to the Members of Parliament for Meath in 1864) of growing fat on confiscated Catholic abbey lands (*Drogheda Argus*, 7 May 1864, p. 5), even though he must have known that Catholics also enjoyed confiscated monastic wealth. But Cogan's abiding historical interests and his huge historical knowlege on local issues allowed this country curate a perspective on Irish affairs which few could match in his time. In that same harangue to the Members for Meath in 1864, Cogan lecturing them on historical matters, was rightly pessimistic for the future, and prophetically pointed to coercion as the one policy resorted to by Britain which would eventually bring the Union down:

> It may be asked and it is often commented upon with surprise and regret, why has the policy of conciliation never been adopted towards unfortunate Ireland? Arms Acts, Coercion

42 Dangan Castle near Summerhill, Co. Meath, the family home of the duke of Wellington became the focus of Wellington mania in the British Press on the death of the duke in September 1852. *Illustrated London News* (16 October 1852) ran a feature on Dangan, the room in which Arthur Wellesley was said to have been born, and the school in Trim which he attended. This passing obsession highlighted the distance between the political and cultural lives of Ireland and Britain in the middle of the century. For Cogan, the place – long since abandoned by the Wellesleys – only 'has attractions' for 'an admirer of English rule' (ii, 386), while in nearby Laracor he noted that 'the neighbourhood still abounds with anecdotes' about Stella, the friend of Jonathan Swift.

Bills, denounciations of the people, have been the order of the day from time immemorial. From the invasion of Henry II till the present, with slight intermissions, the rule of England has been the same—viz., jealous, intolerant, one-sided, cruel. It was so in the exclusive days of the Pale; it was so in the confiscations of Elizabeth and James I; it was so in the bloody days of Cromwell and after the restoration of the ungrateful Charles II; it was so after the wars of the Revolution and in violation of the Treaty of Limerick. It was and is so, for Parliament after Parliament, year after year, has passed away and still the policy is the same—viz., keep down Ireland, discourage her manufactures, diminish her population, set class against class and sect against sect . . . (ibid.).

Anthony Cogan was a child of his time. His deep and abiding love of Ireland and its past emerges from almost every one of the 2000 or so pages of his life's work. His view of that past and his prejudices were conditioned by the religious and political intolerance and residual persecution of his age, and in no small measure by his training in Maynooth. It would be entirely wrong to label Cogan as a bigot, and an oversimplification to describe him as an old-fashioned nineteenth-century Irish nationalist. His scholarly interests were too immense and too dependent on the works of his Protestant and Anglo-Irish predecessors in Irish historical research not to have won his admiration for their work. He himself generously acknowledged that 'much, undoubtedly, has been done, with laudable zeal, by Protestant as well as by Catholic writers, to preserve our records and to chronicle the deeds of our forefathers' (II, ix) and he regularly cited the published works of all the leading Protestant scholars from Archbishop James Ussher, 'the learned Camden' (i, xxix), and Sir James Ware, to William Reeves who had helped to make the sources of Irish history available to antiquaries and local historians. At a speech in the Merchant's Dining Rooms in Liverpool in 1863, Cogan again acknowledged the generous help he had received from Protestant as well as Catholic learned men 'from many of whom he had received the most generous offers to use all books and documents which they had in assisting him in his researches' (*Drogheda Argus*, 12 September 1863, p. 3, col. 4).

It is a remarkable coincidence that Slane was home to both Anthony Cogan and Mervyn Archdall—two men of different faiths who chronicled the monastic history of Ireland in their different

43 Lynally Church, Co. Offaly.

ways. Archdall had died in Slane a whole generation before Cogan was born, but his work and scholarly interests must have held a peculiar fascination for Cogan. Neither man could be described as an historian of the first rank, but then neither was a professional, and both in their different ways provided outstanding service to Irish history. Of the two writers, Cogan's contribution was unquestionably the greater, for while Archdall's *Monasticon Hibernicum* was a poor attempt to emulate Dugdale's *Monasticon Anglicanum*, Cogan's *Diocese of Meath* was a work based (in its later volumes) on primary research, and offered besides, a vast compendium of folklore and tradition. While Cogan could make mistakes as Archdall frequently did, Cogan's researches have taken on postumous importance with the destruction of the Meath diocesan archive in 1909. But for Cogan, Archdall was 'the distinguished author of the *Monasticon*' (iii, 654), and the Protestantism of this adopted Slane man was for Cogan no bar to his membership of the Republic of Letters.

While he inveighed mercilessly in the rhetoric of his time against the Protestant establishment whom he viewed as the despoilers of Ireland's Catholic past, Cogan was generous in his tribute to those members of the Protestant gentry of Meath who had given shelter to hunted priests and who spoke out against the excesses of the Penal Laws. We have already been introduced to the Protestant Mr Webb of Dunshaughlin, who intervened to save the life of a Catholic

95

peasant. Cogan was unstinting in his admiration of patriotic Protestant gentlemen:

> The Irish peasantry have to this day grateful remembrance of the Protestant families that befriended themselves and their clergy in the times of persecution; and there is a traditionary respect for the descendants of these benefactors, which has survived the degeneracy of some of the Protestant gentry. (ii, 355)

Of the Stepneys—Protestant gentry at Durrow, Co. Offaly—Cogan observed:

> The Stepneys were a kind-hearted family, who lived on friendly terms with their Catholic neighbours, and often interposed to prevent persecution. (ii, 548)

Cogan goes on to observe that George Stepney was married to the daughter of the Protestant rector of Mullingar, and that one of his sons shielded the people of Westmeath and Offaly from the worst excesses of reprisals for the Great Rebellion in 1798. He had a strong sense, too, that at a community level in his native Meath, which in his time had a significant Protestant population, relations between people of differing faiths ought to be civilised if not indeed friendly. Thus he notes that after the funeral of Bishop Logan in Kells in April 1830, 'every respect was paid to his memory by Protestants as well as Catholics' (iii, 469). And he writes of individual priests such as Denis Walsh (ii, 250), parish priest of Rosnaree and Donore (died 1849) or Patrick McDermot, parish priest of Castletown-Kilpatrick (ii, 285) who were loved by their Protestant neighbours. Cogan also included a list of the Protestant bishops of Meath as a penultimate chapter in the last volume of his work (iii, 668-9), and he had intended giving an account of the careers of those bishops (ii, 185), had he not been prevented by rapidly failing health from doing so. We have seen how he dealt so leniently with the bizarre career of Bishop Thomas O'Beirne. Cogan tells us himself that Protestants as well as Catholics in Meath had supported his efforts to bring sobriety and a higher moral code to the youth of Navan (*Meath People*, 11 May 1861, p. 1) and we find Protestant supporters and even Protestant clergymen attending an anti-eviction rally addressed by Cogan at Mullagh (*Drogheda Argus*,

15 July 1871, p. 2). At Cogan's funeral (Appendix 9), Protestant friends crowded into Slane Chapel to pay their last respects to a man who had fought against bigotry and intolerance.

Cogan's confused thinking in relation to the political and social rôle of Protestants in Irish life is nicely exemplified in his references to his native Slane. On the one hand, the shadow of '98 still hung over Slane and Meath generally. Cogan collected numerous traditions relating to harassment and savage reprisals against the rebel population in the time of the Great Rebellion, such as the ransacking and desecration of Fr Richard Meighan's chapel in Moynalvy in an abortive search for arms (ii, 372), or the tale of Fr Philip Mulligan who was parish priest of Slane. On one occasion Fr Mulligan was said to have offered Sunday Mass in Slane in the summer of 1798 in defiance of a ban by a Mr G —— who was captain of the local militia (ii, 356), while in another anecdote he is shown hearing the Confession of a peasant mortally wounded by the yeomanry. An officer in that corps is portrayed as a heartless brute endeavouring to ride over the body of a dying man (ii, 357). Yet Cogan adds that another of the officers was a Catholic who was reprimanded by his priest for the 'nice company' he was keeping, and we are told that 'many of the corps were Catholics'. In these anecdotes, Cogan claimed that the parochial house was then near the old church at Gernonstown, and that Mass in the village of Slane

44 Collège des Lombards on the rue des Carmes in Paris, was located in the Latin quarter on the side of Mont Ste Geneviève. Granted to the Irish students by Louis XIV in 1677, its previous occupants included Ignatius Loyola and Francis Xavier. A Kells man, Patrick Joseph Plunket, became one of the four Provisors or senior administrators here in the eighteenth century, and after 26 years in France he returned as bishop of Meath, where he ruled until his death at the age of 89 in 1827.

was celebrated in a barn or outhouse. But in the first volume of his work, Cogan explained how Colonel Conyngham, later the first marquis, took pity on the curate of Slane, Fr Michael O'Hanlon, and provided him with the site for a new church, which he also helped him to build (i, 291–3). The details of the story have elements of a folklore dimension so characteristic of many of Cogan's anedotes. While Fr O'Hanlon was staying at the Irish College in Paris he was supposed to have rescued Colonel Conyngham from a French military tribunal, and that Protestant gentleman later rewarded the priest who saved his life with a splendid chapel in Slane. Once again, the truth of the tale is less important than the general message which Cogan employed it to convey. The Conynghams of Slane Castle, in Anthony Cogan's record, were popular landlords who had befriended the local Catholic community. Cogan was a man to have known the truth of this, having been brought up in the village, and his benign tale of Conyngham generosity comes as all the greater compliment in view of the fact that they had replaced the ancient and Catholic house of Fleming. Cogan's favourable view of the Conynghams is also significant in view of the sectarian troubles in Slane during his early childhood in the 1830s.

One detail does not belong to folklore. The Catholic church in Slane, which houses the grave and a monument to the memory of Anthony Cogan, had its foundation stone laid in 1802 by the young son of Lord Conyngham. The chapel was called Mount Charles in memory of the son of the future marquis*, who gave the ground for the erection of the chapel (Trench, *Slane*, p.12). So, at the very time when bands of yeomanry with a large Catholic membership were supposedly rampaging about the Slane countryside harassing the Catholic peasantry, the Marquis of Conyngham on the other hand was contemplating the erection of a splendid chapel for the Catholic community. Such were the contradictions in Irish life, and they would be nothing more than historical curiosities if they were not symptomatic of a problem which was eventually to have such a destructive effect on the development of modern Ireland. The underlying problem came down to this. Cogan was generous in his praise of those whom he considered to be good Protestants, and merciless in his hostility towards those whom he considered to be

*Henry Conyngham was created a Viscount in 1789, and Marquis of Conyngham in 1816. His son, Henry Joseph, Earl of Mount Charles, was seven in 1802 and died at Nice, in the lifetime of his father in 1824.

bad ones. On the whole, Cogan's notion of what constituted a good Irish Protestant centred on that person's ability to support Catholic political aspirations as well as to guarantee religious liberties. But a major question remained unresolved in Cogan's mind. What role would there be in a future Ireland for those Protestants who did not subscribe to Catholic political aspirations? Indeed, that question was scarcely asked, much less answered. It may be wrong to blame Cogan for ignoring this issue and it would certainly be wrong to expect him to have resolved it. The ills of the Catholic majority were so great, and the struggle for liberty so hopeless and so intense, that the issue of the future of the Protestant minority was low on the Catholic agenda in a county such as Meath. The matter did not seem so pressing in Meath and Westmeath, where unpatriotic Protestants were seen—outside centres such as Kells at least—as an alien élite clinging on to power through coercion. But at the root of the wider issue was a problem which would not go away, and which Catholics of Anthony Cogan's ability had ignored at a cost. In

Ulster, where there was a large loyalist Protestant community, this issue—or its lack of resolution—would demonstrate its destructive consequences into the twenty-first century.

45 High Cross at Durrow, Co. Offaly. Cogan wrote of this place: 'Durrow, Durrow! what associations and holy memories linger around you! Durrow, hallowed by the foot-prints of St Columbkill. ... Durrow no longer exists not a stone of it remains; its glories live in the traditions of the people, and its merits have ascended like incense around the throne of the omnipotent God. Durrow, so long the abode of sanctity and learning, has been torn down and uprooted. ... Yet, in its ruin and loneliness there is a charm, a holy spell around the hallowed site and the surrounding scenery which no earthly power can uproot, and which speaks to the heart ... that here, undoubtedly, was one of the ancient sanctuaries of Ireland' (ii, 543-4).

V

THE MAKING OF A LOCAL HISTORIAN

The conflicting claims of the Protestant and Catholic nations within nineteenth-century Ireland were evident within Anthony Cogan's own family. His father, Thomas Cogan, was a baker, whose shop stood on the main street in Slane and his father's family was undoubtedly steeped in the older Catholic traditions of rural Meath. Thomas Cogan, who died in 1839 at the age of sixty-six, was a young man of twenty-five at the time of the Great Rebellion of 1798. Anthony Cogan's mother, on the other hand, Anne Sillary, had been brought up in the Protestant faith, and came from a well-to-do farming family at Nobber in north Meath. Her family also owned land at Platten near Drogheda in Co. Meath. Anne Sillary became a Catholic on her marriage to Thomas Cogan. She bore him five sons and three daughters, and she outlived her son, Fr Anthony, by seven years, dying in 1879. Anthony Cogan, in the Matriculation Book of Maynooth College in 1845, gave his age as nineteen at last birthday. He was born probably in 1826, but his monument in Slane Catholic Church, giving his age as forty-five on his death in 1872 suggests he may have been born in 1827. One of Anthony's brothers—Francis—was a surgeon-major in the British army. Francis Cogan, whose death at the age of forty-four in 1871 is recorded on his grave-stone in the cemetery on the Hill of Slane, must have been very close to Anthony in age, and died only a year before him. A Cogan family tradition holds that Michael, another of Anthony Cogan's brothers, was also an army surgeon and died in Gibraltar. In spite of his family connections with Protestant Ireland and with the British army, Cogan showed in his confused but passionate thinking on Irish politics in later life, that he was his own man in those matters. He was educated locally in Slane and later at the Seminary in Navan. This was a diocesan school founded by Bishop Patrick Plunket in 1802 which was subsequently moved in

46 The teaching staff at St Finian's Seminary in Navan *c.* 1867. Names as on the back of the original photograph: standing, left to right: Fr Behan, Fr Moore, Dean Cogan (centre), Dr Higgins, [unidentified priest], and the Abbé Meade. Seated, left to right: Fr McCormick and Fr J. Kelly.

Dr Joseph O'Higgins was the president of the school and was later to act as celebrant at Cogan's Requiem Mass. He is identified in the photograph as standing beside Cogan and third from the right. But the man shown in that position was too young to have been the president in Cogan's time. The President must surely be seated at the front. The priest standing third from the right may, then, be Fr Kelly. The front row must include the President, Dr O'Higgins, and the veteran Fr William McCormick, Science and Classics master (expounding from the book?), who was greatly admired by Cogan and who was born *c.*1804. Cogan stands between these two senior colleagues in his capacity as senior dean, a position he held from 1864. Fr Francis Meade (top right) was a master in the school when Cogan was writing his second volume (1862–67) and Fr James Moore (second left) taught the first class and was master of ceremonies at Cogan's Requiem. Fr J. Duff, a teacher at St Finian's who was also present at Cogan's funeral, may have joined the staff after this photograph was taken, or he may be the unidentified priest standing Napolean-like second from the right, who is the only member of the group not wearing a soutane.

47 Anthony Cogan *c*.1867 (detail from
ill. 46). Cogan has been correctly
identified on the back of the original.
His rounded features concur with those
in the portrait of Cogan as a young
priest in the CYMS Hall, Navan (ill. 1),
and with those of the bust in semi-relief
on his tomb in Slane church (frontispiece).

1908 to become St Finian's College in Mullingar. Plunket had
begun fund-raising for this secondary school as early as 1794 (i,
242). The buildings cost about £4000, of which £500 had been
contributed by Matthew Corbally, the grandfather of the M.P. for
Meath during Anthony Cogan's adult life. Plunket raised the
remaining funds for his Navan seminary from the parishes of his
diocese. Cogan in his *Diocese of Meath* was to give pride of place to
this bishop who had founded his old school and who, as a Plunket,
belonged to a family which, like the Flemings, had done so much
for Catholic Ireland in the troubled centuries after the Reformation.
Bishop Plunket's seminary at Navan, where Cogan was educated
and where he eventually returned as dean, was a grammar school
which had given him a solid grounding in Latin and Greek.

The first President of St Finian's had been Eugene O'Reilly who
ended his life as parish priest of Navan and who was responsible for
building the splendid church in that town in 1839, followed by the
parochial house in 1845. Fr O'Reilly died, appropriately, on the
feast of St Finian, on 12 December 1852, and living until his eighty-
fourth year (i, 247), he must have been available for the newly-
ordained Anthony Cogan to gain a fund of information from him on
the past history of Navan and the early days of St Finian's. Cogan
even provided the precise time of Fr O'Reilly's death on that St
Finian's Day, which fell on a Sunday, at 7.30 p.m. The President
during Cogan's schooldays at Navan was Nicholas Power who was

associated with St Finian's for almost forty years (1828-67) and who died as parish priest of Donore. Power's evidence given before the Endowed School Commission in 1854 shows him to have been a keen educationalist who insisted on moral influence rather than corporal punishment to maintain discipline in his school, and who insisted on the teaching of French and (if possible) of German. At the time when Cogan was a pupil in St Finian's, there were four priest masters and two prefects who were perhaps teaching monitors. There were some 65 pupils in all. Because it was the first Catholic school of its kind in Ireland—a diocesan minor seminary—the boarders came from as far afield as Thurles and Dungarvan, Ballinasloe, Loughrea and Roscommon, with an occasional pupil from overseas. Boarders' fees were set in 1826 at £40 a year, while day-boys paid six guineas. Among its early alumni were Archbishop MacGettigan of Armagh (1870-87), Nicholas Callan, the Maynooth scientist (1799-1864), who came from Louth, and John Hand from Oldcastle (1807-46), the founder of All Hallows College, Dublin. Cogan identified two former masters at the school as Fr McEneroe later archdeacon of Sydney, and Eugene O'Connell, bishop of Marysville in California (i, 240), Cogan paid tribute to his old school thus:

> Of all similar establishments in Ireland, few have produced more eminent men, more patriotic or pious priests, more zealous missionaries, many of whom are on the English, Scotch, American, Australian and Indian missions, than St. Finian's seminary of Navan. She can boast of men in the army and navy, at the bar, in the various professions of life ... who were once reckoned her *alumni* (i, 240).

It seems likely that Anthony Cogan's brother, Francis, who was destined for a career in the British army and who was very close to Anthony in age, was also a pupil at St Finian's.

When Cogan matriculated at Maynooth on 26 August 1844, he was entered along with those students for Logic, suggesting that he already had a good Classical education. The other half of his class matriculated into Humanity which required them to read two years' Classics at Maynooth. Cogan would later put his grounding in Latin to good use in translating documents from that language into English (cf. ii, 85n). A Maynooth manuscript volume containing 'Ordinations and Prize Lists 1845–1864' shows that Cogan failed to distinguish himself as a student. He is not mentioned in the prize lists for logic, metaphysics and ethics in 1844–5; or for natural philosophy in 1845–6. He did make *proxime accesserunt* in the theology lists for 1846–7 (no. 18 in his class); for 1849–50 (no. 15 in class) and for Scripture in that same year he was also listed among the *proxime accesserunt* at no. 15. He appears in these records as a worthy student who gradually improved over his time at Maynooth, where he was ordained on 25 May 1850. But Cogan from his writings shows himself to have been a man of sensitivity and imagination and a well organised scholar, capable of sustained effort. He wrote with authority and handled his sources with confidence. As a student, his heart clearly did not lie in ethics or metaphysics and we may surmise that he spent more time day-dreaming on Ireland's past than applying himself to dogmatic theology.

As it happened, there was an established scholar at Maynooth in Cogan's time there, whose interests in Irish history were soon to be fully shared by Cogan. Cogan's days at Maynooth coincided with the career there of Matthew Kelly, who from 1841 had been professor of French and was later (from 1857) to hold the chair of ecclesiastical history. Kelly was a much travelled and learned nineteenth-century scholar, who was steeped in early Irish ecclesiastical history. Cogan acknowledged the interest Kelly was later to show in his work, and saluted his memory as a friend and adviser (i, v). It was this man who must have inspired Anthony Cogan, if not when a student, then certainly as a young priest, to undertake his mammoth antiquarian labours. Matthew Kelly was born in Kilkenny in 1814 and in his childhood had been the pupil of M.S. Brennan, the author of the *Ecclesiastical History of Ireland*. Although educated at Maynooth, he eventually, after ordination, became professor of philosophy and theology at the Irish College in Paris from 1839 to 1841. Kelly is perhaps best remembered as the editor of the Celtic Society's three-volume edition of John Lynch's *Cambrensis Eversus* (1848–52), but in his short life—he died at forty-four—he produced a remarkable flow of editions and translations including Philip O'Sullivan's *Historiae Catholicae Iberniae Compendium* (1850) and M. Gosselin's *Power of the Popes during the Middle Ages* (1853). Kelly's own contribution to historical research centred on Early Irish Church history with his collected essays on *Dissertations Chiefly on Irish Church History* published posthumously by McCarthy in 1864, and at his death he was busily occupied with a continuation of John Lanigan's *An Ecclesiastical History of Ireland*. He had also supervised the publication of Renehan's *Collections on*

48 Romanesque window from Rahan, Co. Offaly.

Irish Church History. Lanigan's *History* which had appeared in 1822 had ended at the beginning of the thirteenth century, while Kelly was preparing a set of *Ecclesiastical Annals* down to the Reformation. Kelly, although more fortunate, less flamboyant, and seen to be more orthodox than Lanigan, nevertheless had much in common with his late eighteenth-century predecessor. Both men had studied and lectured in continental universities (Lanigan held a chair at the University of Pavia until 1796) and both had returned to Maynooth and thrown themselves into research on the Early Irish Church. Through Kelly, Anthony Cogan had immediate access to a long and splendid tradition of post-Reformation Irish scholarship which the Wild Geese and their ecclesiastical kindred had pursued and promoted in the colleges of Europe. Cogan, who had seldom strayed far beyond his native Meath, had clearly travelled in the mind with Irish fugitives to Salamanca, Rome and Paris, and Fr Kelly, once a professor at the Collège des Irlandais in Paris, was just the man to fire the young Meath student's imagination with tales of long-forgotten priests who made heroic journeys and endured immense hardships for the sake of faith and fatherland.

Cogan served as a young priest in the parishes of Johnstown, Beauparc, Dunboyne, Bohermeen and Navan—all of which, apart from Dunboyne—were quite near his native Slane. Dunboyne, on the other hand, was but a few miles from Maynooth, where he no doubt kept in contact with some of his old mentors and availed of its library. His entire ministry was spent in Co. Meath, and since he had also been born there, the western parts of the diocese covering Westmeath and parts of central and southern Offaly must have been unknown territory before he was given leave of absence to travel in those parishes in the summer of 1863. Cogan proved to be a popular and a remarkably active and effective priest. It is clear from contemporary reporting in the local and national press, that apart altogether from his immense historical output, he was a greatly loved and untiring pastor to the youth of Navan, and a champion of the oppressed. We may conclude from the vigour of his writings that he was a formidable preacher with a developed dramatic sense, which must have been appreciated by nineteenth-century congregations. In his writings, he never fails to note the qualities of a priest who was remembered as a good preacher. His reported speeches at functions in Navan and Liverpool, show him to have been a man of the people, who addressed his audience as 'Friends' and who possessed a keen sense of humour. His words lacked pomposity, and allowing for the rhetoric and verbosity of the age, Cogan showed a directness and clarity in his speeches which marked him off from his more exalted contemporaries. He was unquestionably a charismatic figure, devoted to the welfare of the young, who also possessed qualities of leadership in relation to political issues, as well as genuine scholarly ability. The fact that he was in demand as a preacher for Irish congregations in Liverpool also confirms his ability in the pulpit. His preaching assignments in Liverpool must have arisen from personal friendships with priests who settled there. Among such men was the Benedictine monk, James Sheridan. Born in Moylough in 1779, he was educated in Cogan's old school in Navan, and moving on to Ampleforth, he was professed as a Benedictine in 1836 and in 1850 he became parish priest of St Mary's in Liverpool. Dom. James Sheridan died in 1860 and at the inauguration of his memorial in St Mary's Church, Liverpool, on 27 October 1861, Cogan was invited to deliver the panegyric on his old Meath colleague (ii, 335).

The Liverpool dimension to Cogan's career is a fascinating aspect of this Irish country curate's life. Cogan was invited as a celebrity preacher to Liverpool Catholic congregations at regular intervals throughout the Sixties. Granted that the majority of his hearers were Liverpool Irish, it is still a remarkable fact that this scholarly priest, lost in his researches on ancient Meath, and ministering away from the limelight of Dublin and outside its archdiocese, should be sought after by Liverpool clergy as a special preacher. In addition to

49 Clonmacnoise, Co. Offaly.
Founded by St Kieran. In early Christian times, saints' lives and sagas were written
here and annals were recorded here. The Anglo-Saxon Chronicle in King Alfred's
reign acknowledged the scholarly reputation of its scribe, Suibhne. The Irish clung
to this ancient centre throughout the wars of religion and a synod of bishops was
convened here as late as December 1649 to help organise resistance to Cromwell.
Stephen MacEgan, the Dominican who was consecrated bishop of Clonmacnoise by
Pope Benedict XIII in 1725, was transferred to Meath four years later and
continued to administer Clonmacnoise. Clonmacnoise was eventually united to
Ardagh c. 1756.

Cogan's personal contacts in Liverpool, his Slane origins meant he
was familiar with nearby Drogheda. And Drogheda in the middle of
the nineteenth century had closer contacts with Liverpool than it
had with more remote parts of Ireland's interior. John Boyle
O'Reilly's aunt in Preston was married to the ship's master of the
Caledonian which plied between Drogheda and Liverpool, and a
Liverpool contingent of the Young Men's Society sailed to
Drogheda on the *Leinster Lass* in August 1863 to join Father
Cogan's youth rally at Laytown (*Drogheda Argus*, 15 August 1863,
p.4, col.4). The *Drogheda Argus* ran a special weekly column of
Liverpool News all through the Sixties. So Drogheda, in the days of
the British Empire, and in the aftermath of Famine emigration, had
much closer contacts with Liverpool than we might at first imagine.
And consequently, rural Meath, with immediate access to the port
of Drogheda, was not as dependent on Dublin for its outlet to
Britain as it became in the twentieth century.

Some of Cogan's preaching forays into Liverpool were reported
in detail by the *Drogheda Argus*, and it is clear that he was fêted on
these occasions by the Catholic establishment and hero-worshipped

50 Inchcleraun, Lough Ree *c.* 1870. Cogan remarked on the beauty of the scene with its islands, water and woods, complete when he was there, with pleasure yachts sailing among the monastic ruins.

by his Irish emigrant hearers. In September 1863 (when Cogan was only thirty-seven) he preached the Anniversary Sermon at St Mary's in Edmund Street, Liverpool, where we have seen him two years previously. Two thousand people flocked to hear him preach (Appendix 4) for an hour in the morning on the Blessed Virgin, taking as his text *Behold from henceforth all generations shall call me blessed.* At six o'clock that evening, looking fresh and relaxed, he preached yet again on *Honour thy father and thy mother that thy days may be long in the land.* The evening sermon was delivered to boys and girls as well as to the Young Men's Society whose quarters at St Mary's he visited afterwards. Reports of events such as this, show Cogan to have been a thoroughly integrated personality—a dynamic young priest who combined powers of oratory with his burning zeal to serve God, to help the young and the disposessed, and to further the cause of his country.

At a grand banquet given in Cogan's honour in the Merchant's Dining Rooms in Castle Street, Liverpool, a hundred guests heard Martin Rankin, vice-president general of the Catholic Young Men's Society in Britain, praise Cogan's efforts 'to procure for the down-trodden serfs of Ireland the right to live upon the soil whereon they first drew breath'. And Cogan in his reply showed that even so far from home he was still engrossed with the work in hand, and informed his bemused listeners that the First Volume of his *Diocese of Meath* was already out of print and that he hoped to publish his Second Volume in the following year—when he also expected to return to Liverpool. The account reveals that Cogan had been a guest preacher at St Mary's during the previous autumn of 1862. When he addressed the Liverpool Catholic Young Men's Society in '63 'he spoke of the Old Country, her wrongs and hopes, the fidelity of her people and the utter confusion of all the machinations of the world and the devil in their attempts to wrest from her the Faith once planted by St Patrick' (*Drogheda Argus*, 12 September 1863).

For Anthony Cogan, his life as a priest and preacher, his work with the young and his labours for the freedom of Ireland, were all part of the same great enterprise—serving God and his own oppressed people. As a curate in Navan, Cogan was the founder of the Catholic Young Men's Society. A plaque high above the Young Men's Hall in Trimgate Street in Navan, bears testimony to the fact that the building was erected by Cogan in 1863. A painting of Cogan as a young priest still hangs within this building. A report in the *Morning News* (30 December 1859) of a meeting convened in Navan on the previous day to express sympathy for Pope Pius IX in his negotiations with Italian nationalists, mentions that

> a prominent feature in the day's proceedings was the presence of upwards of thirteen hundred members of the Catholic Young Men's Society, who, at an early hour, headed by their estimable and zealous guardian, the Rev. A. Cogan, and preceeded by their excellent band, marched from their rooms and proceeded to their Metropolitan church and took the places allotted for their accommodation. (iii, 520)

The mention of 1300 members is remarkable for such a recently founded body. On an excursion to Laytown on the Meath coast in 1863, Cogan chartered a special train to ferry 700 of his Young Men and their friends out of Navan. That was the occasion on which he also organised a rendezvous with the Liverpool Young Men's Society—no mean achievement in an era when communication and travel were so difficult.

The population of Navan in 1861 was 4214—a drop of nearly 2500 since before the Famine (P. Connell, *RnM*, vi, no.3 (1977), 52). While the reduced population placed less strain on housing resources, it is clear from the *Meath People* and elsewhere that squalor and overcrowding was still a very serious problem in the town. Many of Cogan's young men must have come from the slums of Brews Hill, Chapel Lane and elsewhere. Unemployment was still rife, as was drunkenness and its associated ills. It was Cogan's achievement to take the youth of Navan off the streets. Peter O'Neill in an address to Cogan, reported in the *Meath People* (Appendix 1), stated: 'No right minded man can walk our streets without being impressed with the great social revolution the Young Men's Society has effected. Public intemperance and [im]morality— which were proof against the rigours of the law—have here disappeared before its teaching and example.' All this was thanks to 'the almost superhuman exertions of its devoted founder and spiritual guide', Anthony Cogan.

In his reply (ibid.), Cogan tells us: 'I flung myself heart and soul into the movement, to develop and expand its efficacy. . . . That the blessing of sobriety, morality and Christian charity have been widely diffused through our organisation, Protestants as well as Catholics have given willing testimony.' He ascribed the credit, however, to the work of his predecessors among the clergy of Navan. Social

51 Inis Aingin (Hare Island) Lough Ree. Cogan travelled to the furthest ends of Meath diocese along the banks of the Shannon, where he recorded inscriptions on the gravestones of eighteenth-century priests in the cemetery at Bunown (ii, 526-7). The boundary of the diocese of Meath runs through Lough Ree and Inis Aingin lies in the Meath sector.

reform could never be separated in Cogan's mind from a just political situation, and he went on to claim that the poverty of his countrymen had been induced by their ruthless oppressors who then taunted their impoverished victims with their own wretchedness. Cogan's towering part in the organisation of the youth of Navan in the post-Famine generation cannot be questioned. Numerous tributes and presentations from grateful fathers of the town such as John Mullen, J.P. and Patrick O'Neill, as well as the affection in which Cogan was held by the young men themselves, testifies to his charismatic ministry to the young. The most impressive tribute was paid by the editor of the *Meath People* who wrote of Cogan in 1861: 'Father Cogan made them [the Young Men's Society] what they are. He it was that raised them into life, and watched them in the cradle, that stood by them in their maturity, and that has them now a credit not to Navan alone, but to Catholicity' (*Meath People*, 11 May 1861, p.4).

In addition to serving the spiritual needs of the young, Cogan also provided them with lectures on the history, antiquities and music of Ireland. Cogan himself alludes to the remarkable fact that he had persuaded Professor Eugene O'Curry from the recently founded Catholic University, to join the excursion of the Navan Catholic Young Men's Society at Gormanstown in east Meath in August 1862 (i, xix). What the poverty-stricken youths from the mud-walled cabins of Navan thought of early Irish folktales and their manuscripts, as explained by Anthony Cogan, remains a matter for speculation. While John Boyle O'Reilly was busy planning mutiny and rebellion, Anthony Cogan as a young priest was promoting a social movement which combined his own interests in religion with those of Irish culture, and all in the hope of weaning the impressionable minds of young Meathmen away from secret societies or the more endemic social evils of excessive drinking. But preaching and even the supervision of the social lives of the young were peripheral to Anthony Cogan's main duties. He was employed by his bishop as a master and dean at the seminary school in Navan, where as well as preparing young men for professional life and trying to inculcate the rudiments of civilisation into farmers of the future, he was also preparing young hopefuls for the priesthood, who planned to proceed to Maynooth or to one of the Colleges abroad. And all the while this incredibly busy and committed priest harboured a dream which again he formulated for the columns of the *Meath People*: 'It has been the ambition of my life—as far as in me lay—to revive the memory of our saints and scholars—of our martyrs and confessors—of our warriors and sages—of those who laboured for us in the senate, and those who shed their blood for us in the field' (ibid.).

Half a century later, another devoted Irish nationalist, Patrick Pearse, who also dedicated his life to the education of the young, and who shared Cogan's idealistic view of Ireland's remote Celtic past—and how a knowledge of that past might be conveyed to the young—developed his own ideas on how Ireland might best be served by the sacrifice of her patriot manhood. Modern Irish historians too rashly attribute notions of fanatical dedication and blood-sacrifice to Pearse without allowing for the evolved tradition on which he drew his inspiration. Pearse may well have developed such ideas to extreme proportions and acted out patriotic dreams in the Easter Rising. But a study of Anthony Cogan's views on Ireland's past combined with his perception of Ireland's ills in the middle of the nineteenth century, shows that ideas involving a succession of Irish martyrs who had shed their blood in the cause of faith and fatherland were already firmly in place by the 1860s and indeed long before. Cogan's perceptions were different from those of Pearse if only because he viewed his world from the standpoint of a committed priest. So, Cogan's pantheon of heroic figures who kept the flame of Irish patriotism alight included an endless succession of holy men engaged in a life and death struggle for the Catholic faith. Cogan allowed room in his scheme of things for political heroes as well, but unlike Pearse at the end of the century, Cúchulainn and the blood-bath of the *Táin Bó Cuailgne* were very peripheral to Anthony Cogan's more Christian vision of Ireland's destiny. But while Cogan's story began with St Patrick rather than Cúchulainn, for Cogan the struggle for Faith and its associated violence intensified and coalesced with the fight for fatherland in the eighteenth century. Nationalism had become in Anthony Cogan's day, not just a struggle for political freedom but for social justice and full religious liberty as well. Cogan was a teacher and a social worker, a scholar and a holy man. But he was identified by his Liverpool guests as 'a patriotic Irish priest', with the implication that all his labours were directed towards promoting the cause of Ireland.

At this time Cogan had already begun to fufil his desire to write. He himself tells us that he first began writing for the *Tablet* before he published his history of the diocese of Meath (i, v). Elsewhere in

52 Fennor, Co. Meath, situated to the south of the Boyne and just outside the village of Slane. Fennor, like Slane, rose to prominence as an early Christian centre in the mid tenth century when Congalach mac Máelmithig, the king of Brega who ruled from nearby Knowth, became highking of the Uí Néill. A fragment of a tenth-century high cross from Fennor is presently in the possession of the parish priest of Slane.

his work (iii, 516) Cogan refers in the warmest terms to Frederick Lucas 'late editor of the *Tablet*, a man of great honesty of purpose, and of wonderful ability'. Lucas had been a Member of Parliament for Meath and a champion of Tenant Right—a cause dear to Cogan's heart. He records a Tenant Right banquet given in honour of Lucas in Navan on 17 January 1854—a meeting which Cogan himself almost certainly attended—at which Bishop Cantwell urged unity among the ranks 'of the Irish party of independent opposition' which that prelate saw as 'the only hope for Ireland' (iii, 517). Cantwell like many other Irish bishops had by now moved on from supporting O'Connell's Repeal Association to promoting the interests of those Irish Members of Parliament who would pursue an independent policy aimed at achieving political freedoms and agrarian reform. Cogan also recorded attending a meeting addressed by Frederick Lucas on Tenant Right 'in June or July, 1852' when that orator spoke by the cross in Duleek (ii, 233). 'Few', he noted, 'have loved the church and people of Ireland better.' Even if Cogan had not enjoyed the personal friendship or patronage of Lucas, he most certainly had access to that patronage through the offices of Bishop Cantwell. Frederick Lucas, who died in the year following his

Navan banquet, was one of the leading Catholic writers and pro-Catholic politicians in England of his day. The son of a London Quaker, he became a Catholic, and founded the *Tablet* in May 1840. He espoused the cause of O'Connell and Repeal and later that of Tenant Right in Ireland. He moved the publishing offices of the *Tablet* from London to Dublin in 1849 and became one of the Members of Parliament for Co. Meath in 1852. In the towering figure of Frederick Lucas—a man who personally petitioned Pope Pius IX in his dispute with Dr Cullen, archbishop of Dublin, over the rôle of clergy in political affairs—Anthony Cogan, directly or indirectly, made contact with a world of distinguished Catholic journalists and writers far beyond the confines of Meath. It can scarcely have been coincidental for the development of Cogan's career as a writer, that the editor of the *Tablet* began his brief but distinguished career as a Member for Meath only two years after Fr Cogan's ordination, when both men's very different interests and activities focussed on Navan. Cogan's first contributions to medieval history appeared in the pages of the *Tablet* when he was about thirty and within a year of the death of Frederick Lucas. His earliest work dealt with *The Ancient Diocese of Duleek*, written in five parts throughout 1856 and 1857—the last section of which was published on 28 February 1857 (p. 139). This was soon followed by his *Ancient Diocese of Clonard* which appeared on 25 April 1857 (p. 266) and 23 May 1857 (p. 331). Significantly, Cogan began his researches not only on his own diocese and his own county, but almost on his own parish. Duleek was an ancient bishopric nearest to his native Slane, while the achievement of Clonard was to become a symbol for the diocese at large. These short articles contain some of Cogan's finest medieval research. He had meticulously abstracted entries relating to these ancient centres from the medieval annals and then sought to construct a narrative on the evidence before him. The approach is valid to this day. These contributions were unsigned, but the care with which they were written shows that Cogan, through the pages of the *Tablet*, was gaining valuable experience which was soon to equip him for a more ambitious historical enterprise.

Although he was devoted to championing the cause of the downtrodden masses in mid nineteenth-century Ireland, Cogan's immediate preoccupations were with the people and places of his beloved Meath. His concern for Irish history was unquestionably with its ecclesiastical history and he viewed his world as a Catholic priest who put his Catholicism first, and other cultural considerations second. Yet as we have seen, his political aspirations were conveniently accommodated within his concern for the Catholic past. Cogan's preoccupation with local history and his herculean work on the diocese of Meath shows that his loyalties at a secular level were to his own region that he knew and loved so well, rather than to the wider national stage. Not that Cogan had an narrow or myopic view of the past. His 'Introductory Lecture to the Youthful Reader' in the first volume of his *Diocese of Meath* demonstrates his astonishing breadth of reading and the scope of his learning. In a chapter where we might have expected a pompous and patronising harangue to the young, we are treated instead to a scholarly survey replete with extensive footnotes on the contribution of Ireland's saints and scholars on the Continent of Europe in the Early Middle Ages. In reading this chapter we are allowed to see how Cogan had clearly devoted every spare moment of his time to reading everything he could get his hands on—from the eleventh-century Icelandic *Landnámabók* to Dr Johnson, and from *Duffy's Catholic Magazine* to historians such as Thierry and Wattenbach. Many of his authorities are cited at second hand, but the miracle is that he had read them at all, given the conditions under which he worked. It was this point which struck Eugene O'Curry when he wrote to Cogan in July 1862: 'It astonishes me that, with your distance from public libraries and your heavy parochial duties you managed to make time to collect, from a thousand scattered sources, the

53 St Columkille's House in Kells.

fragmentary history of your ancient diocese' (i, xvii).

Cogan demonstrates in his *Introductory Lecture* his gifts as a synthesizer—so essential for the mammoth task he had set himself—and his ability to organise material and present a coherent argument. He takes his reader on a Cook's tour of the early Irish saints in Europe—'from the Alps to Scandinavia, from the Atlantic to the Carpathians'. And he manages, like all talented historical writers who cite at length from primary source-material, to convey the impression that he is allowing his reader to view all his material at first hand. So, we are treated to lengthy quotations from Carolingian sources on Donatus, bishop of Fiesole in Tuscany, and on Irish scholars in the Francia of Charles the Bald. He even manages to summarise two great debates which had bedevilled early Irish historiography from the time of Archbishop Ussher and which were only petering out in Cogan's own day. The first of these was his refutation of the notion that the early Irish saints had been the forerunners of Protestantism and the second that ancient *Scotia* referred to Scotland rather than to Ireland proper.

VI

OUTSPOKEN CRITIC AND CONSCIENCE OF A DIOCESE

Anthony Cogan, regardless of his talents as a preacher and his duties as a teacher, and despite his successful pastoral programme for the young, was a man obsessed with the past. He was a romantic who longed to recover the story of the lost innocence of Early Irish Christianity and who hankered after the image of Ireland's primeval wilderness inhabited by God-fearing people keeping faith with the countless generations who had gone before. His was an outlook which was as melancholic as it was romantic and conservative. Cogan was by nature opposed to change of any kind which promoted a break with Ireland's past—a past which he himself had so idealised. He was acutely aware of the need to preserve the historical and archaeological records in the face of what he saw as the major upheavals of his time—land clearances, famine, and the death of the Irish language in Meath. It was unquestionably with the fugitive priests and their oppressed people of the seventeenth and eighteenth century that Cogan identified most. His prose acquires an emotional power when describing the 'atrocious Penal Code' (i, ix) and what he calls 'the dread days of Queen Anne' (i, vii) when 'our priests were hunted to the caverns and the wilderness, and the same price was fixed upon them as upon the head of the wolf' (i, lvi).

He gave full rein to his romanticised and idealised image of those saintly priests who risked their lives for their flocks in late seventeenth-century Ireland when (addressing those holy forebears directly) he wrote:

'the mysteries of the saving faith for which you sacrificed all in this world, were celebrated in the lone glen or in the fastnesses of the mountain.'

It was unquestionably in his devotion to the memory of the Penal Day priests of Meath—'the holy men who sleep in our grave-yards' (ii, viii)—that Cogan drew powerful inspiration for his own priestly vocation. His staggering historical output was in part driven by an emotional need to find out all there was to know of the men who had kept the faith alive in days of persecution—of men to whom he realised he owed so much. He tells us how he spent his summer vacations:

> I went from churchyard to churchyard, taking the dimensions of the existing ruins, deciphering the tombs of priests, transcribing inscriptions on the pedestals of the old chalices, searching the registries, gathering old documents and letters of the deceased pastors . . . visiting old crosses and holy wells, and taking notes of every surviving memorial of the faith and piety of the people. (i, viii)

And in 1870 he wrote of visiting 'every holy well, . . . mountain altar [and] ecclesiastical hiding place in the penal times . . . from Birr to county Cavan, from the Shannon to the sea' (iii, viii). This last phrase, incidentially, reveals how steeped Cogan had become in the language of the early Irish annalists as revealed to him through John O'Donovan's edition of the *Annals of the Four Masters* which first appeared in 1848.

But it was above all else to exhume the memory of those priestly predecessors with whom he identified so passionately that Cogan laboured. He rightly cast modesty aside and boldly proclaimed in 1862 that he was the first historian since the Reformation to recover an almost unbroken succession of Catholic pastors from 1690 down to his own time (i, ix). His researches took him to family archives and the unpublished diaries of Bishop Plunket and to recording a multitude of inscriptions. He writes of a custom relating to almost every Meath churchyard and surviving into his own time, whereby he was able to identify the graves and grave stones of priests of an earlier age.

> As very many of our old churches were converted to Protestant uses after the Reformation, the old custom of placing the corpse before the high altar was of course abandoned; and even after the temple had been deserted and permitted to fall into ruin, the people ceased carrying the corpse inside, but selected the grave of some old pastor on which to deposit and unrope the coffin, and chant the *De profundis* previous to interment. (i, viii)

Numerous examples of mourners 'unroping' coffins over the graves of eighteenth-century priests are found throughout Cogan's work, as in the case of Athlumney grave-yard (ii, 239); the grave of Fr Tom Brady (died c.1770) in Ardbraccan (ii, 271); or that of Fr Phillip Reilly in Monknewtown (ii, 308). Fr Reilly whose name occurs in the registration of popish priests in 1704, had been ordained by St Oliver Plunket back in 1674.

Cogan clearly enjoyed explaining to his readers how he 'found many of the tombs erected over the priests of the last century, deeply embedded in the clay, covered with grass and weeds . . . and only remembered in the traditions of the peasantry' (ibid.).

It is not difficult to envisage this eccentric but scholarly country priest toiling in his clerical frock-coat in the wilderness of a Meath churchyard: 'I was obliged to dig with the spade to remove the superstratum of earth, and wash the stone, in order to decipher the inscription' (ibid.)—and all in the cause of rescuing the names of 'these heroic old pastors, whose memories are allowed to die out' (i, ix). Cogan was in hot pursuit of the ghosts of all those persecuted holy men whose lives had fired his own spiritual imagination—great men like Patrick Fleming who had given his life for his beliefs in far-off Bohemia, and more humble priests of no less heroism who brought the Sacraments to an oppressed people otherwise bereft of hope, in an Ireland wracked by penal and sectarian legislation. It was to the memory of these largely forgotten men that Cogan devoted his short life, and it was Cogan the untiring historian of his Penal Day diocese, who supplied the *Sagart Aroon* with his own version of a noble epitaph: 'They sacrificed all the comforts of this world, crossed the seas at the peril of their lives, indifferent to the fearful penalties of the law, graduated in foreign colleges, and, true to their sacred calling, they returned home to be hunted like the wolf—houseless wanderers in the land of their forefathers' (i, ix).

What lends added interest to Cogan's writings is the clear—and what must have been for him worrying—contradiction between his idealised version of priests in the eighteenth century and those of his own time. There is evidence from Anthony Cogan's *Diocese of Meath* for the author's personal frustration with what he perceived as the complacency of his Catholic clerical colleagues in his diocese. While the *Sagart Aroon* had 'sacrificed all the comforts of this world', the same could scarcely be said of the increasing numbers of Maynooth educated and gentrified farmers' sons who were joining the ministry in mid nineteenth-century Ireland. Cogan, knew them well, having grown up and gone to school among them. The reader who searches patiently through Cogan's vast historical output, will be rewarded by the discovery of an occasional broadside fired off by this fearless observer of the system. Cogan cites Fr William Fagan, the then parish priest of Kilbride (ii, 319, 321) as noticing 'a marked superiority in the knowledge and proficiency, in matters of faith, of the old inhabitants over those instructed in subsequent years, thus evidencing greater pastoral care in former times.' Such comments were scarcely calculated to win Cogan friends in the wider circles of his clerical colleagues. He fulminated against the rich who sought to monopolise seats in chapels (ii, 399) and supported notices put up in church by Fr Patrick Healy of Castlejordan, outlawing such practices which, in Cogan's view, produced 'a great amount of bickering and bad feeling'. As an historian of Early Christian Ireland he was regretful that Catholic priests had come to discourage the custom of pilgrimage to ancient holy sites in Meath (ii, 511). It was a sensitive issue, because Cogan knew full well that 'patterns' at holy wells attracted drunken and unedifying behaviour as well as the prayers of the pious. Much more sensitive was the subject of ecclesiastical preferment, but Cogan grasped this nettle—displaying courage of a kind frequently lacking in clergy of all denominations: 'As a general rule, translations of pastors to more emolumentary cures, unless in cases of *superior adaptability* or other *grave reasons* [Cogan's italics], should be discountenanced, as tending to excite inordinate ambition, and thereby to undermine zeal and foster a spirit of diplomacy' (ii, 319).

These were bold words, written it must be said after the death of Bishop Cantwell, and early in the time of his successor, Thomas Nulty. Since translations, in the form of complicated musical chairs, were the order of the day in the Meath diocese, one wonders how this footnote was greeted by Cogan's bishop.

Cogan was no mere eccentric prodding about with his spade and walking-stick among the ruined churches of his diocese. He set about methodically measuring the dimensions of all surviving ruins, providing details in feet and inches; he measured the vertical height of arches to the vertex and he gave the width at the base. The records of those particular measurements constitute a valuable body of evidence for archaeologists concerned with the state of medieval church ruins in mid nineteenth-century Ireland. He likewise tracked down and recorded inscriptions and carvings on stone crosses and medieval fonts as at Stackallen (ii, 303–4) and Culmullen (ii, 351).

Already, when he was a young curate in Johnstown in the Spring of 1853, he tells us that he and Mr Lentaigne 'the present Inspector-General of Prisons' organised the sending of the medieval church font from Kilcairn to the great Dublin Exhibition of that year (ii, 239–40). We may take it then, that by his late twenties, Anthony Cogan had already established a scholarly interest in the antiquities of Meath. His architectural and archaeological surveys were rather haphazard and they were neither sufficiently detailed nor statistically complete to satisfy the highest standards of Cogan's own time. There were important locations in Meath and many more in Westmeath and Offaly which Cogan failed to visit—in spite of his bold claim to have seen them all. Yet for many of the obscure places he did visit, Cogan's precious record is all that survives. He displayed a remarkably professional approach in his ideas on the preservation of medieval structures and of antiquities generally, which was well ahead of his time.

By a happy chance, Cogan's scholarly approach towards the preservation of antiquities coincided with his extraordinary respect for the resting places of the Christian dead. He was merciless in his condemnation of despoilers of holy places in Meath in his own time and in the recent past. The fate of Ireland's Early Christian remains was a complicated saga, and Cogan himself had researched the subject thoroughly enough to have shown that initially, at least, not all blame could be apportioned to the Protestants, and least of all to the Williamite ascendancy. At the dissolution of the monasteries in the time of Henry VIII, many of the important Pale families who held on to their Catholicism nevertheless profited from acquiring monastic buildings and estates. In some cases those estates may have been reverting, after many centuries, to their original owners. Christopher Nugent, the Baron of Delvin, in spite of his known 'obstinate affection to popery' was granted the estates of Fore Abbey and of Inchmore by Elizabeth in 1567. Similarly, the Cusacks appropriated the celebrated monastic site of Clonard and the nunnery at Lismullen, near Tara. These were but two of several Catholic families who profited from the spoliation of the monasteries of Meath and Westmeath. The fate of parish churches at the Reformation was different from that of the monasteries, since the parishes and their church buildings were taken over by the Established Church. But since adherents to the Reformation were in a minority even in the Pale, many parish churches were deserted and left to ruin. But Cogan's concern did not relate to the distant past. It

54 Ardbraccan Church of Ireland, near Navan. Seat of the Protestant bishops of
Meath and mausoleum of Bishops Pococke and O'Beirne. Cogan objected to
renovations which had been carried out here in 1777 which involved the destruction of earlier graves and ecclesiastical ruins. The cedars, still standing at
Ardbraccan in the twentieth century, were planted by Bishop Richard Pococke in
the summer of 1765.

is clear from reading his work, that the already fragile ruins of
medieval Irish Christianity had come under renewed assault in his
own day from road improvements, land clearances and a renewal in
church building. Some of the destruction he blamed on the vandalism of an alien landlord élite, and on greedy cattle graziers,
insensitive to the intrinsic value of early Irish civilization. Some
blame, too, he apportioned to the Established Church which had, on
occasion, shown insensitivity in site clearance during the building
and restoration of some Protestant churches on Early Christian
locations. He disapproved strongly of the site clearance and removal
of burials at Ardbraccan, for the building of the Protestant church
there in 1777 (ii, 259). He fumed against the building of roads

through the Early Christian cemeteries at Clonfad and Kilbride-Pace in Westmeath (ii, 437). Against those who allowed cattle to foul the sanctuary of Moorechurch in Stamullen, he railed: 'Execration on the goths who dishonour the dead! Where will their own worthless bones rest? Are they human beings, or mere cattle in human shape? Have they souls or is it animal instinct that sets them in motion? The only excuse for these monsters is gross ignorance' (ii, 254).

The obvious target for Cogan's outbursts against the demolition of old monuments was of course the ruling class, whom he perceived as turning a blind eye to the destruction of Ireland's already shattered heritage. He had established that a chapel dedicated to St Peter at Moymurthy in Moorechurch parish had been removed together with surrounding tombstones to be used for building purposes, as recently as 1854. Cogan was all the more incensed because he believed that the vault of this chapel had been used as a place for Mass in Penal times.

Why was not *this Vandal* prosecuted and held up to public indignation, for defacing our ancient monuments and dishonouring the dead? If a bough were lopped off a tree—if a hare or pheasant were captured, *by a poor hungry peasant, the rights of property* would be invoked, the game laws quickly set in motion, and *a magisterial rebuke*, followed by pains and penal-

55 Medieval font from Clonard (*c.* A.D. 1500). Among the panels depicted in this drawing from Sir William Wilde's *Boyne and Blackwater* are a bishop with mitre and crozier (top centre, left) and an angel holding an open book (right). The Flight into Egypt is shown in the top panel on the extreme right. Wilde shared all Cogan's indignation at the desecration of places such as Clonard which he believed had been savagely vandalised by 'vestry clerk, parish bumpkin and itinerant architect' as late as the second quarter of the nineteenth century (ibid., pp. 63–7).

ties, administered to the unhappy delinquent; but the dead may be insulted, their bones exhumed, and their monuments broken, without exciting the indignation or moving to action the very class who, in a healthy state of society, would be the protectors of the people, *the guardians and avengers of the honour of their country.* (ii, 255)

For Cogan in this argument, religious sentiment, nationalism and antiquarianism had all merged.

Not all of Cogan's anger was directed against Protestant land-lords. Already by the time he was writing, a significant number of Catholics had joined the ranks of the older proprietors in the post Famine era. A number of these aspiring and gentrified Catholic farmers were regarded as 'grabbers' by their co-religionists who perceived them as usurping the holdings of those who had been evicted or who had emigrated during the Famine. Such aspiring farmers and *nouveaux riches* who had also turned from tillage to pasturage were not likely to respect old and disused burial grounds which got in the way of commercial enterprise. Cogan, as a conservative and an antiquary, reserved his most dire condemnation for his Catholic colleagues who were insensitive to the treasures of their own past. In a remarkable outburst against one of his own clergy, Cogan took a priest to task for having embellished his new chapel at Meedin in Rochford Bridge at the expense of an Early Christian monument:

> No parish priest has authority vested in himself *to tear down the ancient sanctuaries of our country*; and in a healthy state of society such a man would be prosecuted *as a defacer and destroyer of the ancient monuments of Ireland.* If we expect the laity, Protestant and Catholic, to respect *the consecrated walls of ancient worship*, assuredly *we Priests* ought to show the exam-ple. There are stones sufficient in our quarries, without sacrilegiously plundering the old churches that remain. (Cogan's italics. ii, 481–2)

Few modern archaeologists would dissent from the central senti-ments in this harangue. Cogan was implacably opposed from strong Christian sentiment and traditional Irish respect for the dead, to the building of churches—Protestant or Catholic—over existing burials in established grave-yards. So, he severely lectured his Catholic colleagues on what was, for him, the obscenity of building the Catholic chapel at Frankford in Offaly, on what had been part of the old cemetery of Kilcormick:

> This pagan desecration of the dead—this cruel and heartless (if not impious and sacrilegious) intrusion on a consecrated cemetery, where slept the prince and the peasant, the priest and the monk—where generation after generation of the people, for miles around, went to repose in the silence of the grave—cannot be stigmatised in language sufficiently expressive and condemnatory. If no site could be obtained for a chapel, save and except by rudely invading the *graves of our fathers*, by shovelling up the bones of the dear departed, and carting them off as if they were a nuisance or an obstacle—then better indeed, have the Holy Sacrifice offered up, as it was often-times before, on the mountain top, in the secluded valley or by the shady boreen;—better indeed kneel in the green fields with the open canopy of Heaven above us, . . . than, like parricides, to tear open and outrage the tombs of the dead. (ii, 515)

This impassioned outburst was not likely to find favour with those in authority who were busy raising funds for the erection of numerous churches across the diocese.

VII

FRIENDS AND ENEMIES

While Cogan toiled with manic antiquarian zeal digging up the past in country churchyards, his account of the contribution of the Catholic clergy of Meath to his *History* leaps off the page like a blow from his antiquarian spade: 'I solicited neither advice nor assistance from the clergy of the diocese, nor received any . . . I neither consulted them on the compilation of this work, nor received any suggestion or hint whatever' (i, x). There is of course the obligatory statement that he found his brother priests 'disposed to encourage me' but he returns to the attack with renewed and barbed vigour: 'I am fully conscious that there are many priests in the diocese immeasurably more competent for this undertaking than the writer; but as none took the subject in hands, or, as far as I could judge, seemed likely to do so, I may be excused for at least having made a beginning' (i, x–xi).

Consistent with his defiant attitude as a scholarly loner in a world of clerical philistines, is the scarcity of any acknowledgement on Cogan's part of named local historians who helped him at a scholarly level to compile his three-volume work. He acknowledges his debt to two recently deceased scholarly heavyweights in the first volume—Professor Eugene O'Curry of the Catholic University and Matthew Kelly, professor of ecclesiastical history at Maynooth. But only one (Kelly) may have been his teacher, and neither had ever been his colleague. In the third volume he thanked Father Hogan of Clongowes and Dr McCarthy in Maynooth for showing him historical records, and McCarthy was acknowledged in footnotes for showing him an item from the O'Renehan manuscript collection in Maynooth library (ii, 177) as well as letters of Bishop Anthony Mageoghegan (ii, 85). The first volume of Cogan's work was dedicated with conventional Victorian verbosity to Bishop John Cantwell, but there is no mention of that prelate within any of

Cogan's prefaces, apart from a passing mention of his having obtained a few months leave of absence from his bishop to study the parochial records of Westmeath and Offaly in July 1863 (ii, vii). It is clear from his later account of Cantwell's episcopacy that Cogan respected and may even have liked his bishop, whom he described after his death as 'the old ornamented oak of the forest [who] cast a halo round the very name of Mullingar, by his unflinching patriotism' (ii, 477). But the evidence suggests that John Cantwell took little active role in promoting his Navan curate's historical researches, apart from providing a modest leave of absence and formally directing that Dr Plunket's papers be put into Cogan's care (ii, 552). Although Cogan was still relatively young, his promotion within the diocese during Bishop Cantwell's time had been modest. Cantwell's successor, Bishop Thomas Nulty, gained a warmer mention from Cogan with the inclusion (in his third volume) of an episcopal letter written from the First Vatican Council in Rome in May 1870, supporting Cogan's historical enterprise (iii, xii–iii). Both Cantwell and Nulty, however, were two patriotic bishops who publicly supported the Irish Nationalist movements of their day, and it is curious that Anthony Cogan who shared their political aspirations was not more fulsome in his praise of his two superiors. It may be that Cogan, who was forever a man of the people and who was never slow to advise and criticise his leaders, proved too outspoken even in his historical utterances. The solitary colleague from within his own diocese who earned Cogan's gratitude in any of his prefaces was Matthew McAlroy, parish priest and vicar general of Tullamore, who was thanked 'for the vast mass of letters which he, in the most friendly manner, forwarded to me' (iii, xii). It emerges from elsewhere in the *Diocese of Meath* (ii, 552) that the papers in question were those belonging to Dr Patrick Plunket. The honorable mention of Fr McAlroy is conspicuous for its unique quality and it is clear that this priest played a key role in providing Cogan with crucially important archival material on the eighteenth-century Meath diocese.

While Cogan's helpers at a professional level were virtually non-existent, it would be unwarranted to assume that at a personal level he was a difficult man who lacked friends. He was not only a charismatic preacher, but he also knew how to relate to people—especially the young—at a personal level. A rare insight is afforded into Cogan's warmth and humanity from an account of the impression he made on his Liverpool hosts in 1863: 'His rich fund of amusing anecdote, and his graphic powers of description convulsed the assemblage with unbounded mirth.' (*Drogheda Argus*, 12 September 1863, p. 3, col. 4 under 'Liverpool News'). His round, florid face, presented the appearance of a jovial Meath farmer, and in his obituary he was remembered in Meath as a man 'abounding in anecdote and story' who was 'affable, genial and warm-hearted' to clerical and lay friends alike (Appendix 9). Cogan was himself an outspoken admirer of men who were good company, who could tell a good tale, and who were of a naturally friendly and generous disposition. He could never have gathered all the anecdotes and clerical folktales of such a large diocese without the help and friendship of many priests. While such men may not have shared Cogan's scholarly enthusiasm, they nevertheless helped in important ways. Fr Simon Clarke, who was based in Mayne, Co. Westmeath, is thanked for having driven the author 'to several of the neighbouring churchyards' in Westmeath during the summer of 1863, and Fr Michael Mullen a native of Ardmulchan near Navan, provided Cogan with valuable information on the Westmeath parish of Kilbixy, where he was parish priest (ii, 488). Although Cogan spent little time in the field in Westmeath and Offaly, he had constant access to priests who had been brought up in those areas and who were posted near Cogan in Navan. One of these was the young priest, Joseph Coyne, a native of Tyrrellspass, who was ordained as late as 1865 and who joined the staff of the Navan Seminary as bursar and English master, at the time when Cogan was busy working on his second volume. Cogan thanks this man in his account of the parish of Castletown-Geoghegan 'for much valuable information communicated respecting Westmeath' (ii, 420). Fr Patrick Gibney, parish priest of Castletown Kilpatrick is said to have shown a lively interest in the publication of Cogan's work and was thanked 'for the very friendly spirit in which he replied to all his [Cogan's] queries' (ii, 286). Information on Eniskeen (Kingscourt) was supplied by Luke Farrelly, a curate in Rathkenny (ii, 300), which was a parish adjoining Cogan's native Slane. Richard Costelloe of Killglyn is one of the few laymen who is thanked by Cogan for helping, in his case, with information on Kilcloon parish (ii, 365).

At that point where Cogan takes his history of Meath down to his own time he is almost alarmingly outspoken in his praise of personal friends. His lengthy footnote to the record of the ordinations of three priests, Clarke, Rooney and Morgan, on 10 August 1857 is a case in point (iii, 494–5). These three young priests, who were about seven years Cogan's junior in the diocese, clearly occupied a special place in his affection. Fr Clarke, as we saw above, ferried Cogan around parts of Westmeath. Fr John Rooney, had taught in All Hallows College, Dublin, but had returned to his own diocese 'to the joy of all who knew him' and was at the time of Cogan's writing in 1870, in the parish of Frankford, Co. Offaly. But it was Christopher Morgan, a curate in Skryne when Cogan was writing, who was singled out for special attention. Cogan had served with this man for seven years as a curate in Navan and he was 'I will add, [writes Cogan] his bosom friend':

> the memory of happy days gone by, of unbroken friendship, of fidelity, honesty, and sincerity; of a genial, gentle, gentlemanly, highminded, and patriotic confrere, shall never, and could never be forgotten by the writer of these pages. No one can be more dissatisfied at my eulogy than Fr Morgan; for his humility can only be equalled by his worth; but the author wishes to place on record, even against his will, the feelings of appreciation and affection with which he regards his old, faithful and dearly beloved friend and fellow-labourer.

Clarke, Rooney and Morgan had one thing in common which was important to Cogan. All three were natives of Navan or its environs, and all three had been pupils in the school at Navan, where Cogan was then a master and of which he was very proud. Other references to clerical friends of his own time confirm the picture of Cogan's staunch support for the Navan and St Finian's connection. In his diary for 25 January 1853, Bishop Cantwell noted: 'I assisted at the month's mind of Fr Eugene O'Reilly, of Navan. Sixty-six priests attended on the occasion' (iii, 448). If the bishop had been inspired by the sermon, he failed to record that fact, but his editor, Cogan, who was almost certainly present as a young priest, noted: 'The Rev. Michael Tormey, then professor in the diocesan seminary, at present curate in Rathmolyon, preached a magnificent funeral oration on this occasion.'

Cogan never failed to underline the contribution of priests who taught at St Finian's in Navan, such as that of Terence Timmons, parish priest of Duleek, a 'humble and zealous priest' who was educated in Paris and taught at the Navan seminary from 1840 to 1843 (ii, 236). He identified a young contemporary, Fr Francis

Meade, who taught in the Navan seminary when Cogan was writing his second volume, as the brother of a 'late lamented' recently ordained priest (Thomas Meade) who died in March 1858 (ii, 297–8). So too, Fr James Moore, who taught the first class at the Navan seminary, was identified as the brother of Bartholomew Moore (ii, 478), a curate in Multyfarnham who died as a victim of typhoid 'caught in the discharge of his sacred duties'. Cogan reserved his most impressive eulogy for Fr William McCormick, the science and classics master at the Navan seminary. McCormick, who was ordained in 1829, was many years senior to Cogan, and was thanked 'for much information respecting the pastors of Westmeath' (ii, 502). McCormick was a native of Ballimore and had much information to impart. His uncle, Fr Luke Doyle, who also came from Ballimore, was born back in August 1786 and was ordained in 1810. Here was man with personal memories of '98, who had been involved in priestly matters for almost twenty years before Emancipation. His name had been returned as *dignus* (third in line) in the election for coadjutor bishop in 1824. As for Doyle's nephew William McCormick, he had first-hand experience of the parishes of Sonna, Fore, Kinnegad, Castlejordan, Nobber, Killucan and Tubber. Such a veteran was of invaluable assistance to Cogan who went 'over the top' in recording his gratitude to a senior colleague:

> As a scientific scholar he has no superior in Ireland, and his great abilities and vast information are only equalled by his profound humility, simplicity of manner and unostentatious piety. His letters some years back on the usuries of the Loan Fund, and his numerous poems, are well known throughout the Diocese. Few ecclesiastics love the old land more ardently, and few are more willing to make sacrifices for her welfare, than Father McCormick. At the peril of alienating an old friend, the writer is compelled, through a sense of justice, to place on record the many obligations under which he has placed him. (ii, 504)

Cogan mentioned yet another contemporary who had been a pupil at the Navan Seminary and who later served as a curate in Navan before joining the Jesuits. This was Michael Kelly (iii, 495) a mutual friend of Cogan and Christopher Morgan who 'wherever he laboured his name is still a household word, and nowhere more than amongst the good people of Navan.' The Slane man was remembering his own. And when it came to remembering the dead, he was equally partisan when it came to his friends and neighbours. In 1870, he published a list of Meath priests who had died since the publication of his second volume in October 1867. He lists thirteen men who minstered in parishes scattered across the counties of Meath and Westmeath, laconically entering their names, their parishes and the dates of their deaths. In one case only did Cogan add his own eulogy:

> The Rev. Richard Macken, a native of the parish of Slane, an alumnus of Navan and Maynooth, died, in the second year after his ordination, at Arcachon, in France, whither he went for the good of his health, universally lamented for his many excellent qualities, on Christmas Day 1868; and about the same hour, his saintly sister, Sister Mary Gertrude, of the Convent of Mercy, Drogheda, departed this life, and went, with her beloved brother, to enjoy the reward which awaits innocence of life and fidelity in the service of God (iii, 667).

It is true that the circumstances of these two young people were special—brother and sister had died on Christmas Day—but what was most special to Anthony Cogan was that he and Richard Macken and his sister, all belonged to neighbouring families on the same village street in his beloved Slane. It may be significant, too, that the majority of contemporaries who earned Cogan's fulsome praise were younger curates such as Thomas Gavin 'the present zealous, energetic, and patriotic curate of St Mary's, Drogheda' (iii, 499), who had been ordained as late as September 1861 and who was still a young priest when Cogan was writing. Such men were unlikely to get in the way of Cogan's scholarly programme or of his high ideals.

There were, presumably, those who were jealous of Cogan's success and of the limited recognition he had received as historian of his diocese. He himself was occasionally not averse to quoting flattering words in his own favour. He cites Archbishop John MacHale of Tuam (*Freeman's Journal*, 18 January 1867) where that formidable prelate referred to Anthony Cogan 'the learned and industrious annalist of this large diocese of Meath, who has already contributed so much to our ecclesiastical literature' (iii, 530). But in fairness to Cogan, the passage was embedded in a eulogy which MacHale had delivered at Dr Cantwell's month's mind in Mullingar cathedral on 16 January. One sentence only, on the completion of all Cogan's labours in 1870, contemptuously disposed of the inevitable jealousy and indifference of those who failed to share his enthusiasm: 'Difficulties of course, often arose to obstruct me, and obstacles interposed, to which it is needless to make reference now' (iii, ix).

VIII

AN ARCHIVE RESCUED AND DESTROYED

Cogan may have been a scholarly loner, but he had never worked exclusively as an isolated antiquary in the solitude of a distant library or in his parochial study. On the contrary, his professional life was spent among the young as a teacher, and what we might describe today as a youth-club social worker. As a local historian, he was essentially a researcher who worked in the field, and the success of his operation was dependent not only on the co-operation of the few who had access to documents, but on a host of country priests, many of whom may have viewed him as interfering, if not actively prying, into the affairs of their parishes. His silence therefore, about the help or hospitality which he received from parochial clergy in the course of his known travels is understandable. As for the diocesan archives in Meath and elsewhere, it was difficult for Cogan—a mere curate—to confront this problem head-on. But he was profoundly worried about the future safety of the records he had consulted, and he said so, in bold terms. As his monumental work progressed, he gained in confidence in stating what needed to be done. He had latched on to an idea, which he tells us he had picked up from his mentor, Dr Kelly in Maynooth (i, v), of the need to compile the history of each individual Catholic diocese in Ireland before the ecclesiastical history of the country as a whole could be written. He returned to hammer home this idea in his second volume (ii, x) and boldly placed the ball in the court of the Irish Catholic hierarchy by proclaiming that 'in every diocese there are a number of Priests, full of ability, learning, and zeal . . . who if they be duly patronised by their Bishops, will cheerfully and successfully apply themselves to the meritorious work' of compiling diocesan histories.

What was needed, in Cogan's view, was for the Irish bishops 'to *will* it . . . to utter words of *commission* and *encouragement*, and

133

forthwith the names and memories of many of the saints and scholars . . . of Ireland, shall be rescued from oblivion and neglect' (ii, x). Cogan may well have exaggerated for the purposes of his argument, the number of able and eager local historians in the ranks of the nineteenth-century Irish priesthood. But he understood correctly two crucial points. He recognised the fundamentally local aspect of the great majority of Irish historical records prior to the eighteenth century, and the consequent necessity to study them at regional level. This point is still lost on many modern Irish historians. Secondly, Cogan understood that whatever the calibre of local historical scholarship in the ranks of the Catholic clergy, what was desperately needed was a directive from on high to implement and coordinate a policy for the calendaring and preservation of diocesan records.

> If every Prelate in Ireland called on the Parish Priest or Curate of each parish, to prepare carefully a history of his parish for conference, then appoint an archivist to collect and preserve these records, and subsequently take the opinion of the clergy in the selection of a competent historiographer, in order to impart life, shape, and form, to these parochial collections, I have no doubt a volume of interesting materials would be forthcoming, which would reflect the greatest honour and glory on the piety and fidelity of our ancestors, as well as on our predecessors in the ministry. (iii, x–xi)

Cogan had a far-sighted and ambitious programme for the preservation not only of documents, but also of archaeological material. He suggested elsewhere (ii, 327) that 'every diocese in Ireland could have an ecclesiastical museum ... for the preservation of the old chalices, altar-stones, crucifixes, vestments etc. which were used in penal times.' If that were not feasible, he suggested that a central museum be established for this purpose in Maynooth. He was rightly convinced that with the proliferation of new churches in Ireland in the mid nineteenth century 'the next genera- tion shall find it difficult to credit that their ancestors worshipped by stealth' (ibid.). He urged that the thatched chapel at Cruisetown, Nobber, which had been condemned and closed by Bishop Cantwell should be photographed so that 'it would teach the next generation a lesson of respect for the faith and fidelity of their forefathers' (ii, 331). As ever, Cogan understood the value of recording the monuments of his own time in a way that married his archaeological and historical interests to his strongly held conservative Christian faith.

Cogan wrote, not as an armchair historian, but as a researcher and field-worker, whose primary concern was with the preservation and transcription of the records themselves. That approach also tied in with his reputation for being a man of the people. His desire to rescue medieval baptismal fonts, write down the clerical folklore of his time, and compile a photographic record of outdated mud-walled chapels—all sprang from his love of the people and of the past from which they came. By the 1860s, this self-taught local historian had come of age, and writing with extraordinary achievements behind him, he dared to lecture the Catholic bishops not only on what needed to be done, but on what would happen if his advice were not followed. He branded the lack of action on the part of those in authority as 'a national grievance' (ii, ix) and proclaimed that it was 'hopeless to expect a complete ecclesiastical history of Ireland in our own day' (iii, xii) unless action were taken at diocesan level. Bishop Gaffney eventually (and after Cogan's death) acted on Cogan's advice, by ordering that a chronicle of events should be kept in each parish of the diocese of Meath. That order was not observed. Cogan had predicted that if the task 'be much longer deferred, a time will certainly soon arrive when it will be *too late* [his own italics]' (iii, xi). He was not just worried about the death of Ireland's Gaelic oral tradition. Experience—no doubt much of it bitter—had taught him to fear for the very survival of the rudimentary episcopal archives themselves. He tells us that it took him ten years to collect and edit the letters of the late eighteenth-century Bishop Patrick Plunket and that the papers from the Meath diocesan archive catalogued at the end of his third volume would 'if printed at large, constitute a large quarto volume' (iii, ix). But all was not well with that archive as Cogan's concern reveals:

Many of these papers and letters are most important, as they throw great light on the various controversies and subjects of their day; but whether they are destined to perish, or to see the light of publication, must necessarily depend on the public spirit, and love of Irish ecclesiastical history, which animate the clergy and laity of the Diocese of Meath.

Cogan knew his people well and he rightly feared the worst. Even during the time of Bishop Nulty some documents were destroyed. Cogan himself suggests that very recent material had been lost from the archive before his own time. In his catalogue of undated manuscripts which he found in the archive, he lists 'A cover with the following inscription: "Papers concerning Lord Dunboyne"' and he adds the comment: 'Unfortunately the papers have disappeared, at least the writer has never seen them' (iii, 681). Even the papers of John Cantwell—the bishop of Cogan's own time as a priest—seem to have gone missing, for while Cogan had access to Cantwell's diaries (with the exception of that for 1842), he feared for the safety of that bishop's archive: 'his numerous collection of diocesan papers I have never seen; but I experience great pleasure in saving from ruin or oblivion all the materials which have fallen in my way' (iii, 471).

Diocesan disputes in Meath during the late nineteenth century—perceived by some as scandalous—rendered the once neglected Meath archive an embarrassing encumbrance. At the direction of Bishop Gaughran in 1909, virtually the entire diocesan archive for the Catholic diocese of Meath was burned. Fr Richard MacCullen, who later became parish priest of Kells and a monsignor and vicar general of the diocese, had been present as a young priest at the burning, but was not responsible for it. He died in 1975. Cogan listed over two hundred manuscript items in his *Catalogue of Papers and Letters in the Archives of the Diocese of Meath* (iii, 669–81) which he described as 'an immense mass of papers and letters' which were 'too bulky and voluminous' to be included in his *Diocese of Meath*. This material, dating from 1623 to 1826, along with all subsequent archival documents down to the beginning of the twentieth century were destroyed on Gaughran's orders.

Each historian who consults Cogan's catalogue of lost treasures will have his or her special reason to regret this catastrophe. The list is too extensive and too varied to single out any particular loss. Documents vary from tantalising details of local upheavals and disputes, or lists of chapels and clergy, and letters from parsons and demands for tithes, to wider issues such as provision for the education of priests in continental colleges, and matters such as Louis XVIII and the Abbé Edgeworth, or to Mrs Fitzherbert and the Prince Regent. As the eye falls on such items as *Excommunication fulminated by Dr Plunket against some rioters who had disturbed the peace of the town of Navan*, dated 2 April 1780 (iii, 672) or on *A Manuscript on the Pronunciation of the Irish Language* (iii, 680) we realise that a whole people have been cheated out of a record which was primarily theirs, by custodians who proved lamentably unworthy of their stewardship of a Christian heritage. Fr John Brady in *A Short History of the Parishes of the Diocese of Meath*, writing in 1937, labelled the fate of the Meath archive a 'criminal destruction', but he was still too close to those events and to the bishop responsible for them, to lay blame squarely where it belonged. Cogan who laboured in the face of complacency and ignorance, and who predicted what might come, was less afraid to speak out and must be allowed to have the last word in passing judgement:

> A terrible responsibility to God and their country will have devolved on those who could, in times propitious, with little trouble, have preserved the memory of those really great men, the true patriots, and benefactors of their countymen, who were faithful and true in their generation, and whose names in the Book of Life are identified with the sufferings, the sacrifices, the glories, and the triumph of Catholic Ireland. (iii, xi)

Ironically, it was probably Anthony Cogan who established a diocesan archive in Meath in the first instance. He informs us that the papers of Bishop Patrick Plunket (died 1827) were in his care by 1867 (ii, 289), and those papers made up the great bulk of the manuscript collection. When Cogan died, he was referred to on his monument in Slane Catholic church as diocesan archivist. In the early eighteenth century it was neither prudent nor practical for Irish Catholic bishops to preserve information on ordinations to the priesthood, Confirmations, or details on parochial organisation. Not only were their episcopal activities carefully monitored by law, when not actually proscribed altogether, but bishops—constantly on the move—lacked a fixed residence or *caput* within their dioceses. That was very obviously true of early Penal Day bishops such as the first Patrick Plunket (son of the 9th Baron of Killeen) who was translated to Meath in 1669 (ii, 115). A report drawn up for Pope Clement IX claims Plunket 'lay concealed in the woods, on the mountain, and in the cabins of the poor' (ibid.). But even as late as 1765, Bishop Augustus Cheevers was writing to the Bishop of Arras from 'his hiding place' (ii, 166), and later in his life he relied on relatives to provide him with a room. He usually stayed with his niece, Margaret Cheevers, the wife of James O'Neill, at Crackenstown near Ratoath (ii, 166). Towards the end of his life (he died in 1778) he was accommodated by the Everard family in Randalstown (ii, 173). Such a man, who in the words of his own relative, 'was always uneasy for a convenient place in his diocese' (ii, 166) is unlikely to have preserved many documents, and his relatives even less so. The next bishop, the second Patrick Plunket, who was consecrated in Paris in 1779, was responsible for the organisation of the modern diocese of Meath and was the first post-Reformation Catholic prelate to exercise his episcopal duties, for the most part, without undue fear of the law. Patrick Plunket was a conscientious bishop who during his forty-eight years in Meath kept meticulous records relating to his visitations, and he hoarded all letters and documents. With his episcopate, the Meath archive came into being, and on his death in 1827, it was miraculously saved by Fr James O'Rafferty of Tullamore. That priest, who had once served under Bishop Plunket as a curate in Navan, 'observed the vast mass of papers and letters which Dr Plunket had piled on the shelves of his library. . . . He attended the auction of his effects, and, comprehending the loss which the diocese would sustain if these records passed away, collected with pious praiseworthy care, all he could secure, brought them to Tullamore, and guarded them during life from dispersal and destruction' (ii, 552).

James O'Rafferty died as parish priest of Tullamore in June 1857 and his successor, Matthew McAlroy, mercifully 'exercised similar vigilance' towards Bishop Plunket's papers, passing them on to Anthony Cogan 'enjoining at the same time rigorous guardianship over their safety and preservation' (ii, 552). Fr McAlroy lived until September 1892, but it was Anthony Cogan who organised and calendared the papers of Dr Plunket, and it must have been from Cogan's time, or at his death, that an episcopal archive—if such it could be called—was established at Mullingar under Bishop Nulty. Mullingar could not have been a place for the collection of documents prior to the moving of the centre of the diocese from Navan to Mullingar, and the dedication of the cathedral there a few years later, by Bishop Cantwell in 1836. There are several remarkable aspects surrounding the tale of survival and destruction of the Meath archive. It appears that a bishop's documents were regarded as his personal property, and that on his death their fate was more precarious than that of his armchair or his walking-stick. Meath fared better in terms of archival survival, as Cogan reminds us, than many other dioceses such as Armagh, Ferns, Ossory and Tuam. He reminds us, too, that some of the papers of John Thomas Troy,

Archbishop of Dublin (died 1823), 'were found round soft goods emanating from a grocer's shop' (ii, 550). It is clear that there scarcely was a Meath archive as such prior to Cogan's time, and that in spite of his labours, the documents which he had preserved were later left to lie, neglected and unused in Mullingar, rather than form the nucleus of a centre for information or research. It is small wonder that such a manuscript collection should perish. It is to the immortal credit of James O'Rafferty—a man born in Kinnegad in the late eighteenth century—that he treasured Bishop Plunket's memory sufficiently to have rescued his papers back in 1827. We are equally indebted to Fr McAlroy who 'exercised similar vigilance' so that they survived long enough and briefly enough, for Anthony Cogan to bring his great hunger for the past to bear on their precious testimony. The wonder is not that these records were destroyed, but that Cogan ever had an opportunity to consult them and transcribe so many of them.

IX

HARVESTING THE COLLECTIVE
MEMORY OF HIS PEOPLE

It is thanks to Cogan's extraordinary labours that so much has survived the vandals of a later age. This point deserves special emphasis in view of the depressing evidence of scholarly neglect and archival destruction that marred the generation of his successors. Cogan's first volume on the early Irish Church in Meath is now too much of a period piece to merit radical revision. William Hennessy's edition of the *Annals of Ulster* did not appear until 1887—fifteen years after Cogan's death, so Cogan understandably relied on John O'Donovan's edition of the later and less reliable *Annals of the Four Masters*. But Cogan made the maximum use of the early Irish sources then available to him and he studied closely the great mass of topographical information available in the published works of O'Donovan and O'Curry. His own extraordinary knowledge of Meath and Westmeath topography led him to an instinctive under-standing of his early material. His notion, for instance, of there being a set of annals preserved at Trevet in Co. Meath was a remarkable idea which has much to recommend it. He was capable, too, of correctly associating the most obscure places (such as Rathcore in south Meath) with isolated incidents recorded in the early annals. When we realise that Cogan did not have access to the Vatican archives or to more recent State Papers relating to Ireland, we realise how well he succeeded in patching together the scattered later medieval and early modern records of his diocese. His docu-mentary work was based largely on those boxfuls of papers sent to him from Tullamore. That was a fortuitous situation, for the very dearth of his materials forced him to concentrate on those docu-ments which were later destined for the flames. His fundamental achievement—although he did not appreciate it at the time—was to record so much of the vulnerable Meath diocesan archive for posterity. Cogan had an innate respect for documents and because of this he edited and transcribed masses of original material—bishops' diaries and letters—through which he recorded the acts of the Catholic Church in Meath from the Reformation down to his own day. With the loss of the sources from which he worked, Cogan's *Diocese of Meath* has taken on the character of a primary source in its own right. When we bear in mind that several Irish dioceses still await a scholar to write their histories at the turn of the twentieth century, we appreciate something of Anthony Cogan's achievement as a pioneer in this field.

It would be completely wrong to attempt to portray Anthony Cogan as a great historian—something which he clearly was not. It would also miss the point of the man's true claim to greatness. Although he was accurate and methodical with the sources at his disposal, his desire to fill in gaps and to embellish a narrative led him into minor errors of fact when his meagre sources failed him. So we are told priests died at a great age, when on checking, we find they were only in their fifties, and elsewhere we are informed that some pastors died in a given year, when in fact they only retired at that time. On the other hand, Cogan was rarely wrong when he cited a date from an inscription or a document, and he possessed encyclopaedic knowledge of the inter-relationships between the clerical families of Meath. His method of using oral tradition alongside documentary material, which might seem eccentric to us, proved invaluable at a time when pre-Famine traditions were still alive in rural Ireland. Thus, he identified countless locations for Penal Day Mass sites of which all memory would vanish in the generation after his death. Some of these he located with pin-point accuracy, such as the pedestal of a stone cross outside Eniskeen graveyard in Kingscourt (ii, 299), or the 'Mass Hollow' at Glennenerrim at the foot of the Hill of Ballinvally in the parish of Oldcastle (ii, 337). Other 'mass rocks' and priests' hiding places were assigned a more general location, such as the Hill of Mullagh in Dysart (ii, 425); the Ben of Fore and islands in Lough Lene (ii, 430); and on the Erry Hills near Clara (ii, 500). The list seems endless. Obscure and forgotten burial places of saintly Penal Day bishops—so important for Cogan's own understanding of the continuity within the sacramental life of his own community—were recorded with loving care. We read of Dr James Cusack buried at the east end of the old church in Duleek in 1688 (ii, 140); and of Dr Cheevers, buried in Donaghpatrick in 1778 without 'headstone or slab' (ii, 173). An old man whose father had attended that bishop's funeral, pointed out the exact location to the wandering Cogan, and Cogan found an entry in the registry of deaths in Kilberry which confirmed the Donaghpatrick location for Bishop Cheever's burial. Finally, he tells us that the first Bishop Patrick Plunket of Meath (there were two) was laid to rest with his noble ancestors in the east end of the old church of Killeen in November 1679 (ii, 127). That Bishop Plunket's friend and relative, St Oliver Plunket, Archbishop of Armagh, wrote of him: 'although he was the son of one of the first nobility of the kingdom, yet he never pursued any of the vain pleasures of this world' (ii, 128).

Cogan was not critical when it came to evaluating the evidence for the eighteenth century, and his work was too hagiographical to have achieved the objectivity required of a mid nineteenth-century historian. But among his many achievements was to visit the churchyards of his diocese, describe ruins, take measurements, record inscriptions, and jot down all the clerical traditions which he encountered en route. The great wealth of folklore, parish gossip and oral traditions which he relegated to footnotes in his *Diocese of Meath* are more precious today than most of his conscientious labours at writing the history of his diocese. These local traditions, replete with names of farm labourers, peasants, priests and gentry, exhibit all the hallmarks of stories written down accurately in the field. Their accurate recording was facilitated by the fact that Cogan chose to believe so many of them. Cogan presents us in these tales with a mixed bag of important fact and no less important fiction.

While Cogan served as a curate in Ardbraccan in the summer of 1857, he recorded the tale of the proprietor of Dormstown Castle who, while trying to effect the desecration of the old church at Markystown, hacked at his own leg with a spade and died 'miserably' (ii, 259). Far away in Clara, Co. Offaly, he recorded the tale of a man who feigned sickness in order to ensnare the priest who attended him. The ruse backfired on the hoaxer, who became genuinely ill and was dead on the arrival of the priest (ii, 501). It did not trouble Cogan that he recorded the same folktale in the parish of Eglish (ii, 511–2). With these tales we may compare that of Barry Lowe, a notorious priest-hunter from Newtown, Westmeath, who was struck 'stone blind' for his capture of a priest (ii, 419–20). Cogan recorded a tale 'to which the people attach unwavering faith' which centred on Fr John Duffy who became parish priest of Castletown-Geoghegan in 1795. In the aftermath of the 1798 rebellion, a band of Orangemen, marching down the road to Toar

56 Multyfarnham Abbey, Co. Westmeath.
Elizabeth I wrote of this place; 'Likewise, in the diocese of Meath, which is in the
heart of the English Pale, there is suffered to stand untouched a house of friars,
called Multifernam, the only place of assembly and conventicle of all the traitorous
Jesuits (*sic*) of the realm, and where was the first conspiracy and plotting of the
great rebellion.' O'Donnell *Franciscan Abbey of Multyfarnham*, p.25.
The continuity of Franciscan ministry at Multyfarnham was to Cogan a symbol of
the resilience and strength of faith in Ireland. As a secular priest Cogan showed
nothing but admiration for the work of the friars and other orders in the eighteenth
century, and he chose to play down evidence for any friction between regular and
diocesan clergy.

had resolved on murdering Fr Duffy, but the priest's horse, divinely
appraised of their evil intentions, insisted on ferrying his master
home 'by a much more circuitous, and, as the event proved, a much
safer road' (ii, 422–3). Such anecdotes belong more to the world of
medieval hagiography than to nineteenth-century historical writing.
But their presence in Cogan's work has preserved for all time the
collective memory of a diocesan community where fact and folktale
were inextricably mingled in local lore.

Cogan presents us with more straightforward folktales, such as
those relating to church bells, but as is often the case with Cogan,
he mixes in tantalising circumstantial details into these stories,

which leaves them suspended in a realm of half-truth. So, he tells us of the burial of a silver bell at Churchtown, Bective (ii, 348) or the curious tale of a Catholic bell of Killagh, which was also buried, but was later dug up and first offered to the priest. It was afterwards said to have been sold to a parson, who used it in his Protestant church (ii, 315–16). Cogan had a developed dramatic sense, and he could tell a good story. He was at his best in relating the miseries of the Penal Days, and being the good synthesiser that he was, he had a keen eye for the relevant stirring tale. Among his more memorable accounts is that of Fr Mooney's record of his profession as a Franciscan friar while a prisoner in the castle at Ballymore in 1601. Cogan (iii, 594–5) took the passage from Meehan's *Franciscan Monasteries of Ireland* :

> Realise it, to your imagination, dear brother: picture yourself as a young man in the plentitude of his strength, kneeling at the feet of an aged bishop and his provincial, both captives for their loyalty to God and the faith of their fathers, and there in the gloom of that dungeon, pronouncing with unfaltering tongue those irrevocable vows which consecrated him the liege servant of God, and doomed him to the persecution of ruthless laws.

Anthony Cogan had a special interest in such men and in the Franciscan convent of Multyfarnham, in Westmeath, because of the heroic efforts made by the friars to maintain a community there into the nineteenth century. For him, its ruins and its graveyard were a living symbol of the continuity of Faith within the diocese—faith which had been kept at great personal cost and whose story needed to be celebrated by the historian. As a secular priest, he was generous in his praise of those communities of friars who kept the Church alive at a time when diocesan and parochial organisation had all but broken down, and thanks to Cogan we have local accounts of the activities of Franciscans and Dominicans within the diocese in penal times. The smaller communities are of particular interest, such as the Franciscans in the eighteenth century who 'had a farm of land attached to the Friary' in a secluded part of Cully in the parish of Frankford or Ballyboy in Offaly (ii, 514).

Cogan's most memorable tale is that of Bishop Eugene Geoghegan's defence of his house in distant Ballybeg, in the parish of Tubber, in a western corner of Westmeath, which was attacked by a gang of murderous ruffians on the night of 27 March 1776:

> A stone flung through the window, which hit the post of the
> bed on which Dr Geoghegan was sleeping, awoke him; and,
> when he rose to ascertain the cause, he saw a robber with a
> hatchet in his hand attempting to force his way through the
> window. When the bishop asked him what brought him there,
> the ruffian, who was supported on the shoulders of his
> companions, averted his face, took more drink, and continued
> to force himself through the window. The bishop remon-
> strated with him, threatened, but all to no purpose. Now in
> the room there was an old rusty gun, which Dr Geoghegan
> had in his hands that day while walking through his little farm,
> and in which there was an old charge which he endeavoured
> frequently, but in vain to fire off. When remonstrance failed
> with the robber, the bishop took the old gun in his hands and
> presented it at the intruder. More drink was now supplied to
> Allard, and he persevered, hatchet in hand forcing himself in
> the window.

This is Cogan's best story—and as it happened, a true story—which
I leave for the master himself to complete on page 176 of the second
volume of his *Diocese of Meath*. Cogan, with his customary eye for
the kind of local detail, that invested his tales with heightened interest,
named the murderous attacker as 'Mick Allard (pronounced by the
people Ollard), from the hill of Rathconrath' but he embroidered his
account with hagiographical embellishments. The *Hibernian Journal*
(29 March—1 April 1776) reported this incident as an attack by
White Boys in retaliation for Bishop Geoghegan having preached
against their depradations. It identified the bishop's victim as 'a
notorious leader of the White Boys' and claimed the bishop was
prepared for the assault. Cogan must have found it difficult to
accept that this most serious attempt on the life of a Catholic bishop
was perpetrated not by 'bigots' but perhaps by members of his own
congregation. He did not discuss the embarrassing political or
religious affiliations of the would-be murderers.

Bishop Geoghegan was not the only clergyman whose life was
put at risk in those violent times. Fr John Hoey, parish priest of
Castlejordan, was stoned to death in a faction fight on St Patrick's
Day, 1732. The unfortunate pastor, then in his late eighties, had
intervened to put an end to the fracas (ii, 397). In the century before

57 The castle of Donore, Co. Meath, near the Dominican friary. Dominican priests continued to minister to the people of this parish throughout the eighteenth century. Richard Ennis, one of Cogan's priestly heroes, was parish priest here until his death in 1854. Fr Ennis was remembered for ministering to cholera victims in Navan in 1832, and as a founder member of the Tenant League in Meath. He was a firm supporter of Fredercik Lucas, seconding his nomination in the election of 1852 (ii, 380-1).

(c.1645), Fr Gargan of Nobber had been stoned to death by Puritans at Robertstown (ii, 332). Fr Richard Ennis was remembered by the people of Navan for his untiring efforts to console cholera victims during a terrible outbreak of the disease in that town in 1832 (ii, 380), while Cogan's friend, Denis Walsh, parish priest of Donore, died of cholera in 1849. Cogan's pages are replete with records of holy men in nineteenth-century Meath whose memories were revered for sanctity of life by their people. We read of Fr Thomas O'Reilly from Hayestown near Navan, who was buried in Ardmulchan graveyard in 1779 and whose grave became a place of pilgrimage for his people and to whose intercession 'many miracles were attributed' (ii, 300). Fr George Barnewall, parish priest of Moynalvy c.1750, had died from a fall from his horse, and the place of his death was marked by a roadside cairn at which was recited the *De profundis* in Cogan's day (ii, 372). Perhaps Cogan's greatest testimony to the sanctity of one of his own colleagues was his comparing Fr George Leonard of Oldcastle to the Curé of Ars. Cogan was impressed most of all by this priest's dedication to the service of his people: 'He has not slept six nights out of his parish for the last thirty-four years', and then only when he was absent on the diocesan retreat (ii, 339). There is a real sense from reading Cogan's records that many of these men had indeed given up all in

146

their devotion to the priestly calling, and hagiographical rhetoric apart, Cogan's eighteenth- and early nineteenth-century Meath priests appear to have experienced genuine hardship and deprivation. One of their number was the thirty-five year old Richard Gosson, a curate in Mountnugent, who was buried in Moyagher cemetery in 1806 after he 'got a wetting while attending a station [Mass], sat hearing confessions in his wet clothes, and caught a severe cold' (ii, 261). 'Stations' were organised as venues for Mass and Confession in certain houses in remote areas of a parish which provided a base for the priest to attend his scattered people. While attempting to reach one such outpost in Drumconrath, 'Rev. Mr Fleming or his successor [Fr O'Reilly], I don't know which, had a narrow escape from being drowned, crossing over the swollen stream to attend a sick call or discharge some duty in Innismot' (ii, 295). Fr Thomas Fleming mentioned in this record, had been ordained at the hands of St Oliver Plunket in 1684. Fr Patrick Geoghegan, parish priest of Tullamore (Durrow and Kilbride) died after a lengthy decline in March 1799. He was believed to have suffered from exposure while hiding from yeomen in a cornfield during the Great Rebellion in '98 (ii, 549).

Cogan's great historical enterprise underlines above all the intimate bond which existed between priest and people in Ireland in the eighteenth and early nineteenth centuries. For Cogan, it was a bond which was never to be severed, either by emigration or even in death. There is evidence, for instance, that the mass exodus of people from Meath to Britain and the United States did not, in the initial stages, sever the bonds between emigrants and their communities in the parishes back home. Irish emigrants in England

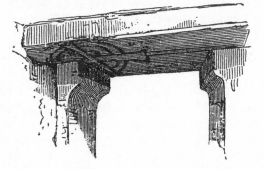

58 Doorway of church at Ardmulchan showing an early Christian cross-slab reused as a lintel. Cogan records that Fr Thomas O'Reilly from Hayestown near Navan was buried here in 1779 and that his grave became a place of pilgrimage where miracles were reported by those who sought his intercession (ii, 300).

contributed the substantial sum of £470 to Fr Andrew McAlroy when he was a curate in Navan (1827–37), for the church in that town (ii, 438). Fr Leonard's erstwhile parishoners from Oldcastle sent him back a beautiful chalice from New York (ii, 339). Many Meath priests also travelled to England and to the United States, some of whom ended their days there. There was Fr William O'Brien who ran into debt trying to build his church at Ballymore, and who ended his career as a priest in Wisconsin in about 1859 (ii, 495). His successor, on the other hand, was not surprisingly a financial wizard who had collected £1000 in the United States for the building of Rosemount chapel in Tubber (ibid.). One of Cogan's own 'College companions', William Barry from Cookstown, near Batterstown, died as a priest in Louisiana in 1863 (ii, 362–3). Cogan tells us that when Fr Edward Gargan, parish priest of Castlepollard died in Birmingham in 1829, he was secretly exhumed after burial in Birmingham and his body was spirited back to Ireland where 'it was waked for a night in the chapel of Athboy' by his old friends from Navan, as the cortège made its way to Castlepollard (ii, 404–5).

There was a price which occasionally had to be paid by bishops for the power which individual priests derived from their extraordinary popularity with their people. Thomas Hitchcock, a Dominican friar was suspended by his bishop, Patrick Plunket, in 1810, from his job as administrator of the newly-formed parish of Longwood. The Dominicans from the nearby friary of Donore were popular with the people. Fr Hitchcock refused to stand down. 'He continued contumacious, and led into schism a number of the parishoners' (ii, 367). The dispute dragged on, with Dr Plunket being summoned before the Quarter Session at Trim, on another matter relating to Fr Hitchcock, in July 1812. The strong-willed Dominican eventually relented and 'died an edifying death'. In Cogan's own time, one of his friends 'the venerable and saintly Father Mullen', was prevented from taking up his duties as parish priest of Ballinacargy or Kilbixy in October 1825. Cogan passed over this embarrassing episode with the comment: 'A faction closed the chapel doors against him, resolved to admit no one as pastor except Rev. Edward Duffy, their former curate. By degrees this absurd combination crumbled away, and all became reconciled to their learned and zealous parish priest' (ii, 487).

It is clear, however, from the pages of the *Drogheda Journal* (12 October 1825) that the bishop's decision to remove Fr Duffy against the wishes of local people caused major unrest within the parish, including outrages committed against the property of people who were believed to have been instrumental in the curate's removal. The church in Ballynacargy was placed under a self-imposed interdict which Anthony Cogan felt it was inappropriate—out of loyalty to his friend, perhaps—to record:

> They assembled on the Sunday following, subsequent to the removal of their pastor, to the number of several hundreds, barricaded the doors of the chapel with stone and threatened to destroy any clergyman who should attempt to enter. The consequences have been that no worship has been performed there ever since; and so determined are the people to oppose what they believe an act of tyranny that they will not even allow the rites of their church to be administered to any individual in the parish or by any priest until Fr Duffy is restored to them. The peasantry have also assembled in great numbers and at different times came to the chapel of this town [Mullingar] and uttered threats to the Parish Priest here [Fr M. McCormick], against any clergyman who should go to officiate in Ballynacarig, and remonstrated against his interference in the affair. (*Drogheda Journal*, 12 October 1825)

Fr Mullen eventually took up his duties as parish priest. Fr Duffy did not return to his people, and later died as parish priest of Ballynabracky.

The overall picture which emerges from Cogan's extraordinary wealth of clerical portraits is that of a team of strong-willed patriarchs who occasionally displayed an independence of mind which ran contrary to the wishes of their bishop, but whose personal integrity and dedication to their calling was rarely in doubt. A striking feature, which has a bearing on this independence of mind, is the fact that well into the middle of the nineteenth century a very sizeable proportion of Meath priests had been educated in colleges scattered over France, Spain and Italy as well as in the more recent foundations of Maynooth and Carlow. While nearly all the younger generation had been schooled in Navan, by no means all had gone on to Maynooth, which as far as Meath was concerned, had not yet tightened its uniform grip on the making of Ireland's Catholic priests. Even for those who had been trained in France, Paris had not been their exclusive home. George McDermott, parish priest of Oldcastle (died 1832), had been a student at Bordeaux (ii, 338–9);

John Masterson, a friend of Cogan, had studied at the Sulpician house of Toulouse, and was ordained in Meaux cathedral in 1828 (ii, 382), while the veteran Patrick McDermott had served as a chaplain to the Irish Brigade at Fontenoy before ending his days as parish priest of Castletown-Kilpatrick (ii, 285). Peter O'Reilly, the parish priest of Kingscourt who championed Tenant Right, had studied at Nevers in France and was ordained in Rome in 1837. Among other exotic personalities who pass before our gaze are John Hackett, 'The Old Spaniard', parish priest of Longwood (1842-54), who had trained in Salamanca (ii, 367); and Awly McAuley, whose career had led him to Rome and back to remote Frankford in Offaly, and from there back again to Parma, and the United States, ending his days in 1824 as administrator in Castletown-Geoghegan (ii, 519). These men and many others like them, such as 'The Baron O'Donoghue', parish priest of Rathmolyon, who was drowned in Liverpool in 1836, do not convey the impression of colourless conformists who carved out a farming career from their rural ministries. A few of them may have done, but the great majority appear in Cogan's pages as well educated roundly formed person-alities who had travelled far, and seen more of life than most of the Protestant gentry of Meath and Westmeath. Their bishop, the aristocratic Patrick Plunket, had spent twenty-six years in France, prior to an incredible forty-eight years in the episcopacy in Meath. During his long stay in France he had become one of the provisors at the Collège des Lombards—centre for the Irish students in Paris. On his consecration in Paris as bishop of Meath in 1779, he was said to have been presented with an episcopal ring by Marie Antoinette. Plunket was certainly recommended for the bishopric of Meath to the pope, Pius VI, by the archbishop of Paris and the French Court. We have already encountered this aristocratic Irishman withdrawing 'in grief' before the prospect of the rebellious upheavals in Meath in '98. But we must not forget that another priest, Fr John Murphy, legendary leader of the Men of Wexford, also in that Great Rebellion, had not spent all his days at Boulavogue. Fr Murphy, like Patrick Joseph Plunket, had also studied overseas—in the case of the Wexford priest, at Seville in Spain.

There were veteran priests in Cogan's time whose memories of their continental training took them back into the late eighteenth century and who clearly held a special fascination for him. Such a man was Fr Gough, 'the worthy and venerable pastor of Curraha, in whose society the author has passed some of his happiest hours' (iii,

59 The Sorbonne, Paris, *c.*1650. Nearly 2000 Irishmen took degrees at the University of Paris in the seventeenth and eighteenth centuries. The story of this remarkable band of exiles, some of whom settled in France, joining the army and the professions, and others of whom returned to penal-day Ireland as priests, is one that has been sadly neglected by all but the specialist. Among the many works by Irishmen, or about Ireland, produced in this Paris community was the *Histoire de l'Irlande* written in three volumes by Abbé Ma-Geoghegan in 1756. Its author was one of the last of a family of kings, bishops and scholars which had ruled in Westmeath and Offaly from the seventh to the seventeenth centuries.

458). Gough had been a student at the Irish College in Paris in the early 1820s and his personal memories of Irishmen studying in France went back twenty years beyond those of Dr Matthew Kelly of Maynooth. Gough is mentioned as a student in Paris in a letter written by Fr Hugh O'Reilly to Bishop Plunket of Meath from St Roch in Paris (25 November 1824), in which the writer also describes how he [O'Reilly] 'was amongst the last to take a parting view of Lewis XVIII' before 'he was laid in the tomb.' Yet another veteran, 'one of our most distinguished priests, Father Kelly of Kilskyre, no ordinary judge indeed' conveyed to Cogan his personal memories of Bishop Logan's ability as a preacher (iii, 468). Fr Kelly's memories of Bishop Logan had to predate that prelate's death in 1830. Perhaps the most remarkable link between that era of holy men who had been trained abroad and those who lived in an easier age, was in the person of Patrick McDermott, parish priest of Castletown Kilpatrick who died at the age of 111 in 1814. Cogan had heard from the parish priest of Oldcastle that he had served Fr McDermott's Mass as a boy when the old patriarch was then 108. On this reckoning, Cogan had a colleague who knew a priest who was born in 1703. That same Fr McDermott had served as a chaplain to the Irish Brigade in the Battle of Fontenoy (1745).

It is a small wonder that Cogan tells us such men as Fr McDermott were invariably sought out by the gentry to grace their dinner tables (ii, 279, 285). These claims, that the company of cultured priests was sought by the Protestant gentry, may in part reflect the inferiority complex of a writer whose people was colonised by a Protestant élite, and who was at pains to show that his side could hold its own at a social level. On the other hand, the claim has much to recommend it, if for no other reason than it runs counter to the dubious stereotype in Cogan's popular tales of relentless conflict between hunted priests and their bigoted oppressors. The contradiction between the image of the *Sagart Aroon* out on the hillside attending his down-trodden flock, and the Paris-trained *abbé*, recounting tales after dinner to his Protestant host, was a product of the very different kinds of source material employed by Cogan. There must be truth in both of these apparently contradictory images, when applied to different circumstances and to different times. But by Cogan's day, the mythology of conflict between the religions had gone so deep, that more sober realities were swamped in the rhetoric attached to set positions adopted by protagonists on both sides. Consequently, the more enduring image we retain from Cogan's *Diocese of Meath* is, significantly and regrettably, one of conflict and oppression.

Cogan emerges not just as an historian, but as a great repository of clerical lore in mid nineteenth-century Ireland. He seems to have begun his researches as an antiquary, set on the task of writing up separate accounts of the early Christian monasteries and churches of his midland diocese. Initially, he had set himself the task of following in Archdall's footsteps. His discovery or introduction to the papers of Bishop Patrick Plunket, preserved in Tullamore, was probably the single major factor which transformed his labours. His imagination was fired by the great mass of letters and diaries relating to the eighteenth century, and he formed the ambition to preserve as much of this material as possible for posterity, and to recover if possible the unbroken succession of Catholic clergy in Meath since the Reformation. This quest led on, in turn, to his tour of graveyards and presbyteries in search of records and inscriptions, and by way of a side dish he recorded in his footnotes that wealth of clerical folklore and gossip which forms a unique collection for the Irish midlands. In a strangely unobtrusive way, this scholarly curate, allows us view the world of late eighteenth- and early nineteenth-century Meath through his eyes. It is a world where bishop and priests formed a close-knit and eternal family, succeeding each other in their generation, exercising a mandate handed down from an Apostolic Age, and in which all were united with those who had gone before in faith. It was a world rich in tragedy and political drama, where drunken villains rubbed shoulders with men who rivalled Oliver Plunket for sanctity; where faction fighters, Orangemen, priest-hunters, proselytisers, and ordinary ruffians, transformed the task of the country priest into a heroic struggle for spiritual mastery. It was a world filled with the horrors of famine and disease, in which Ireland's old order was swiftly passing away. Cogan, who had a masterly sense of the importance of detail, knew how to make that world come alive, by sharing with us the seemingly trivial mementos and reminiscences of the ordinary people whom he encountered on his travels. So, we are informed that the pocket watch of Fr Christopher Betagh (*fl.* 1778)—'a time-piece of the old style is in the possession of Mr Peter Saul of Drumconragh' (ii, 244), and we are introduced to an old man who remembered seeing Bishop Owen Geoghegan's horse tied to a tree 'while he was administering Confirmation in the old chapel at Durrow' (ii, 547). Bishop Geoghegan died in 1778.

Cogan not only lifts the veil on the lives of his priestly colleagues and their people. He also allows us to experience the contradictions in his own mind—contradictions that were beyond resolution, and which still trouble the lives of modern Irish men and women. We see his fascination with the world of culture and learning, and his genuine respect for the leisured Protestant élite who enjoyed that world. We also see his bitterness and anger directed against bigots and those whom he perceived as persecutors of his people. His formal denunciations of Ribbonmen and their secret organisations of terror was at odds with his romantic views of manly peasants thrashing the life out of priest-hunters in the century before. And he reserved his angriest and most inflammatory words for those who evicted the poor from their country cabins or the Navan slums. His confused hopes for an independent Ireland did not allow a place for those who shared a different dream, and although he stood proudly in the tradition of O'Connell and his constitutional goals, much of Cogan's rhetoric might be used as ammunition for more violent agitation. Many of his confused notions on Irish nationhood persist to this day, but in Cogan's writings the contradictions are particularly vivid. That is not because Anthony Cogan was more confused than others, but because he was writing at a turning point in the evolution of modern Ireland. Cogan was writing on Irish history at precisely that crucial point in time between the collapse of Repeal and the birth of new movements in Irish political life, when men of the next generation would make a choice between the old constitutional formulas of O'Connell on the one hand, and revolutionary violence on the other.

Cogan, weary with a work which he struggled to finish, rather self-consciously took his farewell of his reader:

> If my humble labours tend to awaken a spirit of antiquarian research, if they be any way insrumental in urging a brother in the ministry to take up his pen and record the "Gesta Dei per Ibernos", the sufferings and triumphs of our Church, and the unswerving constancy of our people, under innumerable trials, to the faith of their fathers, then I will not have written in vain (i, xi).

Anthony Cogan had not written in vain. There were others in Meath who followed his splendid example. Eoghain O'Growney, an Irish writer and grammarian in the heyday of the Gaelic League, and Paul Walsh, a formidable scholar of early Celtic Ireland, were two Meath priests who cannot have escaped the spell of Cogan's great work which adorned the shelves of every Meath library and presbytery in their days. O'Growney had absorbed all of Cogan's romantic love of the Gaelic past and Walsh had inherited Cogan's preoccupation with local history. By concentrating on the Celtic history of Mide and Brega—those early Irish territories within the diocese of Meath—Paul Walsh correctly understood that the starting point for all early Irish historical research must be at a local or territorial level. Cogan's *Diocese of Meath* was never revised or rewritten, but he did find a continuator in Fr John Brady of Dunboyne, who in 1937 published his *Short History of the Parishes of the Diocese of Meath.* Brady began his work on the parishes where Cogan had left off in 1867.

Anthony Cogan's own life was relatively brief. He mentions in his final volume that illness had prevented him from publishing a map of the diocese of Meath to accompany that third volume in 1870. But the map was apparently completed 'copious and satisfactory, embracing the sites of the old monasteries [and] churches' (iii, xi). The third and final volume of Cogan's *Diocese of Meath* lacked an index and failed to contain a promised appendix (ii, 278) which was to have included a poem by Fr Christopher Cheevers of Kilbeg (died 1789). Cogan's diocesan map was never published—in spite of the fact that Cogan himself tells us he had 'made every arrangement' for its publication (iii, xi), and it most likely perished in the general destruction of the Meath diocesan archive in 1909. For one who was still relatively young there is a note of weariness in Cogan's final preface. He tells us 'that it has cost me ten years of the best part of my life to collect the various letters embodied in the illustration of the Life of Dr Plunket' (iii, ix). His own life was run, and a final illness was to follow. John Brady in his *Short History of the Parishes of the Diocese of Meath* (1937, p.3), reports that Bishop Nulty while in Rome for the First Vatican Council obtained an honorary doctorate of divinity for Cogan from the pope 'but it was never conferred as it was feared that the excitement of the announcement might have a harmful effect on the dying man.' The suggestion is surely naive. Cogan was never so honoured in his lifetime or posthumously. He was too outspoken—and therefore too dangerous a man—to receive honours or promotion too early in life. Any curate who could lecture his bishop on the evils of clerical diplomacy and ambition, and who believed his Catholic colleagues should be prosecuted if they damaged ancient Christian ruins in their keeping, was unlikely to be treated with anything other than caution. But he had already drawn in and saved his rich harvest—the collective memory of a great diocese at a crucial stage in the making of modern Ireland. He died from a heart condition in his family home in Slane on 28 December 1872. He was 45.

Anthony Cogan's Requiem Office and High Mass was celebrated in Navan at 11 o'clock on Monday 30 December 1872. 'The Young Men's Society of Navan, with scarfs and hatbands carried the remains of their beloved Director in procession round the Chapel.' When it came to John Boyle O'Reilly's turn to lie in state before the high altar in St Mary's Church in Charlestown in 1890, the same

Young Men's Catholic Assocation—but this time from Boston College—made a floral tablet of an open book with the words wrought in violets: 'A sower of infinite seed was he, a woodman that hewed toward the light'. The Meath community which knew of Anthony Cogan through his work for youth, or had heard his voice from Tenant Right platforms across the county, or who had read his *Diocese of Meath*, felt as though (Appendix 9) they had lost a member of their own family. The celebrant of his Requiem was his old colleague Joseph O'Higgins, President of St Finian's. The funeral procession moved back to Slane in the early afternoon, and there in the presence of a great crowd of Catholic and Protestant mourners alike, Anthony Cogan's body was laid to rest inside the church where he had prayed as a boy, on the Gospel side and near the Virgin's altar. A splendid wall memorial in Italian marble was erected by the firm of James Pearse—the father of Patrick Pearse—in Slane Catholic Church to his memory:

> Pray for the soul of the Rev. Anthony Cogan, who died in Slane his native town on 28th December 1872 aged 45 years. Father Cogan was spiritual director of the Navan Young Men's Society, Dean of the Navan Seminary, author of the Diocese of Meath Ancient and Modern and diocesan achivist. This good and faithful servant of God was endeared to all who knew him by his piety, simplicity and evident innocence and purity of life. His memory shall ever live in the souls of the people of Navan amongst whom he laboured for 14 years, whilst generations yet unborn will appreciate his worth as a devoted patriot, a gifted preacher and a learned historian. May he rest in peace. Amen.

Cogan's short life had been crowded out with some of the greatest events in Irish history. He was born before Emancipation. His earliest childhood coincided with serious outbreaks of sectarian and agrarian violence in Slane and in Meath generally, brought on by the excitement caused by Emancipation and by eviction, famine and want. As an older child in Meath 'in the summer of 1840 or '41' he recalled hearing the Irish Apostle of Temperance, Fr Theobald Mathew, preach by the side of the old medieval cross in Duleek (ii, 233). We have seen him sitting in the crowd addressed by O'Connell on Tara in August 1843. He later tells how he attended O'Connell's funeral at Glasnevin. Cogan was then still a student in the summer of 1847. He spent all that day at the Liberator's funeral in the company of a saintly neighbour, Fr Denis Walsh of Donore, whom Cogan tells us had fasted from the midnight before. Fr Walsh did not break his fast until returning via the last train to Drogheda, he reached his house at ten the next evening (ii, 250). Famine was by now raging in Ireland. Walsh died on 10 July 1849, having contracted cholera from victims of the hunger. Cogan went on to ordination and out into the world of Tenant Right and Fenians. He did not live to see his dreams of an independent Ireland—however vaguely he had formulated them—realised. But before he died he had witnessed the disestablishment of the Church of Ireland in 1869 and Mr Gladstone's first Land Act in the following year. Modern Ireland had come into being.

Little of Cogan's achievement or of his short life was remembered within his own diocese or by his clerical successors. His friend and fellow historian of Dublin, Fr John O'Hanlon, believed (Appendix 10) that because of his labours and his personal sanctity 'in aftertime his grave shall be sought by many a pilgrim and from many a distant land.' But twentieth-century Ireland, languishing in the petty politics of the post Civil War era, and blinkered by an exclusive sense of remembrance of the heroes of 1916, allowed the memory of men such as Anthony Cogan to fade and die. A housing estate in Navan was named after Dean Cogan but few could explain the significance of the name. By 1990, in spite of the presence of the monument on the wall of Slane church, all memory even of the whereabouts of Cogan's grave had vanished. Those who claimed to know, believed he was buried somewhere in Navan parish, and only among Cogan's immediate collateral descendants had any memory of the man survived. In spite of latter-day ignorance and confusion regarding the exact whereabouts of Anthony Cogan's grave, contemporary accounts clearly state that he was buried within the Catholic church in Slane and most likely beneath his monument on the wall in that church. The very thing which Anthony Cogan had laboured so hard to prevent had now happened. Ireland was losing its collective memory—ironically not under a foreign oppressor, but under its own complacent independent regime.

The loss of that collective memory in Meath was accelerated by a conscious policy on the part of its late nineteenth-century bishops to shift the centre of the diocese from the Pale into the heart of the Midlands at Mullingar. Bishop Patrick Plunket had lived in 'the chapel lodge'—a modest place, perhaps over stabling—in the chapel yard in Navan (Brady, *A Short History* p. 105) until his death in 1827. His successor, Robert Logan, had been consecrated coadjutor in Duleek, and on his death in 1830 he was buried in the chapel in Kells. John Cantwell was consecrated in Mullingar in September 1830, and that bishop set out to make Mullingar the *caput* of the diocese. Cantwell chose to live in Mullingar, and in his diary from 1838 he referred to his church in that town as his cathedral. This may partly account for the failure of the Meath clergy to erect a monument or even mark the grave of Bishop Plunket in the old chapel in Navan—a situation justly branded by Brady as 'an ungrateful act of omission' (ibid., p. 98). By 1901, Plunket's grave had to be 'pointed out' to then administrator, Fr James Poland, by 'an old man' whose evidence amounted to little more than hearsay (ibid.). The identification of the grave of Bishop Plunket at so late a time must have been conjectural because the site of the old chapel where he was buried had by then been incorporated within a new church, which had been built in 1839. So, remarkably, the grave of this tireless bishop who had dragged the diocese of Meath out of its Penal Day past and established its modern form, had been forgotten by his own clergy. The shift of the centre of the diocese to Mullingar was completed in 1908, when St Finian's College was closed down in Navan and relocated in spacious buildings and grounds outside Mullingar. The move was not without problems. Navan was deprived of its secondary school until 1930, and in spite of apparently magnificent facilities, the nature of the old Navan school was transformed in its new Westmeath home. Elocution, drawing and even French had been dropped from the curriculum by the 1950s, and Fr Power's enlightened policy of discipline through moral influence had been abandoned in favour of a much more rigorous regime of corporal punishment from the earliest days at Mullingar. Although the buildings of Cogan's old school in Navan were partially re-occupied for the use of St Patrick's Classical School in 1930, neglect for tradition was allowed to proceed unchecked. The chapel of the old St Finian's, where Dean Cogan once led his boys in prayer, had become the paint spray-shop of the Navan Engineering Works, while over in the new St Finian's in Mullingar, even the name of Cogan was unknown among its pupils. There is ample evidence within Cogan's *Diocese of Meath* to show that its author had undertaken the work to combat the forces of neglect as early as 1860 and to salvage records from the eighteenth and early nineteenth centuries from oblivion. Cogan's praise for his

60 Detail of engraving on the silver handle of a walking-stick presented to Anthony Cogan in 1862. This cane, now in the possession of the Cogan family, was most likely presented to Dean Cogan by the Navan Branch of the Catholic Young Men's Society. That same group had presented Cogan with a gold watch and chain in May, 1861.

61 'Presented to a Good Mother from her affectionate Son. The Author.' Anthony Cogan's personal dedication of Volume II of his *Diocese of Meath* for his mother, Anne Cogan (*née* Sillary). His mother outlived him by seven years.

school in Navan and for his colleagues who taught there shows that he regarded that place as an oasis of learning and culture in a changing world where, not only had his bishop moved far into the west, but old cultural values and the high idealism of men such as Bishop Plunket and Eugene O'Reilly were coming under increasing threat.

Cogan's *Diocese of Meath* alone survived on presbytery and farmhouse shelf alike, where it stood, too often like an icon, with its leaves uncut. But although scarcely read by the people for whom he had laboured so hard to provide it, it was and remains his true memorial. And even for the many who possessed the three volumes of the *Diocese of Meath*, and who never read them, their iconic association with a beloved scholar called 'Dean Cogan', had its own power, capable of being tapped through an accidental encounter with the thought-world of the book. Such a man, so dedicated in the remembrance of others, ought never himself to have been forgotten. But his own historical writings had ensured that the memory of his life and labours could be rediscovered by those who cared to read them. And so, in spite of the neglect of several generations, what Anthony Cogan wrote of his friend and neighbour, Fr Denis Walsh, we also may write of him:

The memory of the just man will live forever.

62 Section of the Apostle font from Kilcarne (cf. ills. 2 and 21). One apostle is allocated to each niche, while two are squeezed in together on the left. St Andrew, with his distinctive cross is shown on the extreme right. The bowl of the font is dodecagonal in form and dates to the late fifteenth century.

Appendix 1: Testimonial presented to Anthony Cogan by Navan Young Men's Society, 1861*

Summary: Testimonial presented to Fr Cogan at a general meeting of the Navan Young Men's Society. John Mullen, Esq., JP, in the chair. The address was signed by John Mullen, President, and by Patrick O'Neill, Secretary, and was presented by Peter O'Neill.

Cogan was complimented on the social reforms which his organisation of the Young Men's Society had achieved in Navan: 'No right minded man can walk our streets without being impressed with the great social revolution the Young Men's Society has effected. Public intemperance and [im]morality— which were proof against the rigours of the law—have here disappeared before its teaching and example.' All of this had been achieved thanks to the Young Men's Society and to 'the almost superhuman exertions of its devoted founder and spiritual guide'.

The President presented Anthony Cogan with a gold watch and chain and a purse containing £20. The watch was made by Donegan of Dublin: 'On the dial is a beautifully carved likeness of the front of St Peter's Church [sic], Rome; the other side has deeply cut the following inscription: "Presented by the Navan Young Men's Society to Rev. Father Cogan, as a token of grateful acknowledgement and affectionate remembrance.—1861".'

Fr Cogan replied. He speaks of what has been achieved by the Young Men's Society and of its ideals for moral renewal which meet with approval by both Catholics and Protestants. He points out that he alone is not responsible, and pays tribute to the generation of clergy gone before him. He tells of his ambition to write his *Diocese of Meath* and of its religious and patriotic motivation. He launches into a political commentary on Ireland as a country reduced to slavery by ruthless oppressors who have then blamed their victims for the very poverty they have inflicted upon them.

The editiorial comment on p. 4* ascribes the entire success of the Young Men's Society to Cogan. A *soirée* is reported on, which concluded the evening's proceedings. Two hundred guests attended a banquet followed by speeches and signing.

Appendix 2: Letter from Archbishop John MacHale to Anthony Cogan, January 1863†

THE DIOCESE OF MEATH ANCIENT AND MODERN

We have great pleasure in inserting the following magnificent testimony of his grace, the great Archbishop of the West, to the merits of the above-mentioned publication and to the deserved eulogium bestowed on the author, the Rev. Anthony Cogan, C.C. of Navan.

* Report in the *Meath People and Cavan and Westmeath Chronicle*, vol. iv, no. 42, Saturday, 11 May 1861, p. 1.
† *Drogheda Argus*, 17 January 1863, p. 4, col. 6.

St Jarlath's, Tuam
9th January 1863

Rev. Dear Sir,
It is high time, you will allow, to return you thanks for your kindness in presenting me with your valuable book on your native Diocese of Meath, Ancient and Modern. For the tardiness of my acknowledgement I will not plead the frequent apology of the want of time or the pressure of various duties.

Though having an average share of business to dispatch, I could not deem any such a sufficient excuse for delaying to convey to you the gratification I derived from the perusal of the greater part of the interesting volume.

I was anxious to read the entire before writing and now beg to thank you, not so much for the compliment of sending me your book, as for giving such a rich contribution to the ecclesiastical literature of our country.

It passes that in which books of much pretention are often deficient in facts of deep and permanent interest, and while productions relying on fashion alone for their ephemeral currency, will be forgotten, the simple annals of the diocese of Meath will be remembered and referred to with grateful curiosity. Compared with the vague and general narratives to which I have alluded, leaving but little of distinct impressions on the reader's mind, your book reminds one of the distinct and defined figures that are found in the artless annals of Muratori which you look for in vain in the more ambitious productions of the recent histories of Italy.

Your industries and talents have been well devoted to the advantage of our religion and our country. You have given an example, too, which will kindle a generous emulation in the young priesthood of Ireland to illustrate the annals of their respective dioceses, and to rescue from oblivion the names and deeds of their fathers in the Faith – the heroic confessors of the time of trial to whom, under God, we are indebted for their religious trophies which no other nation, however eminent in arts or arms, can display.

Meath was assuredly a rich ground to engage and reward the toil of a diligent ecclesiastical labourer, forming the earliest of those deep fountains which our Apostle so profusely planted throughout the land, as it was likewise the most ancient and time-honoured centre of the civil polity of Ireland. Meath abounded in materials which even a less skilful hand could not fail to render interesting. If in deciphering some of the monuments of the past you laboured under embarrassments which you freely alluded to, created by the forcible destruction of our native language and insidious substitution of that of the stranger, such loss was no fault of yours, but the misfortune of the times.

To the credit of Meath, be it recorded that though amongst the earliest districts to be brought within the dominion of the Pale, it was one of the last to adopt its foreign dialect.

The ancient language still survives in some of the most remote parishes, but though the language of the country has at length decayed, its spirit is there in full vigour, for the soil of Meath was too well saturated with the native seed ever to yield to the growth of exotic and anti-national influences.

It is a source of great gratification to the historian of the Ancient and Modern Diocese of Meath to feel that the one has not degenerated from the other. It must be gratifying to the biographer of the ecclesiastics of both, to find in their estimable qualities such perfect harmony. Nay, whilst writing this brief epistle I am rejoiced beyond measure that your native diocese can boast of a bishop and clergy worthy of the best as well as the worst times of Ireland, who while delighted to be left in the loneliness of the sanctuary as long as their flock is safe, can come out as they have done last week and boldly remonstrate against the misgovernment that is reducing to a state of mendicity and serfdom a moral and industrious and high minded people, and labouring by their sweeping evictions of our old and faithful Irish race, to turn into a wilderness one of the fairest portions of the vineyard of Christ.

Wishing you health and perseverance in the second portion of your estimable work.

I am, Reverend Dear Sir,
Your Very Faithful Servant
+ John, Archbishop of Tuam

Rev. A. Cogan

Appendix 3: Young Men's Excursion to Laytown organised by Anthony Cogan, August 1863*

Summary: Fr Cogan chartered a special train with a remarkable number of carriages to transport 700 members of the Young Men's Society with their friends on a weekend excursion to Laytown, Co. Meath. Details of catering refer to a sandwich lunch and the prohibition of whiskey. A Liverpool contingent of Young Men's Society sailed to Drogheda on the *Leinster Lass* to join the Meath party at Laytown.

Appendix 4: Grand Banquet to Father A. Cogan, of Navan, in Liverpool†

LIVERPOOL NEWS
(From our Correspondent)

WEDNESDAY.—The Church of St Mary, Edmund Street, was on Sunday filled with one of the largest congregations ever assembled within its sacred walls. The occasion was the preaching of the anniversary sermons by the learned and patriotic Father Cogan, C.C., of Navan. From the great anxiety displayed on former visits of the gifted preacher by the Catholics of Liverpool to be present, and as his fame has been wafted throughout the United Kingdom by the publication of his invaluable work on the ecclesiastical history of the diocese of Meath, the Fathers of St Mary's Church improved the resources of the church by fixing a higher price for admission on Sunday than was their wont to do hitherto.—Notwithstanding this, the spacious church was crowded in every part, and at the lowest calculation there could not have been fewer than 2,000 people within the sacred edifice.

* Reported in the *Drogheda Argus*, 15 August 1863, p. 4, col. 4.
† *Drogheda Argus*, Saturday, 12 September 1863

To add additional *eclat* to the day's proceedings the 64th Royal Lancashire Volunteers (Irish Brigade), under the command of Lieutenant-Colonel Bidwill, Captains Powell (2), Hore, O'Donnell, and Adjutant Greaves, with the band of the regiment, were present. The corps mustered about four hundred and fifty rank and file. The regiment assembled at the rendezvous at ten a.m., and having formed into line marched to the church, in doing which it had to pass through most of the leading thoroughfares, the band playing Irish national airs. Those only who witnessed the processions which in the days of O'Connell's Repeal Agitation were to be seen in Ireland, can form any idea of the enthusiastic bearing of the people, as they proudly—nay defiantly—walked along the streets. The streets along the route were thronged with spectators.

The sacred ceremonies commenced with a solemn High Mass, the Rev. S. Almond being High-priest [*sic*], and Fathers Bartley and Shepherd as Deacon and Sub-deacon; the Rev. Father Stuart, Master of Ceremonies. A full and efficient choir rendered Wether's Grand Mass in an enchanting manner.— After the first gospel, the Rev. Father Cogan ascended the pulpit, took for his text the inspired words of the Magnificat—'Behold, from henceforth, all generations shall call me Blessed.' For more than an hour did the gifted preacher, in a strain of the most cogent and convincing argumentation, place before the vast assemblage the truth conveyed in his text, the universal practice of Catholics in all ages of designating the Mother of God as the Blessed Virgin, and the conduct of all heretics in omitting that prophetic title. He graphically described the proceedings of the Council of Ephesus in the beginning of the fifth century, called together to condemn the heresy of Nestorius, who denied that the Blessed Virgin was the Mother of God. When he came to that part of the Council's proceedings wherein St Cyril stood at the door of the Cathedral of Ephesus and proclaimed that Nestorius was condemned amidst the enthusiastic shouts of the assembled thousands, it was with evident restraint the congregation of St Mary's was prevented from giving expression to the feelings of veneration and joy with which his words had overpowered their hearts.

Long will his discourse be remembered, and many were the prayers offered up by his auditory, that length of days may be granted to him to combat heresy and error, and ground in firm faith the love of Catholics towards the ever Blessed Mother of God.

At six o'clock in the evening Father Cogan was again in the pulpit, and preached from the decalogue, taking for his text—'Honour thy father and thy mother, that thy days may be long in the land.' The great exertions made by the learned ecclesiastic in the morning had not left a single trace of fatigue or exhaustion, and those young men and maidens who heard his beautiful sermon must have imbibed wholesome sentiments of parental love and regard.

Immediately after evening service Father Cogan visited the Rooms of the Young Men's Society. When he entered the rooms a shout of exhultating joy and welcome made the neighbourhood resound, again and again renewed. The restraint in the church in the morning was now taken off, and from the manly breasts of nearly seven hundred Irishmen a right royal 'ceade mille failthe' [*sic*], 'soggarth aroon', made the welkin ring. To do Father Cogan justice it must be said that the warmth of his reception had evidently deeply impressed itself upon his generous heart. He spoke of the old country, her wrongs, and her hopes, the fidelity of her people, and the utter confusion of all the machinations of the world and the devil in their attempts to wrest from her the faith once planted by Saint Patrick. His rich fund of amusing anecdote, and his graphic powers of description, convulsed the assemblage with unbounded mirth.

The friends and admirers of Father Cogan regretted upon the occasion of his visit here last Autumn, that owing to his early return to Navan, they were denied the gratification of testifying in some public manner, the sense of the obligations under which his cheerful compliance had placed them to him. This year they took active steps to carry out their kind wishes, and accordingly Father Cogan was on Monday evening entertained at a public banquet in the Merchant's Dining Rooms, Castle Street, at which more than 100 of the worthy and patriotic Liverpool Irishmen were present. The dinner was served up in a style in keeping with the character of the establishment. The Rev J. Shepherd O.S.B., occupied the chair, and had upon his right the rev. guest of the evening. The Revds Fathers Duggan and Magrath, of St Joseph's sat upon the left of the chairman. The Rev. Father Alban (Passionist) of Sutton, was also present, whilst amongst the general body sat Messrs. Crilly, Rankin, Donnelly, M.D.; Trenor, Campbell, proprietor of 'Northern Press'; Kelly, the world renowned butterman; O'Leary, Ternan, Drogheda Steampacket Company; P. McEvoy, Captain Boden, Brian Boiraimhe; E. Kelly, Kearney, Tormey, S. McArdel, Hood, Hegarty, Corcoran, etc., etc. The good things provided having been disposed of, and grace having been said by the Rev. Father Duggan, M.R., the rev. chairman rose and in a few brief but apposite sentences proposed "Long life to our Holy Father Pope Pius the IX. The health of 'Her Majesty and the Royal Family'. 'The English and Irish Hierarchy' followed. In responding to the last sentiment the Rev. Father Magrath spoke in eulogistic terms of the English Hierarchy, and second order of the clergy. He alluded to the glowing account of the progress of Catholicism in England, lately read at the Catholic Congress at Malines by his Eminence the Cardinal Archbishop of Westminster. In alluding to the latter portion of the sentiment, the rev. speaker depicted in loving phraseology the labours and self-sacrifices of the Irish bishops and priests. He urged upon their rev. guest to tell the bishops and priests with whom he might come into contact that the love and devotion of the poor exiles of Erinn in the United Kingdom towards their pastors of the Church at home, was not surpassed by the most fervid of the residents in the great land of the west.

The Chairman now introduced Mr Martin Rankin, Vice-president General of the Catholic Young Men's Society of Great Britain, and President of the St Mary's Branch in this town, to propose the toast of the evening.

Mr Rankin in an eloquent and feeling address, pointed out the many titles to respect which their honoured guest, Father Cogan possessed, and dwelt with forcible and just laudation upon the service rendered to Church and Fatherland, by the publication of the Ecclesiastical History of his native diocese. He spoke of the efforts which their rev. guest and his brother priests were making to procure for the downtrodden serfs of Ireland the right to live upon the soil whereon they first drew breath. After continuing in a fervid train of affectionate language, Mr Rankin brought his remarks to a close by proposing 'Long life and prosperity to Father Cogan'.

Sang by Mr McArdle, editor of the 'Northern Press', 'The Harp that once thro' Tara's Hall'.

Father Cogan rose to respond, and was received with rounds of applause, which having subsided, he said that the picture drawn of him by his friend, Mr Rankin, was too flattering; so much so that he was quite sure they would have some difficulty in tracing in his person those features which the inventive genius of their friend had portrayed. He accepted the compliment which they had so handsomely paid in the splendid entertainment got up that evening, not as having been paid to himself, but as the embodiment of that love which the faithful Irish people have ever shown towards the 'Soggarth Aroon'. Whatever labours he had undergone in ʋɩe bringing forth of the ecclesiastical history of his native diocese had been more than compensated for by the cordial manner in which his humble labours had been spoken of by the Hierarchy of Ireland, and the too flattering notices of the Press of all parties. His ambition was to render himself useful in his day to his beloved country, and to rescue from oblivion the evidences of the past glories of their saintly forefathers. He saw that as time was going on, the traces of Irish archaeology becoming gradually obliterated, and was urged by a sense of justice, no less than by a love of truth, to do the little he could to save the records of the past from decaying away. In this labour he was preceded and accompanied by many able and learned men, both of the Catholic and Protestant religion, from many of whom he had received the most generous offers to use all books and documents which they had, in assisting him in his researches. He pointed out the necessity of consulting the local seers by him who would attempt the task of writing an exact history of the people of Ireland, for by such means alone could full justice be done to the memories of their dear departed ancestors, whose struggles for the right were entwined around the inmost core of the hearts of the Irish peasantry. The love of religion, which the faithful people of Ireland have maintained in all the dark days of their cruel persecutions, is only equalled by the tenacity with which the traditions of the martyrs are cherished and preserved, from generation to generation. Every holy well, lone tree, broken cross, ruined abbey and mountain cavern, each and all, have their reminiscences of the days, and men, who withstood the ruthless hands of the devastating spoliators. His first volume had a most rapid sale, being now out of print, and he trusted that ere he paid them his usual visit next year, that the second volume would be before the public. As for what the priests of Meath were doing to benefit the tenant farmers they were only following in the footsteps of the late lamented Frederick Lucas. He was proud of being associated with such a body, and they had resolved never to cease their exertions until ample justice was rendered to the tenant farmers of Ireland. After thanking them for the cordial manner in which they had received him, and assuring them that no efforts on his part whereby the Church and people of St Mary's could be benefitted, would be withheld, his reverence sat down amid the loud applause of the assemblage.

The Chairman next proposed 'Prosperity to Ireland' coupling with the sentiment the name of Mr H. Caraher, who upon rising to respond to the toast was most warmly received.

Mr Caraher pointed out in a few pithy words the difference between Ireland prosperous as given up to cattle, and Ireland filled with a bold and self reliant people. He condemned the policy that would set man, the best work of his Maker's hands, below the value of the brute that perisheth.

The Rev. Father Duggan gave the next sentiment, 'The clergy of St Mary's', and in doing so offered them his thanks for the opportunity they had afforded the Catholics of Liverpool to meet Father Cogan and to make his valuable acquaintance.

Mr E. Kelly gave the 'Institutions of St Mary's Parish', and dwelt for some time upon the many meritorious works carried out by the congregation of St Mary's.

The 'Press' was proposed by Mr Alfred Crilly, who took occasion to pass a well merited compliment, upon the proprietor and the editor of the 'Northern Press,' who were present amongst them.

Mr Campbell being loudly called upon, rose and said, that for all that had been said in praise of the 'Northern Press' he was deeply grateful. He promised to leave nothing undone, which it was in his power to do, to make the paper worthy of the cause it espoused. Mr McArdle, editor of the 'Northern Press,' also [. . . illegible line of text . . .] made of his name.

Messrs Keating, O'Leary, Campbell, etc., enlivened the evening's proceedings by singing patriotic and other songs. The company separated at a late hour highly pleased at the agreeable and delightful manner in which the affairs of the banquet were carried out.

Appendix 5: Letter from Anthony Cogan protesting against evictions in the town of Navan*

TO M.E. CORBALLY AND E. McEVOY, ESQRS., MEMBERS OF PARLIAMENT FOR THE COUNTY OF MEATH

Parochial House, Navan, April 29, 1864

GENTLEMEN —As you have contracted an obligation towards the inhabitants of this county, undertaking to represent their wants and wishes in the imperial parliament, and as I have been one of your consistent supporters, I feel [it] my duty to bring under your notice how some of your humble constituents have [been] dealt with in the town of Navan, within the last few days. In doing so, I am actuated by no feelings save those of humanity, as landlord and agent are personally unknown to me, but the victims in this instance being the defenceless poor, who have few friends unless the priest, I feel called upon to raise my voice to protest against their immolation. Amongst the proprietors whom this town acknowledges we must reckon Lord de Ross – a gentleman who seems to take little interest, at least here, in the welfare of his tenantry, and who has as agent, a worthy exponent, in this respect, of his master's neglected duties – a Mr Graham Johnston. A few days ago a ukase went forth from this quarter for the demolition of part of Brewshill street, and although at first it was not credited that an act so outrageous on the town was seriously contemplated, yet on Friday, the 15th of this month, it was carried into effect, in [the] presence of the sheriff and a large body of the police, by the unroofing of fourteen houses, the eviction of fourteen families, and the consequent flinging on the roadside, and scattering houseless and homeless, sixty-four of her Majesty's subjects. In what country in the civilised world dare such Vandalism be perpetrated save in oppressed, down-trodden Ireland?

* *Droghda Argus*, Saturday, 7 May 1864

Surely in a healthy state of the land law, and under the influence of a sound public opinion, the levellers of the homesteads of the people would be denounced and anathematised as enemies to the crown and tyrants over the people by whose industry they are supported. If such ruthless warfare against the poor of Christ occurred in the Papal States or in any Catholic country, what an outcry of indignation would be raised throughout the civilised world! How the unprotected serfs would be sympathised with! How the government that tolerated such barbarity would be denounced and declared to have forfeited all recognition! How the exterminators would be held up to the execration of mankind! But such would not be permitted; and if it were, in addition to well-merited denunciation, the daggers of Mazzini's friends, the Carbonari, would make short work of the oppressors and slayers of the people. The motive assigned for such cruelty is as unique in its way as the act was unchristian; it deserves to be chronicled in the annals of Irish landlordism, and is quite in keeping, in cool effrontery, with many of the paradoxes which figure in the history of the present land code. It is urged, as a motive for demolishing part of the street, that the people were not good, and that the remainder of the town would be benefited by their removal. The people were not good (how very virtuous some landlords and agents are!), and therefore their houses must be levelled! If these rules were applied to the lordly and rich, how many of their habitations would remain standing? Who constituted Lord de Ross or Mr Johnston judge or censor over the morals of the people? If family history or pedigree were pried into, would more virtues be discovered and less vices be conspicuous in the exterminators than in the evicted poor of Brewshill-street? If there have been evil-doers amongst us in '64, is the law not able to vindicate itself? Are the police unable or unwilling to discharge their duty? Are the magistrates leagued to connive at the violation of the law? Are those whom God and man placed over the people unfit for, or inattentive to, their charges, and must a landlord and agent assume the office of judge, jury, and executioner? If tenants be unwilling to pay a fair rent (which can't be proved in this case), let them by all means be evicted, and let their habitations be set to the solvent; but surely there is no excuse for levelling the streets of our towns, and thus cutting off all hope of our country's regeneration. The state of Ireland at this moment is calculated to alarm the statesman and the philanthropist. Our artizans are idle, our labourers are unemployed, the cream of the population is flying abroad, and the remnant at home are awaiting remittances from their exiled friends to take them away from the land of their birth. All hope or confidence in parliamentary legislation seems to have left the hearts of the people. They complain that cattle-shows of every description, even 'dog shows', are presided over by the representative of royalty, as if in mockery over the miseries of the people; that parliament is occupied with foreign questions, such as the Bombardment of Sonderborg, or again, in enacting new laws for the protection of game, and all this time her Majesty's subjects are allowed to perish, their houses are levelled, and their petitions for justice disregarded! What wonder if, in such a state of things, the mass of the population were disloyal and longing for a change? Loyalty has its correlative duties. No man, however humble, should be tempted beyond his strength. Give the masses, by good government, an interest in upholding the constitution, and you can calculate on their loyalty without apprehension. Let me suppose that the homes of the gentry were liable to be assaulted and demolished by the people, and that the law was so constituted that the police were obliged to look on as spectators (I will not say assistants), would the gentry be loyal? Let me suppose that they appealed repeatedly to parliament for legal protection, and that their claims were derided, and met with sophistry and special pleading; that their prayers for fair play were rejected amidst 'Oh's and laughter', how long would the gentry remain loyal? Ah, just so long as would suit their convenience. Let the landlords do to others as they would wish to be dealt with. Let them remember that many of themselves are high in this world, inheriting abbey lands and Catholic Church property, because their forefathers bartered their faith for the flesh-pots of Egypt, and that many luxuriate in titles purchased by treason to Ireland in the unholy sale (at the Union) of the independence of our country. Let them bear in mind that there is instability in all human affairs; that revolutions are often followed by revolutions; that what was won by the sword can be lost by the sword; that the lordly and great may be low on tomorrow; and that one of the surest and most durable guarantees of stability is justice to their fellow man, mercy to the poor, to live in the grateful recollections and affections of the people. It may be asked, and it is often commented upon with surprise and regret, why has the policy of conciliation never been adopted towards unfortunate Ireland? Arms Acts, Coercion Bills, denunciations of the people, have been the order of the day from time immemorial. From the invasion of Henry II till the present, with slight intermissions, the rule of England has been the same—viz., jealous, intolerant, one-sided, cruel. It was so in the exclusive days of the Pale; it was so in the confiscations of Elizabeth and James I; it was so in the bloody days of Cromwell, and after the restoration of the ungrateful Charles II; it was so after the wars of the Revolution, and in violation of the Treaty of Limerick. It was so, and is so, for parliament after parliament, year after year, has passed away, and still the policy is the same—viz., keep down Ireland, discourage her manufactures, diminish her population, set class against class and sect against sect, *divide et impera*—'set O'Donnell against O'Neill' a traditionary Cabinet watchword which Queen Elizabeth is said to have invented and handed down. The result of such impolicy is natural. The people who, under just laws, would have been the bulwark of the empire, fly from Ireland with an intense, burning hatred of England. The enemies of Great Britain are thus multiplied over the world, and however she may just now afford to despise their threats and to dispense with their services, the day may come when she may miss their strong arms, and when her statesmen like George II, may have reason to curse the land laws that deprived her of such subjects. Whoever reads the signs in the times, or is acquainted with the feelings of our emigrants, can easily conclude that the exiled Irish will form the vanguard of any assault on British supremacy. The retribution, the Nemesis, may be nearer hand than is anticipated; and it may be found, when too late, that the right arm is withered, that the old nursery is uprooted, that the policy of extermination had over reached itself, that it was calamitous and suicidal. It has been often a subject of grievous complaint that many of our Irish representatives have exhibited callous indifference towards the wants and miseries of their country, after lavish promises of fidelity, and at the sacrifice of hecatombs of votes. Of course, gentlemen, in this recreant category, we'd not reckon you, or a chosen few, who, amidst wholesale defection, have remained faithful to covenants. But others have been elected by a too-confiding people, and carried triumphantly at great sacrifices and against fearful odds, of whom we may say with truth, better that Ireland were disfranched than be thus misrepresented. If these men were seriously anxious for the welfare of their country—if the public good, and not personal favour, be the object of their ambition, then why not meet together, wait on the Premier, present their ultimatum for a Tenant Compensation Bill—for employing the poor labourers in bringing to cultivation the waste lands of Ireland, numbering upwards of six millions of acres, and for other remedial measures; and if such were refused, then separate from the so-called Liberal party, wield the constitutional weapon placed in their hands by their confiding countrymen, and drive from office a government whose settled policy seems to be the total disregard of Irish grievances, the extermination of the Irish people, and the conversion of our country into a grass-walk? Let them remember that the government under whose inspiration the most satisfactory Tenant Right Bill was ever introduced into parliament was that of which Lord Derby was head, and Mr Napier Attorney-General for Ireland; and let me assure them too that the most thoughtful and experienced, the prudent guides and most trusted in Ireland are, at this moment, looking forward to the advent of that party to power, as comprising the only statesmen from whose comprehensive measures the Irish people are to be saved from annihilation. Apologising for this lengthened address, my only excuse being a feeling of sorrow for my poor countrymen, I am, gentlemen, with great respect, very faithfully yours,

A. COGAN, C.C.

Appendix 6: Very Rev. Dean Cogan—'The Diocese of Meath'*

The second volume of Dean Cogan's great and valuable work - 'The Diocese of Meath, Ancient and Modern' - has issued from the press. It will be received by the Catholic and literary world as a grand contribution to Irish Ecclesiastical History. It is indeed worthy of Father Cogan's high reputation, his loving patriotism, and splendid intellectual gifts. We hope to be able to give a notice and some extracts from the book in our next issue. Meantime we have much pleasure in placing before our readers the high testimony borne by 'The great Archbishop of the West' and other distinguished authorities, to the value of the work and the masterly ability with which Father Cogan has accomplished what may be truly called 'his labour of love':

Tuam, Nov 27, 1867

Dear Father Cogan—You must be rather surprised at my tardy acknowledge-ment of your second volume of the 'Diocese of Meath'. On its arrival here I was [... ...] for some days, and delayed writing until I should have the pleasure of its perusal. It has not lost any of the interest created by the first volume and has thrown additional light on perhaps the darkest and dreariest period of our ecclesiastical history of the 17th century. The last and not the

* *Drogheda Argus*, Saturday, 14 December 1867, p. 4

least important chapters of your work, devoted to the lives and labours of the three last bishops of your diocese, will be expected with impatience, and will be the crowning of your dutiful homage to the noble diocese of Meath, and through it to the entire Church of Ireland. I have read with a melancholy interest your repeated wishes that similar works would be speedily undertaken for the respective dioceses by your contemporaries, but as yet your pious and patriotic anxiety has not been realised. It is when it will be too late such works may be less perfectly essayed. It is now several years since the late author of 'The Round Towers' paid his first visit to the Churches of Clonmacnoise, even then in ruin: but a ruin in such a state of integrity as easily to restore to the eye of taste a perfect image of that ancient splendour. In twenty years after he visited it again, and what did he find ? Not even the cyclopean [?] stones of the sanctuary; for they almost disappeared, adopted, nay, profaned to the meanest and most incongruous purposes of building cattle sheds, or of repairing broken fences; not unlike those holy records of our old ecclesiastics to which you allude, torn up for the service of some village hucksters. Wishing you a successful term of your valuable labours, with the hope that other talented ecclesiastics throughout Ireland may, ere the surviving monuments and traditions of the olden time are gone, be stimulated to the imitation of your laudable industry. I remain, with great esteem, your faithful and obliged servant,

+ JOHN, Archbishop of Tuam

Rev A. Cogan, Dean of the Diocesan
Seminary of Navan

St Edward's College, Liverpool, 26th October, 1867
Dear Rev. Sir—I write to thank you for a copy of your learned work on the 'Diocese of Meath', from the perusal of which I promise myself much pleasure. For many years I have been endeavouring to collect materials for [a] history of my diocese, and very happy shall I be if Divine Providence will raise up some future scholar, like yourself, to put into order my scattered notices. With many thanks and every best wish, I remain truly yours in Christ.

+ ALEXANDER GOSS
[Bishop of Liverpool]

[A short congratulatory letter to Dean Cogan from John Derry, bishop of Clonfert, illegible on microfilm, intervenes.]

Dundalk, Nov 8th, 1867
REV. DEAR SIR—Many thanks for the second volume of the Ecclesiastical History of Meath, of which I have already read the greater part with pleasure and profit. I have read of course with the greatest interest those portions of it which touch on the history of Armagh. Hoping that God may preserve your health to continue your valuable labours in the cause of the Irish Church, I am, with great esteem, your obedient servant,

+ M. KIERAN
[Archbishop of Armagh]

Cavan, Nov 18th, 1867
MY DEAR DEAN COGAN, – Accept my sincere thanks for your great kindness in sending me a copy of your history of the 'Diocese of Meath', a

work which reflects the highest credit upon your talents and industry, and which will contribute much to rescue the Ecclesiastical History of Meath from that obscurity and darkness which characterise the Church History of Ireland. I sincerely hope that your example will be followed by a zealous and talented priest in every Diocese in the land, and thus bring to light our Ecclesiastical Annals which will necessarily add another gem to the crown of Catholicity. Thanking you, my old friend for thinking of me, I am, my dear Dean Cogan, very sincerely yours,

+ NICHOLAS CONATY

To Very Rev Dean Cogan   [Bishop of Kilmore]

Appendix 7: The Mullagh Meeting— Turn out from Navan*

A correspondent sent us the following interesting particulars, but his letter reached us too late to make use of it last week:

The procession which turned out for this meeting on Thursday, June 29, was of a most imposing nature.—Shortly after ten o'clock the town was all astir with preparations for the great meeting, expressive of sympathy for the threatened tenant farmers, and indignation for the parties who in these days would bring woe and desolation on so many peaceful homesteads. The band of the Navan Young Men's Society, headed by the patriotic Father Cogan, lead off in the van, followed by some 40 or 50 cars and vehicles containing a most respectable assemblage from the town and country.—Conspicuous amongst all was the large four-wheeled vehicle of the Messrs. Clayton, woollen manufacturers, Navan. This van was handsomely decorated with evergreens and appropriate banners and devices and contained not less than 40 of the employees of the woollen mill. The greatest good will pervaded the entire proceedings; and it was especially noticed that men of all creeds joined heartily in the movement, and this gave significance to the procession from Navan. The creature comforts were amply provided for, and, altogether, everything passed off in the best manner.

Another correspondent says:

The route lay from Navan to Kilcairne, then to Bellinter, then by Ringlestown into Kilmessan, by the Protestant Church, across the railway bridge, and wheel sharp to the left, skirting the fox-covert of Kilcarty, and then, leaving Swainstown to the left, where a good view was had of Dunsany Castle, Killeen Castle, and Warrenstown (to which latter place the pilgrims are busily repairing, in the expectation of getting cured of some of their bodily afflictions at the renowned well of St John); then on to Kiltale; from thence out on the Dublin road leading to Trim; then a turn to the left which brought the *magnificent pasture fields* of Mrs Murphy, of The Grange, into view, while to the right her fine mansion drew attention; thence on to Batterjohn cross roads, where a turn to the right brought us in a few moments in view of the old churchyard of Derrypatrick; leaving Mr Marmion's to the left, and up College

---

* *Drogheda Argus*, Saturday, 8 July 1871, p. 3

Hill, where creature comforts were to be had at Mulligan's 'big bush'; and then to our left at the top of College Hill, and on straight down to Moynalvy Chapel, where The Mullagh, only a stone's throw before us, reared its green acclivity.

THE MULLAGH MEETING
(Nation)*

On Thursday of last week, at a veritable 'monster meeting' held on the Mullagh, county Meath, a startling verdict was passed on Mr Gladstone's Land Bill. An assembly of ten thousand persons in that county now means a gathering of the entire population of districts where in byegone times full thirty thousand had their homes. Extermination has done its dreadful work in Meath. Driving to the scene of last week's demonstration, by whatever road approached, one passes for miles and miles through a once thickly populated district, now one vast stretch of pasture land, unbroken by ridge or furrow of cultivation—miles of solitude undisturbed by human voice save the herdsman's shout. Standing on the crest of that singular mound whereon the assemblage gathered, the eye could sweep for leagues on every side over an extensive plain of richest natural beauty. But, except for the smoke of the parsonage house near at hand – where dwells the kindly-hearted Protestant Rector, Rev. Mr Kempston – and the indications of barely one or two other human habitations menaced by destruction to-day, the scene might be in the untrodden wilds of Central or Southern America. The landscape was beautiful; but, though it smiled in the sunshine, a chill seized the beholder. Something told him its richness and beauty were like the luxuriant verdure of a cemetery. The desolator had been there. Crumbling, hidden amidst those leafy groves, stood many a solitary gable or tattered wall to tell its tragic tale. The people who once dwelt upon those fertile fields were gone—gone for ever, 'like the snow on the mountain, the foam on the river'. Such was the scene of a demonstration intended as a protest against a further extension of the eviction system. In many respects the meeting was singular. The Catholic clergy—the clergy of the people—the shepherds who had seen their flocks so terribly decimated or dispersed—were there, resolute to save at least the remnant so far spared. Indeed it was to their exertions the meeting owed its existence. But there were there also, joining in the protest of the day, the Protestant clergymen of the district; yielding to none in their sympathy for the peaceable and industrious people now threatened with expulsion. Many hundreds of the agricultural population of Meath walked between twelve and twenty miles to the meeting, and an equal distance returning to their homes. Drogheda, Navan, Kells, Trim, Athboy, Summerhill, all sent their contingents who marched undeterred to the rendezvous amidst a war of the elements, rain and tempest. The cause of all this excitement was in some respects singular too. The fee or head-landlord rights of Mullagh have quite recently reverted to a Mr Keena, a gentleman from whom most persons acquainted with him would have expected considerateness in dealing with a tenantry. Scarcely had he succeded, however, to the reversionary interest which he had purchased in the Mullagh property, than he commenced proceedings to eject the tenantry; all of whom are honest, solvent, respectable, peaceable, and industrious men, punctual in the payment of their

* *Drogheda Argus*, Saturday, 15 July 1871

rents; many of whom expended considerable sums on the improvement of their holdings; and all, or nearly all, of whom have been themselves or their forefathers, tenants of the same homesteads respectively for probably two centuries. Many harsh and hurtful things were said of Mr Keena, naturally enough, at the meeting last week; yet we find it hard to accept the belief that he will pursue to its bitter end his dreadful purpose of evicting the Mullagh tenants. Even as it is, he stands deeply pledged, by the assurances and representations of his agents, not to remove or disturb the tenants resident on the property. But this assurance seems to us to cover an intention quite unworthy of such a man as Mr Keena has hitherto been supposed to be. One or two of the tenants—one of them, certainly whose forefathers had their home on the Mullagh, and who themselves were born and lived to manhood there, have entered into business in Dublin, still farming the family holding, to which, with increased means, they look forward to returning as to the home of their childhood. These are the tenants who, by their better means and their greater spirit, have so far saved all from sudden and complete eviction. By taking equitable defences at law, they stayed the ejectments and averted for all the evil day. It would be a pitiful and shabby revenge for Mr Keena now to compound, as it were, with conscience and public opinion, by yielding something as regards the other tenants, and sacrificing the one or two but for whom all would be on the roadside to-day. His dogged determination bodes the worst. Even on the day when the priests of his own faith and the people of his own kin were assembled on the Mullagh deprecating his threatened evictions, he was busily at work in the law courts pushing things to extremities; and on Tuesday last he succeeded in obtaining a verdict, subject to some points reserved against the hapless tenantry. 'But what of their rights under the Land Bill?' it will, naturally, be asked. The facts which make answer prove the truth of the resolution moved, seconded, and adopted at last week's meeting, that the 'protection' afforded by Mr Gladstone's Land Bill is little better than a cruel mockery. Owing to the sudden dropping of a life in a middleman's lease, most of these people may be flung ruined on the roadside without redress or 'compensation'. But even had it been otherwise, the fundamental principle of Mr Gladstone's Bill is a disastrous blunder. Instead of preventing eviction, unless for statutable causes, it fully warrants unjust and unequitable eviction as of old, but offers the landless tenant a chance, by litigation, of attaining a 'compensation' that is little better than a mockery. All the harm and all the ruin must be wrought and accomplished before the famous Gladstone Land Bill can be put into operation. The victim must be decapitated first; the claim for 'compensation' may then be litigated. One year has sufficed to ruin the reputation of that Land Bill which the Ministerial *claqueurs* would persist in lauding as the Irish Tenants' Magna Charta—a measure whereby Mr Gladstone was 'to do for Ireland what Stein and Hardenberg did for Prussia'. The 'Longfield' scheme, which had the singular merit of uniting in its praise Irish landlords and tenants, Catholics, Protestants, Liberals, Conservatives, and Nationalists, was too simple and too-much opposed to the English ideas whereby Mr Gladstone rules Ireland, to have any chance of adoption. We know of no class of Irishmen—save, indeed, a sleek and obsequious parliamentary following of the great Liberal dispenser of patronage—who approved the cumbrous, complicated, and inefficient scheme of Mr Gladstone. True, all admitted that it would in some respects achieve good results—and so it has—just as allowing Catholics to take thirty years of bog land was a partial relaxation of the penal laws, though it was not Emancipation. But it may fearlessly be stated that Irish public opinion was unanimous in declaring the Gladstone Land Bill a failure and an abortion, judged by the necessities of the case. To the principles laid down at the Mansion House Conference, every day's additional experience points as the only basis for a satisfactory and enduring settlement of the Irish Land Question. Mr Gladstone and his majority bore down all expostulation with the noisy assurance that time would show the superiority of his plan and convert us all into admiration of its perfection. Time is but increasing and strengthening the convictions of Irishmen, that the Irish Land Question is yet to be settled. This is the plain meaning of the action take by the priests of Meath; the men on whom of old fell the brunt of the struggle in fighting that question. The sentiments so forcibly and courageously enunciated last week by the Very Rev. Father Duncan, by the Vicar-General Dr Nicolls, by Father Tormey, and Father Behan, and by the erudite and patriotic historian of Meath, Dean Cogan, were no opinions of yesterday. They were the creed of Meath—priests and People—in 1852 as they are in 1871. Whoever changed, whoever fell away, whoever has need to adjust their positon now, Meath stands just where it always did, upon the great question of the Land. And the other and the greater question still—the question that includes and comprises all other political issues, great and small, for us Irishmen—the question of our National Emancipation— found noble advocacy also on the Mullagh platform. The ovation that hailed the appearance of Mr Martin—the deafening cheers that greeted Mr Smyth—would in themselves have eloquent meaning, even if the speeches of the day did not in more than one instance expressly proclaim the resolve of Meath to stand by the great national struggle on which our country is now entering. In truth, issues of magnitude too great to be affected by the result of Mr Keena's action were powerfully served by the great demonstration of last week. It may avail nothing to soften the heart of an obdurate landlord, but it will assuredly deter many an evil project of a like nature with his, now contemplated, from being put into execution. If it avail not to save the Mullagh victims, assuredly it will be the salvation of hundreds of others whose ruin would be pursued could it be done in safe and comfortable silence. And lastly, that splendid demonstration of priests and people, standing side by side in their ancient and holy union of mutual affection and duty, has spoken out the resolve of Royal Meath to take the van once more in the cause of of Ireland's freedom.

Appendix 8: The Family of Anthony Cogan

MONUMENT TO ANTHONY COGAN'S PARENTS AND
BROTHERS IN THE CEMETERY ON THE HILL OF SLANE

A large horizontal grave slab in the north aisle of the ruined Franciscan Friary church on the Hill of Slane bears the following inscription:

63. Charles Cogan (1830–1907), youngest brother of Anthony, who farmed at Shalvanstown House near Slane, and whose descendants still live there.

Erected to the memory of Mr. Thos. Cogan of Slane who died 16th Feb 183(9) aged 66 yrs.
Also his son Patrick aged 17 yrs.
Also Surgeon Major Francis Cogan who died March 11th 1871
aged 44 yrs.
Also Mrs Anne Cogan relict of the above named Thos. Cogan
who died 25th Jan. 1879 aged 77 yrs.
And their son Charles Cogan who died 17th April 1907.
His wife Claire who died 7th Sept 1884.
And their son Thomas who died 13th June 1877.
And Charles who died 19th March 1931.
His son Charles Philip who died 2nd March 1975 aged 50 yrs.

THE FAMILY OF ANTHONY COGAN
AND HIS COLLATERAL DESCENDANTS

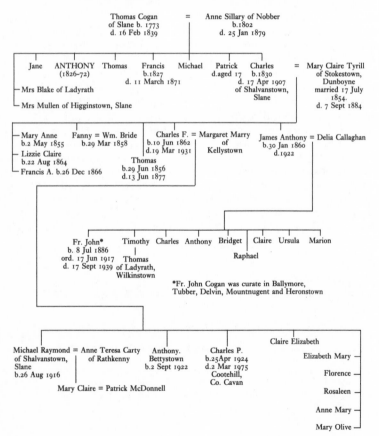

Thomas Cogan of Slane b. 1773 d. 16 Feb 1839 = Anne Sillary of Nobber b.1802 d. 25 Jan 1879

Jane
— Mrs Blake of Ladyrath
— Mrs Mullen of Higginstown, Slane

ANTHONY (1826–72)

Thomas

Francis b.1827 d. 11 March 1871

Michael

Patrick d.aged 17

Charles b.1830 d. 17 Apr 1907 of Shalvanstown, Slane = Mary Claire Tyrill of Stokestown, Dunboyne married 17 July 1854. d. 7 Sept 1884

— Mary Anne b.2 May 1855
— Lizzie Claire b.22 Aug 1864
— Francis A. b.26 Dec 1866

Fanny = Wm. Bride b.29 Mar 1858

Charles F. = Margaret Marry b.10 Jun 1862 of d.19 Mar 1931 Kellystown

Thomas b.29 Jun 1856 d.13 Jun 1877

James Anthony = Delia Callaghan b.30 Jan 1860 d.1922

Fr. John* b. 8 Jul 1886 ord. 17 Jun 1917 d. 17 Sept 1939

Timothy Thomas of Ladyrath, Wilkinstown

Charles Anthony Bridget

Claire Ursula Marion

Raphael

*Fr. John Cogan was curate in Ballymore, Tubber, Delvin, Mountnugent and Heronstown

Michael Raymond = Anne Teresa Carty of Shalvanstown, of Rathkenny Slane b.26 Aug 1916

Mary Claire = Patrick McDonnell

Anthony. Bettystown b.2 Sept 1922

Charles P. b.25Apr 1924 d.2 Mar 1975 Cootehill, Co. Cavan

Claire Elizabeth

Elizabeth Mary —
Florence —
Rosaleen —
Anne Mary —
Mary Olive —

176

Appendix 9: Reports of Anthony Cogan's Last Illness and Death

ILLNESS OF DEAN COGAN*

'With extreme regret we learn that Dean Cogan of Navan is seriously ill. We have not heard the particulars further than the information of the lamentable fact that he is stricken with serious illness. To his many friends and admirers at home and abroad, this will be sad news, while earnest prayers will go forth for the recovery of the good and gifted Dean, and that he may be long spared to the Church, of which he is an ornament, and the county that he served and loves so well. Although the accounts we have received as to his illness are of a gloomy character, still let us trust for the best—trust for the restoration of the zealous and able Dean to his wonted vigour. The voice eloquent to plead in the cause of the people and denounce the wrong doer, and the pen that rescued from passing oblivion, so many of the rich memorials of the diocese of Meath, may yet, we sincerely trust, have years of active exercise in the service of faith and fatherland.'

THE DEATH OF THE REV. ANTHONY COGAN†

'He had returned to his natal spot to breathe the last breath where he had first breathed the vital air. Amidst the beautiful scenes of his youth, close to the hill on whose summit, Patrick had kindled the Paschal light of the Church in whose ministry Father Cogan was a zealous labourer, his pure spirit winged its flight to the kingdom of the blest. While the Christmas altar at which he sacrificed was decked in the floral emblems of the season, the soul of the good priest was called to receive its just reward. Called away in the very maturity of his high intellectual powers, there was earnest and wide lament for his death amongst the people whose cause he ably espoused on many a platform throughout true-hearted Meath. Long will his name and fame be a household word through Royal Meath, the diocesan history of which he rescued from passing oblivion.'

The *Drogheda Argus* includes an extensive extract from the *Freeman's Journal* on Cogan's life and work: That newspaper reported 'the unexpected demise of this gifted clergyman' from 'fatty degeneration of the heart' which had been diagnosed a few months before. Cogan's illness had taken a dangerous turn on Sun. 22 Dec. 1872 when 'his friends abandoned all hope of his recovery' and he died on the following Saturday. Fr Cogan had 'entered his missionary career' in his 24th year; he died in his 46th year and after 22 years in the priesthood. The natural beauty of Slane and its important historical associations were believed to have been important in the formation of Cogan's 'historical sensitivities'.

The *Freeman's Journal* continues: 'There are few instances even in Catholic Ireland, in which the "Soggarth Aroon" acquired a stronger hold on the affections of the people among whom he laboured. As a public orator, Father Cogan was highly distinguished. He was lucid, logical and peculiarly fervent in

---

Drogheda Argus, Saturday, 28 December 1872, p. 4.
†*Drogheda Argus*, Saturday, 4 January 1873, p. 4.

manner'. Fr Cogan was frequently invited to preach in the parishes of St Mary's and St Patrick's in Liverpool, where his 'eloquent appeals told (forcibly) upon the hearts of those thousands of Irish exiles' who came to hear him preach. Fr Cogan had been Senior Dean at St Finian's diocesan seminary for the last eight years of his life.

The *Drogheda Argus* (loc. cit.) continued with its account of Dean Cogan's life: The first volume of his *Diocese of Meath* had been out of print before his death and he had hoped to reprint it. 'It is strange,' he often observed to his friends, 'I believe that I had a vocation to write this work, and I should not be surprised if God would call me soon, since I have finished my labours.' 'Father Cogan was a good conversational speaker, abounding in anecdote and story. In his intercourse both with his clerical and lay friends, he was affable, genial and warm hearted. His death has deeply affected his many friends, by whom his kindly words, his friendly smile, and cordial welcome are not likely soon to be forgotten.'

Dean Cogan's funeral—described by the *Argus* as an 'impressive scene'— took place on Monday, 30 December 1872. The Requiem Office and High Mass were held in the Catholic Church in Navan at 11 a.m. 'The Young Men's Society of Navan, with scarfs and hatbands carried the remains of their beloved Director in procession round about the chapel.' Fr T. Lynch, parish priest of Painstown and vicar foraine of the diocese presided. Dr Joseph O'Higgins, President of St Finian's seminary in Navan (Cogan's school) was the celebrant. Fr C. Keogan, curate of Trim, was the deacon, and the sub-deacon was Fr E. Horan, a curate in Navan. The master of ceremonies was Fr J. Moore, a colleague of Cogan's from St Finian's. Among a lengthy list of priests from Navan and the surrounding parishes in the choir were Fr William McCormick—another of Cogan's colleagues from his school in Navan—Fr John Kelly, parish priest of Skryne; Fr P. Clarke of Kilskyre and Fr Luke Hope a curate of Skryne.

THE BURIAL OF DEAN COGAN
Monday 30 December 1872*
An immense and most respectable congregation of Catholics and Protestants, from Navan, Johnstown, Walterstown, and Yellow Furze, where he had officiated so long and so worthily, were in the church. The remains were interred in the chapel in Slane, at the gospel side of the altar.

Appendix 10: The Dean Cogan Memorial

Moves to erect a memorial to Anthony Cogan were afoot almost as soon as his death was announced. Within two weeks of his death, the *Drogheda Argus* (Saturday 11 January, 1873, p. 5) ran a feature on the establishment of a Memorial Committee headed: *In Memory of Father Cogan*. The feature opened with the statement that 'many in Meath, and particularly in Navan, feel [his death] almost as a family bereavement'. The people of Navan were determined

* *Drogheda Argus* Saturday, 4 January 1873, p. 4.

to raise a monument to the memory of a man who had left them his own enduring monuments in stone and literature—a reference to his *Diocese of Meath* and to the [Catholic Young Men's] Hall he has erected and founded in the town of Navan.

Would it not be hideous libel on the gratitude of this generation, and particularly on the people of Navan, whom he so loved and revered, to permit his saintly remains to sleep in their grave, neglected and forgotten, like the remains of Dr Lanigan at Finglass, or the Franciscan O'Clerys, (the Four Masters), in Donegal—without a monument and an epitaph that shall be as lasting as the works he has left us are imperishable' (loc. cit.).

The Dean Cogan Memorial Society was constituted as follows:

John O'Neill, Hon. Sec., Market Square, Navan.
William Rothery, Hon. Teasurer, Market Square, Navan.
John Mullen, Esq., J.P., President of the Society.
Rev. Dr Higgins, St Finian's Seminary, Navan.
Rev. J. Moore, do.
Rev. J. Duff, do.
R. D. Nicholls Esq., M.D.

The list also included four priests from Navan Parish and 24 other men from the Navan area.

The *Drogheda Argus* ran regular reports on the progress of fund-raising for Dean Cogan's memorial, and included letters from distinguished contributors to the fund. On Saturday, 1 February 1873, the *Argus* (page 4) published two contributions—one from Lord Athlumney of Mountjoy Square, Dublin, and the other from Fr John O'Hanlon, curate at SS Michael and John, Dublin. John O'Hanlon had just succeeded in publishing his marathon ten-volume series of *Lives of the Irish Saints* in the very week in which Anthony Cogan had died. He was clearly a good friend and admirer of Cogan whose work is quoted frequently in O'Hanlon's *Lives*. O'Hanlon remembered Cogan as a man 'so untiring in labour, so simple in habit, so unassuming, and yet so excellent in character, so true a lover of his church and his country'. He concluded: 'Poor Father Anthony Cogan sleeps peacefully in his own native town and within that temple where many of his devotional hours were spent. In after time his grave shall be sought by many a pilgrim, and from many a distant land' *Drogheda Argus*, Saturday, 1 February 1873, p. 4).

DEAN COGAN'S ANNIVERSARY MASS AND THE COMPLETION OF HIS MEMORIAL, JANUARY 1874

The first anniversary of Anthony Cogan's death was marked on Tuesday 20 January 1874, perhaps because the true date (28 December 1873) was too soon after Christmas to assemble clergy, who would normally have taken their break after the Christmas services had been completed

The *Drogheda Argus* (24 January 1874, p. 4, col. 3) reported that the Anniversary Mass of the Rev. Dean Cogan 'of Navan' was celebrated in the Chapel of Slane, with Dr Nulty, Bishop of Meath, presiding.

'Near the Virgin's altar and over the remains was conspicuous a very beautiful monument which has been lately erected by Neill and Pearse of Great Brunswick Street, Dublin, in gothic style of Italian marble, two columns with caps, neatly carved, representing the vine and supporting the arch. There is a lifesize likeness of Fr. Cogan in a circular panel in pediment. Between the columns is the inscription plate in a richly moulded panel. On the pilasters are deeply sunk shamrocks in each corner, and resting on the base is an open book with the words *Diocese of Meath: Ancient and Modern*. All is supported by heavy marble corbels and surmounted with a handsome pediment, corniced, spired and finialed.

The text of the inscription is given in the *Drogheda Argus* (ibid.) in full. See page 156.

This monument to Anthony Cogan was executed by James Pearse, the father of Patrick Pearse, who at this early and modest stage in his career was in partnership with a fellow Englishman named Neill, at 27 Great Brunswick Street, Dublin. James Pearce had recently converted to Catholicism and was busy building up a successful business which was supported by the boom in post-Emancipation church building and embellishing throughout the Catholic dioceses of Ireland. James Pearse was at this time married to his first wife, Emily, who died in 1876. Pearse later married Margaret Brady, a woman of Meath extraction who was the mother of Patrick and Willie Pearse who were executed in the aftermath of the Easter Rising in 1916. James Pearse soon separated his business from that of Neill, and entered into a new partnership with his foreman, Edmund Sharp. Their work as architectural sculptors was recognised by a first class award for their exhibit of an altar at the Dublin Exhibition in 1882. The high altar of the parish church in Navan also bears an inscription to the memory of Anthony Cogan, who spent most of his ministry in that town.

Appendix 11: Extract from Mr and Mrs S. C. Hall's *Ireland* on conditions in Meath and Offaly* (King's County) in 1842

MEATH:

The county of Meath is the great grazing ground of Ireland, and consists almost entirely of pasture-land, vying in its external aspects with the richest of the English counties, and, perhaps, surpassing any of them in fertility. The hedges are remarkably luxuriant; the trees (of which there is an unusual abundance) are of extraordinary growth; and the fields have, at all times and seasons, that brilliant green so refreshing to the eye, and so cheering to the mind when associated with ideas of comfort and prosperity. There is, indeed, no part of Ireland where the Englishman will find himself so completely at home; for, added to great natural beauty, he sees, on all sides, the beneficial results of careful cultivation, and marks, in every direction, the ordinary consequences of industry directed by science; while the poverty and wretchedness that are elsewhere forced upon his attention, is here seldom perceptible; and 'the clamorous voice of woe' rarely 'intrudes upon the ear.' Much of this

* Halls' *Ireland*, ii, (1842), 373-4.

64 'The Day after the Ejectment' (*Illustrated London News* 16 Dec. 1848). Although evictions were reported as 'accompanied by an amount of human misery that is absolutely appalling', the artist managed to sanitise the injustice and personal tragedy under a cloak of smug Victorian romanticism.

apparently prosperous character is, however, hollow and unsubstantial: the large farmers are indeed wealthy, but of small farmers there are few or none; the policy of the 'graziers' has been, for a long time, to devote the produce of the soil to the raising of cattle; and the 'clearing of estates' in Meath has, therefore, been proceeding at a very disastrous rate. We quote the words of a common labourer with whom we conversed on the subject — 'The land is given over to the beasts of the field!' The small plots of ground are 'wanted for the cattle'; and as the cabins cannot exist without them, they are in rapid course of removal. The consequence is, that although misery is not to be encountered upon highways, or adjacent to pleasant meadows, the towns, into which the poor have been driven, are thronged with squalid countenances; starvation stalks at noon-day through their streets; and perhaps in no part of the world could be found so much wretchedness 'huddled' together into an equal space, as the tourist may note in the single town of Navan. All about the suburbs, the cabins are filthy to the last degree; a very large proportion of them have no other outlets for smoke but the broken windows; the roofs of many have partially fallen in; and we examined several from which every available piece of wood had been taken for firing, at periods when the pressure of immediate want had rendered the unhappy inmates indifferent to the future. We entered some of these hovels — within a dozen steps, be it remembered, of the centre of a town, and not hidden by distance and obscurity from the sight of sympathising humanity — and were shocked to find their condition wretched almost beyond conception, and certainly beyond credibility. The scene appalled us the more because of the lovely and plentiful land we had previously passed through; the fat cattle feeding upon pastures so fresh and green; the huge stacks; the full barns; the comfortable houses, midway between mansions and farmsteads — the air of luxury, indeed, that pervaded every object within our ken! It was a sad contrast; to be witnessed without heart-ache only by those who have become familiar with it, and have learned indifference from habit.

Halls' *Ireland*, ii, (1842), 373-4.

OFFALY (formerly KING'S COUNTY):

[Note: The Halls travelled by a horse-drawn canal 'fly-boat' from Dublin to Shannon Harbour].

The passage through the bog of Allen, although dreary and monotonous, is by no means without interest; and as the recurrence of locks enables the passenger occasionally to walk on land, the 'voyage' will amply repay curiosity. The aspect that surrounds him on all sides is very singular; huge 'clamps' or stacks, of turf border the canal, and here and there a cabin rears its roof a few feet above the surface, from which it can scarcely be distinguished. It is hardly possible to imagine more wretched hovels than those which the turf-cutters inhabit. The man rents usually from two to five acres; the turf he cuts with his own hands, and conveys to market as he best can. When settling, his first care is to procure shelter from the wind and rain; he selects, therefore, a dry bank, a little beyond the influence of floods; here he digs a pit, for it is, nothing more, places at the corners a few sticks of bog-wood , and covers the top with 'flakes' of heath, leaving a small aperture to let out the smoke. Yet the inhabitants of this miserable district, existing in this deplorable manner, are by no means unhealthy; and around their huts we saw some of the finest children we have seen in Ireland.

. . .

When internal peace, in Ireland, has been followed by prosperity, the expenditure of capital will certainly convert this immense waste, which contributes so little to the national wealth into fertile and productive fields; the next generation may see the merry harvester taking the place of the miserable turf-cutter, and smiling and happy cottages occupying the sites of the now wretched hovels that would be contemned even by the bushmen of southern Africa.

Ibid., ii, 190-1.

[Note: The hovels described here by the Halls were not confined to the Bog of Allen. Similar tepee-like structures were depicted from the south of Ireland in the *Illustrated London News* on 16 Dec. 1848 and 22 Dec. 1849. The Halls' account of hovels erected over pits in Offaly, recalls the 'dug-outs' or shelters erected over dry ditches in Co. Meath by the destitute and homeless as late as the 1950s. Such miserable structures—quite apart from encampments of tinkers and other travellers—must have been a common feature by Irish roadsides in the century before. Modern reconstructions of nineteenth-century cottages in Irish folk-parks portray an optimistic and fanciful view of a past whose reality was too grim to inflict upon today's tourist.]

Appendix 12: The Conynghams of Slane

Maj. Gen. Henry CONYNGHAM of Slane, Co. Meath and Mount Charles, Co. Donegal. Slain in battle, Spain, 1705-6. **=** Mary WILLIAMS only daughter and heiress of Sir John Williams (2nd Bart) of Minster, Isle of Thanet, Kent. Widow of Charles (PETTY), Baron Shelburne.

Henry CONYNGHAM [1st baron] 2nd and posthumous son, succeeded elder brother, William, 1738. Created Baron Conyngham of Mount Charles, 1753; Viscount, 1756; Earl 1781. Died without issue, 1781.

Mary **=** Rt Hon Francis BURTON of Buncraggy, Co. Clare

William died without issue, 1738

Francis Pierpoint BURTON [2nd baron] succeeded his uncle by special remainder as Baron Conyngham of Mount Charles. Took name of Conyngham, May 1781. Died, Bristol, 1787. Inherited estates in England and Co. Limerick. **=** Elizabeth CLEMENTS daughter of Rt Hon Nathaniel CLEMENTS and sister of Robt. 1st Earl of Leitrim. Married March 1750. Died Ramsgate, Kent, Oct. 1814, aged 83.

William BURTON also took the name CONYNGHAM. Inherited estates in Co. Donegal and Slane Castle, Co. Meath. Died unmarried, 31 May, 1796, when estate reverted to peerage.

Henry CONYNGHAM [3rd Baron and 1st Marquis] born London, 26 Dec. 1766. Maj.Gen. 1808. Created Viscount 1789; Earl, 1797. Viscount Slane 1816; Marquis Conyngham 1816; Baron Minster of Minster Abbey, Thanet, 1821. Constable of Windsor Castle 1829 until his death in Hamilton Plce, Mddx, 1832, aged 66. Buried 4 Jan. 1833, Patrixbourne, Kent. He gave land for the building of the Catholic church in Slane in 1802. **=** Elizabeth DENISON married July 1794. Elizabeth was daughter of Joseph DENISON, banker. Mistress of George IV. Died, Bifrons, near Canterbury, 11 Oct. 1861, aged 92.

Henry Joseph CONYNGHAM Earl of Mount Charles 1795-1824. Died unmarried, at Nice, in the lifetime of his father. The Catholic church in Slane was named in his memory.

Francis Nathaniel CONYNGHAM [4th Baron and 2nd Marquis] second but first surviving son. Marquis Conyngham in the peerage of the kingdom of Ireland and Baron Minster in the peerage of the United Kingdom. Born 1797. Died 1876. From whom the titles descend.

The details of this pedigree have been taken from G[eorge] E[dward] C[okayne], *The Complete Peerage: or a History of the House of Lords and all its members from the Earliest Times*, ed. Vicary Gibbs, H.A. Doubleday, et al., (London, 1910-40) 13 vols. iii (1913), 410-13.

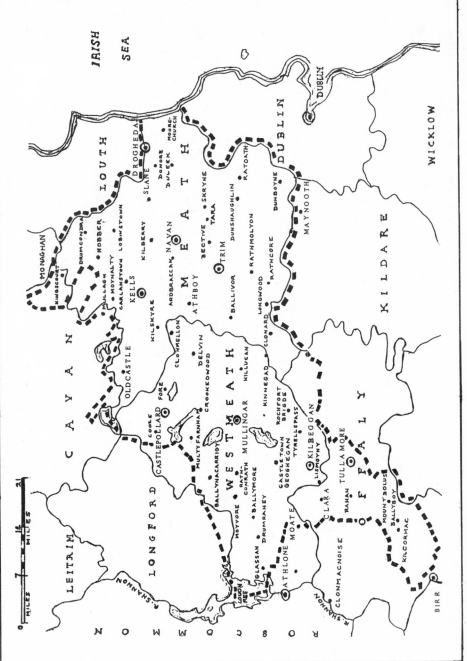

I   THE DIOCESE OF MEATH

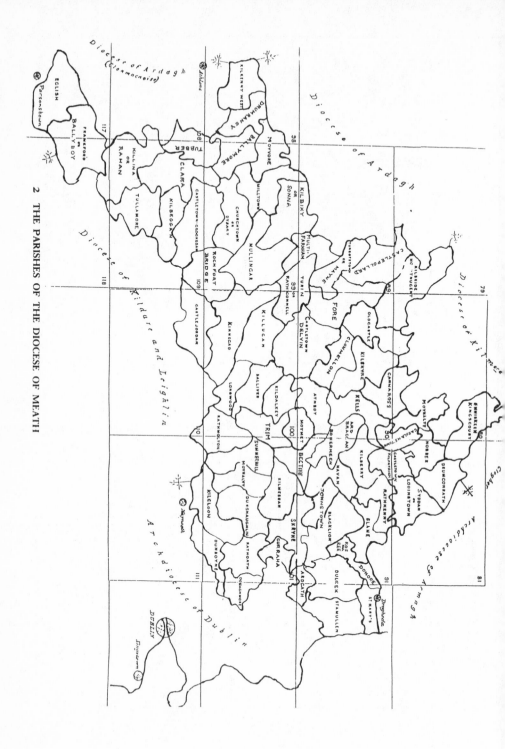

2 THE PARISHES OF THE DIOCESE OF MEATH

3 DETAIL OF SLANE AREA FROM BEAUFORT (1816)

187

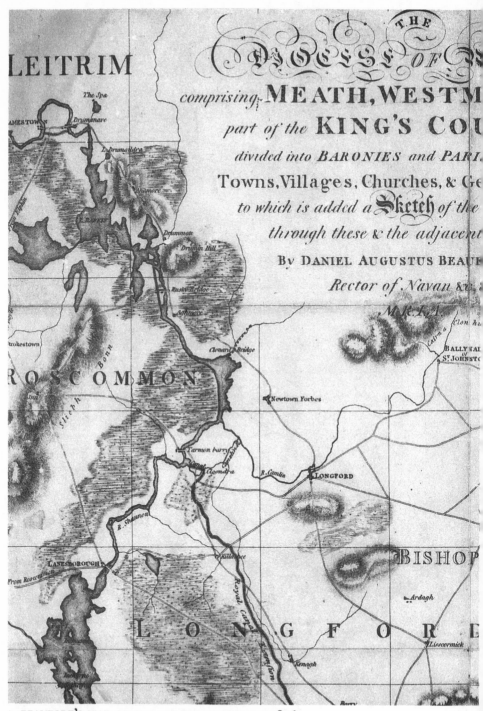

4 BEAUFORT'S MAP OF THE DIOCESE OF MEATH, 1816
NORTH–WEST SECTION

SOUTH–WEST SECTION

190

NORTH–EAST SECTION

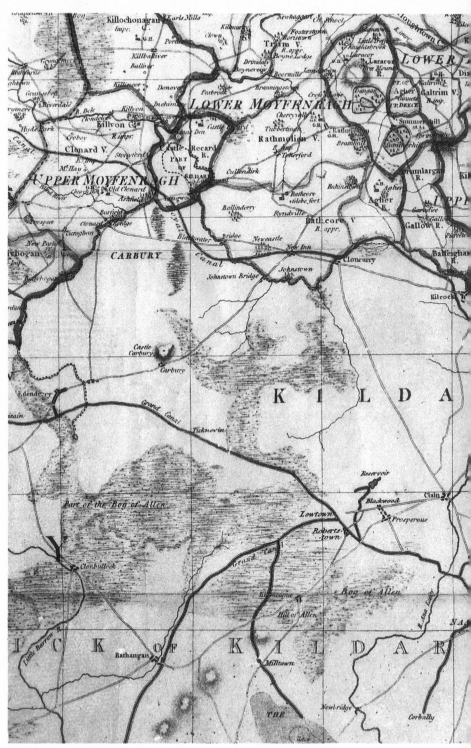

SOUTH-EAST SECTION

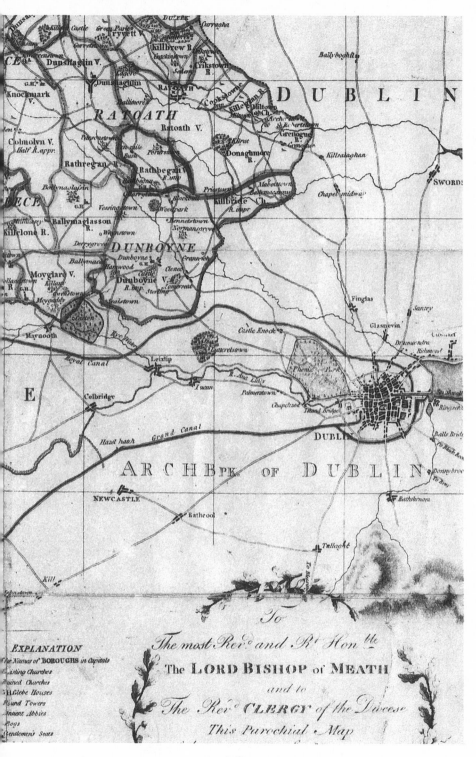

The most Rev.^d and R.^t Honble
The LORD BISHOP of MEATH
and to
The Revd CLERGY of the Diocese
This Parochial Map

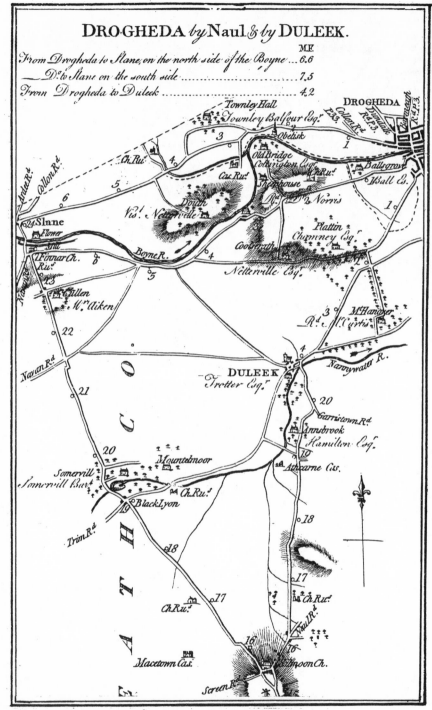

DROGHEDA by Naul & by DULEEK.

ME

From Drogheda to Slane, on the north side of the Boyne ...6.6

—— Do. to Slane on the south side 7.5

From Drogheda to Duleek 4.2

5 TAYLOR AND SKINNER'S MAP OF ROADS IN SLANE AREA, 1777

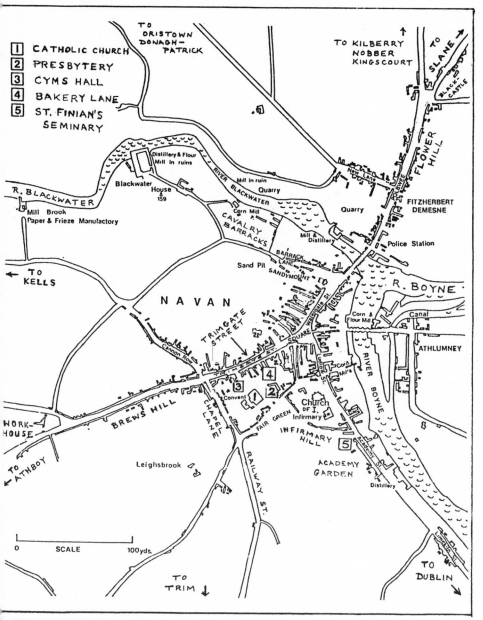

1	CATHOLIC CHURCH
2	PRESBYTERY
3	CYMS HALL
4	BAKERY LANE
5	ST. FINIAN'S SEMINARY

THE TOWN OF NAVAN, *c*.1840 (with grateful acknowledgement to the research of Peter Connell, *Ríocht na Midhe* vi (1977), 39–59).

SELECT BIBLIOGRAPHY

Anthony Cogan studied the diocese of Meath from its early medieval origins up to 1867. The following select bibliography of general and regional studies concentrates on works relating primarily to Cogan's own time and to his interests in the seventeenth century.

GENERAL WORKS

Adams, W.F., *Ireland and the Irish Emigration to the New World from 1815 to the Famine* (New Haven, 1932).

Bartlett, T., and Hayton, D.W., eds. *Penal Era and Golden Age: Essays in Irish History 1690-1800* (Belfast, 1979).

Beames, M., *Peasants and Power: The Whiteboy Movements and their Control in Pre-Famine Ireland* (Brighton, 1983).

Beckett, J.C., *The Making of Modern Ireland (1603-1923)* (London, 1966).

Bowen, D., *The Protestant Crusade in Ireland 1800-1870: A Study of Protestant-Catholic Relations between the Act of Union and Disestablishment* (Dublin, 1978).

Brady, J., and Corish, P.J., *The Church under the Penal Code* in *A History of Irish Catholicism*, IV, ii (Dublin, 1971).

Brady, J., *Catholics and Catholicism in the Eighteenth-Century Press* (Maynooth, 1965).

Burke, W.P., *The Irish Priests in the Penal Times (1660-1760)* (Waterford, 1914).

Chart, D.A., *Ireland from the Union to Catholic Emancipation* (London, 1910).

Clarke, A., *The Old English in Ireland 1625-42* (London, 1966)

Clark, S., and Donnelly, J.S., eds., *Irish Peasants: Violence and Political Unrest 1780-1914* (Manchester and Madison Wis., 1983).

Comerford, R.V., 'Ireland 1850-70: Post-Famine and Mid-Victorian' in Vaughan, *Ireland Under the Union, I, 1801-70*, pp. 372-95.

'Churchmen, Tenants and Independent Opposition, 1850-56', ibid., pp. 396-414.

'Conspiring Brotherhoods and Contending Elites, 1857-63', ibid., pp. 415-30.

'Gladstone's First Irish Enterprise, 1864-70', ibid., pp. 431-50.

Comerford, R.V., *The Fenians in Context: Irish Politics and Society, 1842-82* (Dublin, 1985).

Connell, K.H., *The Population of Ireland, 1750-1845* (Oxford, 1950).

Connelly, S.J., *Priests and People in Pre-Famine Ireland 1780-1845* (Dublin, 1982).

Connelly, S.J., *Religion and Society in Nineteenth-Century Ireland* (Studies in Irish Economic and Social History No.3, Dundalk, 1985).

Corish, P.J., *The Catholic Community in the Seventeenth and Eighteenth Centuries* (Dublin, 1981).

Corish, P.J., ed. *A History of Irish Catholicism* (16 fascicles. Dublin and Melbourne, 1967-72).

Corkery, D., *The Hidden Ireland: A Study of Gaelic Munster in the Eighteenth Century* (Dublin, 1925)

Cullen, L.M., *The Emergence of Modern Ireland 1600-1900* (London, 1981).

Davis, R., *The Young Ireland Movement* (Dublin, 1987).

Devoy, J., *Recollections of an Irish Rebel* (New York, 1929).

Dickson, D., *New Foundations: Ireland 1660-1800* (Dublin, 1987).

Donnelly, J.S., 'Famine and Government Response, 1845-6', in Vaughan, *Ireland Under the Union, I, 1801-70*, pp. 272-285.

'Landlords and Tenants', ibid., pp. 332-49.

'Excess Mortality and Emigration', ibid., pp. 350-6.

'A Famine in Irish Politics', ibid., pp. 357-71.

Dunne, T., 'Haunted by History: Irish Romantic Writing 1800-1850' in Porter, R., and Teich, M., *Romanticism in National Context* (Cambridge, 1988).

Edwards, R. Dudley, *Patrick Pearse: the Triumph of Failure* (London, 1977).

Edwards, R. Dudley, and Williams, T.D., eds., *The Great Famine: Studies in Irish History, 1845-52* (Dublin, 1956).

Fitzpatrick, D., 'Emigration, 1801-70' in Vaughan, *Ireland Under the Union, I, 1801-70*, pp. 562-622.

Foster, R.F., *Modern Ireland 1600-1972* (London, 1988).

Foster, R.F., 'Ascendancy and Union' in *The Oxford Illustrated History of Ireland* ed., Foster, R.F., (Oxford, 1989), pp. 161-211.

Froude, J.A., *The English in Ireland in the Eighteenth Century* 3 vols. (2nd. edn. London, 1881).

Giblin, C., 'Catalogue of Material of Irish Interest in the Collection Nunziatura di Fiandra, Vatican Archives' *Collectanea Hibernica*, I-XV (1958-72) in 11 parts.

Giblin, C., *Irish Exiles in Catholic Europe, A History of Irish Catholicism*, ed., Corish, P.J., IV, iii (Dublin, 1971).

Gwynn, D., *Young Ireland and 1848* (Cork, 1949)

Hall, S.C. [Mr and Mrs], *Ireland, its Scenery, Character, etc.* 3 vols (London, 1843).

Hanly, J., ed., *The Letters of Saint Oliver Plunkett 1625-1681, Archbishop of Armagh and Primate of All Ireland* (Dublin, 1979).

Healy, J., *Maynooth College: its Centenary History* (Dublin, 1895).

Kerr, D., *Peel, Priests and Politics: Sir Robert Peel's Administration and the Roman Catholic Church in Ireland 1841-44* (Oxford, 1982).

Larkin, E., 'The Devotional Revolution in Ireland 1850-75' *American Historical Review*, lxxvii, no.3 (June 1972), 625-52.

Larkin, E., *The Historical Dimensions of Irish Catholicism* (New York, 1981).

Lecky, W.E.H. *History of Ireland in the Eighteenth Century* 5 vols. (London, 1892).

Lee, J., *The Modernization of Irish Society 1848-1918* (Dublin, 1973).

Lovett, R., *Irish Pictures drawn with pen and pencil* (London, 1888).

Lyons, F.S.L., *Ireland Since the Famine* (London, 1971).

Lyons, F.S.L., and Hawkins, R.A.J., eds. *Ireland Under the Union: Varieties of Tension. Essays in honour of T.W. Moody* (Oxford, 1980)

MacDonagh, O., 'The Age of O'Connell, 1830-45' in Vaughan, *Ireland Under the Union*, I, *1801-70*, 158-68.
  'Politics, 1830-45' ibid., pp. 169-92.
  'The Economy and Society, 1830-45', ibid., pp. 218-241.

MacDonagh, O., 'The Politicization of the Irish Catholic Bishops 1800-1850' *The Historical Journal*, xviii, no.1 (Cambridge, 1975)

McDowell, R.B., *Public Opinion and Government Policy in Ireland, 1801-1846* (London, 1952).

McDowell, R.B., ed., *Social Life in Ireland, 1800-45* (Dublin, 1957).

Macintyre, A., *The Liberator: Daniel O'Connell and the Irish Party, 1830-1847* (London, 1965).

McCaffrey, L.J., *Daniel O'Connell and the Repeal Year* (Lexington, Kentucky, 1966).

Miller, D.W., 'Irish Catholicism and the Great Famine', *Jn. Soc. Hist.*, ix, no.1 (1975).

Mokyr, J., *Why Ireland Starved: A Quantative and Analytical History of the Irish Economy 1800-1850* (London, 1983).

Moody, T.W., *Thomas Davis, 1814-15* (Dublin, 1945).

Moody, T.W., Martin, F.X., and Byrne, F.J., eds. *A New History of Ireland, VIII. A Chronology of Irish History to 1976* (Oxford, 1982).

Ibid. IX, *Maps, Genealogies, Lists* (Oxford, 1984).

Moody, T.W., and Vaughan, W.E., eds. *A New History of Ireland IV. Eighteenth-Century Ireland 1691-1800*, gen. eds. Martin, F.X., Byrne, F.J., et al. (Oxford, 1986).

Morris, W. O'Connor, *Ireland 1798-1898* (London, 1898).

Norman, E.R., *The Catholic Church and Ireland in the Age of Rebellion, 1859-73* (London, 1965).

Nowlan, K.B., *The Politics of Repeal: A Study in the Relations between Great Britain and Ireland, 1841-50* (London, 1965).

Nowlan, K.B., *Charles Gavan Duffy* (Dublin, 1964).

O'Brien, G. *The Economic History of Ireland in the Eighteenth Century* (Dublin, 1918).

O'Brien, G., *The Economic History of Ireland from the Union to the Famine* (London, 1921).

O'Brien, W.P., *The Great Famine in Ireland and a Retrospect of the Fifty Years 1845-95* (London, 1896).

Ó Catháin, D., 'Charles O'Conor of Belanagare: Antiquary and Scholar', *Journal of Roy. Soc. Antiquaries of Ireland*, cix (1989), 136-63.

Ó Cuiv, B., ed., *A View of the Irish Language* (Dublin, 1969).

Ó Fiaich, T., 'The Registration of the Clergy in 1704', *Seanchas Árd Mhacha*, VI, i, (1971), 46-59.

O'Hanlon, J., *Lives of the Irish Saints with special festivals, and the commemorations of holy persons* (Dublin and London, n.d. [1872]).

O'Leary, J., *Recollections of Fenians and Feniansim* 2 vols. (London, 1896).

O'Sullivan, D., *Carolan: The Life, Times and Music of an Irish Harper* 2 vols. (London, 1958)

Ó Tuathaigh, G., *Ireland Before the Famine 1798-1848* (Dublin, 1972).

Packenham, T., *The Year of Liberty: The Story of the Great Irish Rebellion of 1798* (London, 1969)

Pomfret, J.E., *The Struggle for Land in Ireland, 1800-1923* (Princeton, 1930).

Power, T.P., and Whelan, K., eds. *Endurance and Emergence: Catholics in Ireland in the Eighteenth Century* (Dublin, 1990).

Ryan, D., *The Phoenix Flame: A Study of Fenianism and John Devoy* (London, 1937).

Simms, J.G., *Jacobite Ireland 1685-91* (London, 1969).

Simms, J.G., *The Williamite Confiscation in Ireland 1690-1703* (London, 1956).

Senior, H., *Orangeism in Ireland and Britain, 1795-1836* (London and Toronto, 1960)

Sheehy, J., and Mott, G., *The Rediscovery of Ireland's Past: the Celtic Revival 1830-1930* (London, 1980).

Stokes, M., *Early Christian Art in Ireland* (London, 1894).

Swords, L., ed., *The Irish-French Connection 1578-1978* (Paris, 1978).

Vaughan, W.E., ed., *A New History of Ireland, V. Ireland Under the Union, I, 1801-70* gen. eds. Martin, F.X., Byrne F.J., et al. (Oxford, 1989).

Wall, M., *The Penal Laws, 1691-1760: Church and State from the Treaty of Limerick to the accession of George III.* (Dundalk, 1961).

Wall, M., *Catholic Loyalty to King and Pope in Eighteenth-Century Ireland*, Proceedings of the Irish Catholic Historical Committee, 1960.

[Ware, J.] *The Whole Works of Sir James Ware concerning Ireland*, ed. by W. Harris (2 vols. Dublin, 1764).

Whyte, J.H., *The Independent Irish Party (1850-59)* (Oxford, 1958).

Whyte, J.H., 'The Appointment of Catholic Bishops in Nineteenth-Century Ireland', *Catholic Historical Review*, (April, 1962), 12-32.

Woodham-Smith, C., *The Great Hunger: Ireland 1845-9* (London, 1962)

SPECIALISED WORKS AND WORKS ON LOCAL HISTORY

RnM = *Riocht na Midhe: Records of Meath Archaeological and*

Historical Society beginning with Vol. I, i in 1955 and continuing to the present, provides an invaluable series of articles on all matters relating to Meath and Westmeath prehistory, medieval archaeology and history, as well as to the modern history and folklore of the region.

A full index to all articles in *Ríocht na Midhe: Index 1955-1989* compiled by Julitta Clancy, with a foreword by Elizabeth Hickey, is an essential point of departure for all Historians working on Meath and Westmeath.

Archdall, M., *Monasticon Hibernicum : or an History of the Abbies, Priories, and other Religious Houses in Ireland* (Dublin, 1786).

Beaufort, D.A., *[Map of] The Diocese of Meath comprising Meath, Westmeath, and a great part of King's County etc. etc. divided into baronies and parishes . . . to which is added a sketch of the principal roads* (n.p. 1816).

Brady see also: *Ó Brádaigh*

Brady, J., *A Short History of the Parishes of the Diocese of Meath, 1876-1937* (Navan, 1937).

Broderick, J.F., *The Holy See and the Irish Movement for the Repeal of the Union with England, 1829-47* (Rome, 1951).

Cawkhill, J. and F., 'Carolan, a Co. Meath Composer', *RnM*, v (1974), 33-9.

Cogan, A., *Diocese of Meath: Ancient and Modern* 3 vols (1862-70) reprint with introduction by A.P. Smyth (Dublin, 1992).

Connell, Paul, 'Repeal and the Roman Catholic Clergy in Co. Meath, (1840-45), *RnM*, vii (1984), 44-60.

Connell, Paul, 'The Rise and Fall of the Repeal Movement in Co. Meath, 1840-45' *RnM* vii (1982-83), 90-113.

Connell, Peter, 'The Changing Face of Navan in the Nineteenth Century' *RnM* vi (1977), 39-59.

Connell, Peter, 'Famine and the Local Economy, Co. Meath 1845-55' *RnM* vii (1985-86), 114-25.

Connell, Peter, *Changing Forces Shaping a Nineteenth-Century Irish Town: a Case Study of Navan* (Maynooth, 1978).

Connell, Peter, *An Economic Geography of Co. Meath, 1770-1870* (Maynooth, thesis, 1980).

Conway, M., 'The Boyle O'Reilly Stone', *RnM* iv (1968), 3-7.

Conway, M., 'The State of the Poor in 1834' (Document in Meath Co. Library), *RnM* i (1958), 69-74.

Coogan, T., and Gaughran, J., *Charlesfort: the Story of a Meath*

Estate and its People 1668 to 1968. (Navan/Kells, 1991).

Cox, L., 'The Mageoghegans (Geoghegans)' *RnM* iv (1969), 63-86.

Cox, L., 'O'Molloys of Fircall' *RnM* v (1973), 14-45.

Ellis, P.B., *The Boyne Water: the Battle of the Boyne, 1690* (London, 1976).

Ellison, C.C., 'Bishop Dopping's Visitation Book 1682-85' *RnM* v (1971), 28-39; (1972) 3-13; (1973), 3-11; (1974), 98-103; vi (1975), 3-13.

Ellison, C.C., 'Dangan, Mornington and the Wellesleys: Notes on the Rise and Fall of a great Meath Estate', *RnM* iii (1966), 315-7; iv (1967) 3-25.

Fagan, P., 'The Decline of the Irish Language in Westmeath', *RnM* vii (1984), 94-101.

Fenning, H., 'The Dominicans of Mullingar: 1237-1610', *RnM*, iii (1964) 105-14.

'The Dominicans of Mullingar: 1622-1654' iii (1966), 299-314.

'The Dominicans of Mullingar: 1667-1696' iv (1968), 20-32.

Fenning, H., 'The Dominicans of Trim: 1683-1710' *RnM* ii (1961), 3-8.

'The Dominicans of Trim: 1713-1833' *RnM* ii (1962), 21-32.

'The Dominicans of Trim: 1263-1682' *RnM* iii (1963), 15-23

Fenning, H. 'Dominican Nuns in Meath' *RnM* iii (1965), 201-3.

Fitzsimons, H., 'Slane: A forgotten Graveyard' *RnM* vi (1975), 65-8.

Flynn, G., 'Bishop Thomas Nulty and the Irish Land Question' *RnM* vii (1984), 14-28; (1985-86), 93-110.

Grose, F., *Antiquities of the County of Meath, with illustrations of its principal abbeys, castles etc.* (Dublin, 1833).

Hanly, J., 'The Beginnings of Meath's First Weekly—*The Meath Herald*' *RnM* iv (1967), 55-60.

Healy, J., *History of the Diocese of Meath* 2 vols. (Dublin, 1908).

Hickey, E., 'Monument to Sir Thomas Cusack' *RnM* v (1971), 75-91.

'Some Notes on Kilbixy, Tristernagh and Templecross, and the Family of Piers who Lived in the Abbey of Tristernagh in Westmeath' *RnM* vii (1980-81), 52-76.

Kenny, M., 'Conacre in pre-Famine Westmeath' *RnM* vii (1982-83) 33-41.

Kenny, M., 'Employment and Wages in Pre-Famine Westmeath' *RnM* viii (1987), 71-92.

Kenny, M., 'Land Tenure in East Westmeath and its Influence

upon the State of Agriculture, 1820-1840' *RnM* vi (1978-79), 33-48.

Kenny, M., 'State of the Poor in Pre-Famine Ireland: Conditions in Co. Westmeath' *RnM* vii (1984), 67-85.

Lewis, S., *A Topographical Dictionary of Ireland* (2 vols with atlas. London, 1837).

McCarthy, D., ed., *L.F. Renehan, Collections on Irish Church History* (2 vols. Dublin, 1861, 1874).

McGreevy, C., 'Some Early Irish Battle Sites Identified', *RnM* vi (1977), 60-1.

Mooney, D., 'The Origins of Agrarian Violence in Meath, 1790-1828' *RnM* viii (1987), 45-67.

Mooney, D., 'A Society in Crisis: Agrarian Violence in Meath, 1828-1835' *RnM* viii (1988-89), 102-28.

Morris, H., see *Ó Muirgheasa, E.*

Murphy, I., *The Diocese of Killaloe in the Eighteenth Century* (Dublin, 1991).

O'Boyle, E., *The Battle of the Boyne* (Duleek Hist. Soc., 1990)

Ó Brádaigh see also *Brady*

Ó Brádaigh, T., 'An t-Athair Pól Breathnach' *RnM* iii (1966), 285-9.

O'Donnell, T., *Franciscan Abbey of Multyfarnham* (The Abbey, Multyfarnham, 1951).

Ó Gallchóir, S., *Séamus Dall Mac Cuarta: Dánta* (Baile Átha Cliath [Dublin], 1971).

Ó Loinsigh, S., 'The Rebellion of 1798 in Meath' *RnM* iii (1966), 338-50; iv (1967), 33-40; (1968), 33-49; (1969) 3-27; (1970) 30-53; v (1971), 62-74.

Ó Muirgheasa, E., *Amhráin na Midhe: cuid a h-aon* (Baile Átha Cliath agus Corcaigh, [Dublin and Cork], 1934)

[Ordnance Survey] *Letters containing information relative to the Antiquities of the county of Meath, collected during the progress of the Ordnance Survey in 1836*. ed. M. O'Flanagan (Bray, 1928) [typescript].

[Ordnance Survey] *Letters containing information relative to antiquities of the county of Westmeath collected during the progress of the Ordnance survey in 1837*. 2 vols. ed. M. O'Flanagan (Bray, 1931) [typescript].

O'Reilly, John Boyle, see *Roche, J.F.*

O'Reilly, M., 'The Barnwalls', *RnM* i (1957), 64-8.

O'Reilly, M., 'The Plunket Family of Loughcrew' *RnM* i (1958), 49-53.

Perry, G., ed., *A Window on the Past* (Rathfeigh Historical Soc., 1991)

Rice, G., 'Attitudes to the Counter-Reformation in Meath, 1600-1630' *RnM* v (1972), 54-63.

Rice, G., 'Extracts from Meath Priests' Wills, 1658-1782' *RnM* iv (1967), 68-71.

Rice, G., 'Thomas Deace, bishop of Meath, and some questions concerned with the rights to ecclesiastical property alienated at the Reformation' *RnM* vi (1975), 69-89.

Roche, J.F., ed., *Life of John Boyle O'Reilly together with his complete Poems and Speeches edited by Mrs. John Boyle O'Reilly* (London, 1891).

Roe, H.M., *Medieval Fonts of Meath* (Meath Archaeolog. and Hist. Soc., 1968).

Sheehan, J., *Westmeath as Others Saw It* (Moate, 1982).

Simms, J.G., 'Meath Landowners in the Jacobite War' *RnM* ii (1962), 55-8.

Snoddy, O., 'Notes on the Volunteers, Militia, Yeomanry and Orangemen of Co. Meath' *RnM* vi (1978-9), 3-32.

Steen, L.J., *The Battle of the Hill of Tara, 26th May 1798* (Trim, 1991).

Swan, L., 'Fennor, Co. Meath', *RnM* v (1972), 64-9.

Sweetman, P.D., 'Trim Castle Archaeological Excavations: Preliminary Report' *RnM* v (1974), 69-77.

Taylor, G., and Skinner, A., *Maps of the Roads of Ireland Surveyed 1777* (London and Dublin, 1778)

Trench, C.E.F., 'Fleming and Conyngham of Slane' *RnM* vii (1982-83), 69-75.

Trench, C.E.F., 'William Burton Conyngham: "Profound Scholar and Antiquary", 1733-96' *RnM* viii (1987), 113-28.

Trench, C.E.F., *Slane* (Dublin, 1976).

Waters, Ormonde D., 'John Boyle O'Reilly and the Catalpa Ballad' *RnM* v (1971), 3-13.

Wilde, W.R., *The Beauties of the Boyne and its tributary, the Blackwater* (Dublin, 1849)

Wilson, T.M., 'The Great Landowners of Meath, 1879' *RnM* vii (1980-81), 99-110.

JOURNALS

Analecta Hibernica, including the Reports of the Irish Manuscripts Commission (Dublin, 1930–).

Archivium Hibernicum, or Irish Historical Records (Catholic Record Society of Ireland, Maynooth, 1912–).

Collectanea Hibernica: Sources for Irish History (Dublin, 1958–).

Historical Studies: Papers read before the Irish Conference of Historians (London, Dublin and elsewhere, 1958–).

Irish Ecclesiastical Record (Dublin, 1864–1968).

Irish Historical Studies (Dublin, 1938–).

Proceedings of the Irish Catholic Historical Committee (Dublin, 1955–).

Reportorium Novum: Dublin Diocesan Historical Record (Dublin, 1956–)

NEWSPAPERS AND MAGAZINES

The following list does not include publications with a national circulation and is provided as an aid for Local Historians who wish to research further into the world of the Irish Midlands in the nineteenth century. Publication runs with no end-dates given indicate that the paper continued publishing up to or beyond c.1900.

Cavan Observer no.1, 11 July 1857 – 29 October 1864. (Cavan).

Cavan Weekly News no.1, 16 December 1864— (Cavan)

Conservative no.1, 16 June 1849 – 20 February 1864 (Drogheda).

Drogheda Advertiser (formerly *Drogheda Conservative*) 7 October 1908 - December 1929.

Drogheda Argus and Leinster Journal no.1, 19 September 1835— (Drogheda).

Drogheda Conservative (formerly *The Conservative*) 27 February 1864 – 3 October 1908.

Drogheda Conservative Journal no.1, 24 June 1837 – 30 December 1848 (Drogheda).

Drogheda Independent 4 January 1890— (Drogheda).

Drogheda Journal January 1823 – 4 March 1843 (Drogheda).

Drogheda Sentinel no.1, 6 July 1861 – 1 April 1865 (Drogheda).

Duffy's Irish Catholic Magazine 1847–48 (Dublin).

King's County Chronicle [Co. Offaly] no.1, 24 September 1845— (Parsonstown [Birr]).

Louth Church of Ireland Parochial Magazine (incorporating St Peter's Drogheda parish magazine. Nineteenth-cent. Dundalk).

Louth Free Press no.1, 18 March 1829 – 21 August 1830).

Meath Chronicle: Cavan and Westmeath Herald no.1, 1897— (Navan).

Meath and Louth Advertiser (continuation of *Drogheda Journal*).

Meath Herald no.1, 15 February 1845— (Kells).

Meath People no.1, 1 August 1857 – 28 November 1863 (Navan).

Meath Reporter 18 March 1871 – 21 October 1871 (Trim).

Midland Reporter 23 Sept 1897 (formerly *The Westmeath Nationalist*).

Westmeath Examiner no.1, 23 September 1882— (Mullingar).

Westmeath Guardian and Longford News Letter no.1, 8 January
     1835— (Mullingar).

Westmeath Herald no.1, 30 April 1859 – 28 April 1860 (Athlone).

Westmeath Independent no.1, 13 June 1849— (Athlone).

Westmeath Journal 27 May 1813 – 1 May 1834 (Mullingar).

Westmeath Nationalist 30 April 1891 – 16 September 1897 (Mullingar).

While productions relying on fashion alone for their ephemeral currency, will be forgotten, the simple annals of the diocese of Meath will be remembered and referred to with grateful curiosity.

John McHale, archbishop of Tuam, on Cogan's *Diocese of Meath*, 1863

INDEX

NOTE: Anthony Cogan's *Diocese of Meath: Ancient and Modern* is provided with its own separate index for each volume

ABBREVIATIONS: C.C. = curate; Mth = Meath; O.F.M. = Order of Friars Minor (Franciscan); O.P. = Order of Preachers (Dominican); O.S.B = Order of St Benedict (Benedictine); P.P. = parish priest; Wmth = Westmeath

All Hallows College, Dublin, 103, 129
Allard, Mick, of Rathconrath, 145
Ampleforth College, N.R. Yorkshire, 106
amusements, 55
Anglo-Irish élite: see *Ascendancy.*
annals, early Irish, 114, 118, 140
Anne, English Queen, 26, 44, 117
antiquarianism, 21-2, 48
Arcachon, Les Landes, France, 131
archaeology, vandalism of ancient monuments, 122-3, 166; Cogan as recorder of monuments, 118-25, 134-5, 171
Archdall, Mervyn, antiquary, 36-7, 38, 47, 94-5, 152
archives: see *Meath Diocese* and *Vatican.*
Ardagh diocese, 89, 107
Ardbraccan, Mth, 119, 122, 142
Ardcath, Mth, 57
Ardmulchan, Mth, 22, 146, 147
Armagh, diocese, 20, 27, 103, 142, 171
Ars, France, 146
ascendancy, 20, 36, 39, 44-5, 52-3, 84, 91, 92, 121
Ashbourne, Mth, 28
Assumption, feast of, 31, 32
Athboy, Mth, 75, 148, 173
Athlumney, Lord, 179
Athlumney, Mth, 26, 119
Aughrim, battle of, 36, 42, 91
Augustinian friary, 47

Australia, 51, 54, 103

Bakery Lane, Navan, 72
Ballinacargy, Wmth, 148-9
Ballinasloe, Galway, 103
Ballinvally, Hill of, Mth, 141
Ballybeg, Wmth, 144
Ballyboy, Offaly: see *Frankford.*
Ballymore, Wmth, 130, 144, 148, 176
Ballynabracky, Mth, 149; see also *Castlejordan.*
Barnewall, Andrew, P.P., Clonmellon, 40-1.
Barnewalls, family of, 44, 57
Barrack Lane, Navan, 48
Barry, William, priest from Cookstown, 148
Batterjohn, Mth, 172
Batterstown, Mth, 148
Beaufort, Augustus, map of, 187-90
Beauparc, Mth, 105
Bective, Mth, 25, 144
Bedford, Duke of, 72
Behan, Meath priest, 75, 101, 175
Belanagare, Roscommon, 37
Bellinter, Mth, 172
bells, 85, 143-4
Benedict XIII, pope, 107
Benedictines, 106
Betagh, Christopher, P.P., Johnstown, 153
Bettystown, Mth, 176
Bible Society, 88-89

bigotry, 63
Birmingham, England, 148
Birmingham, Fr, P.P., Turin, 85
Birr, Offaly, 118
Blacksmiths, 65, 66
Blake, of Ladyrath, 69
Bobbio, Italy, 35
Bodenstown, Kildare, 28
bogs, 182
Bohemia, 35, 119
Bohermeen, Mth, 105
Bordeaux, France, 149
Boston College, U.S.A., 156
Boston, U.S.A., 53, 54, 81
Boyne, battle of, 36, 39, 42, 44, 84, 90, 91
Boyne Meadow, Mth, 42
Boyne, river and valley, 31–3, 87, 113
Brady, John, diocesan historian and priest of Dunboyne, 14, 137, 154–5, 158
Brady, Margaret, mother of Patrick Pearse, 180
Brady, Tom, P.P., Ardbraccan, 119
Brega, kingdom of, 27, 33, 113, 154
Brennan, M.S., historian, 104
Brews Hill, Navan, 48, 72–4, 110, 167–8
Brighton, England, 39
British Army, 54, 63, 84
British Empire, 63
Brugh na Bóinne, Mth, 32, 33
Brunswick Street, Great, Dublin, frontispiece, 179, 180
Bunown, Wmth, 110
burials: respect for, 121, 122, 124–5; unroping of coffins, 118–19; of priests, 28, 117–19; body of priest exhumed, 148; of Catholic bishops, 141–2, 158; of Church of Ireland bishops, 122
Burton, Francis Pierpoint, second Lord Conyngham, 36–7, 38
Burton, William: see Conyngham.
Bush, The Big, Mth, 173

California, 103
Callan, Nicholas, Maynooth scientist, 103
Camden, William, antiquary, 94
Canada, 54
Cannistown, Mth, 43
Cantwell, John, bishop of Meath, 49–

50, 61, 62–4, 92, 113, 120, 126–7, 129, 131, 134, 136, 138, 158
Captain Rock, secret society, 66
Carbonari, 168
Carders, secret society, 55, 66
Carlow, 149
Castle Street, Liverpool, 108, 165
Castlejordan, Mth and Offaly, 120, 130, 145; see also Ballynabracky
Castlepollard, Wmth, 88, 148
Castletown-Geoghegan, (Castletown-Kindalene, Vastina), Wmth, 128, 142, 150
Castletown-Kilpatrick, Mth, 96, 128, 152
Catholic Emancipation, 52, 63, 80, 156
Catholic hierarchy, 70–1, 165; interest in archives, 133–6; synod, 107
Catholic landlords, 75, 124
Catholic University, Dublin, 111, 126
Catholic Young Mens' Society; Boston, 155–6; Navan, 16, 50, 69–70, 75, 90, 102, 107, 109–11, 155, 159, 161, 163; Liverpool 50, 107, 108–9, 163, 164–5
cattle: see graziers.
cattle shows, 168
Cavan, 27, 42, 43, 71–2, 118, 171
Cenél Fhiachach, lords of Moycashel, 35
chalices, 118, 148
Chapel Lane, Navan, 72, 110
Charles the Bald, Frankish ruler, 116
Charles II, English king, 94
Charlestown, U.S.A., 155
Chevers, Augustus, bishop of Meath, 137, 141–2
Chevers, Christopher, P.P., Kilbeg, priest and poet, 41–2, 155
Chevers, family of, 26
Chevers, Margaret, of Crackenstown, 137
children, 182
churches: seats in, 120; measuring ruins of, 120; new buildings, 122, 125, 180; photographing abandoned chapels, 134; raided for arms, 97; cathedrals, 138
Churchtown, Mth, 144
Cistercians, 25, 33
Clara, Offaly, 141, 142
Clare county, 38
Clarke, P., priest of Kilskyre, 178

Clarke, Simon, C.C., Mayne, 128, 129
Classics, 103
Clayton, Navan family of, 172
Clement IX, 137
Cletty (Cleitech) Mth, 33, 58
Clonard, Mth, 114, 121, 123
Clonfad, Wmth, 47, 123
Clonfert, Galway, 171
Clongowes Wood, Kildare, 126
Clonmacnoise, Offaly, 35, 36, 89, 107, 171
Clonmellon, Wmth, 41
Cloyne diocese, 78
Cogan, Anne: see *Sillary*.
Cogan, Anthony, monument (frontispiece), 29, 156, 178–80; childhood, 65, 100; family of, 175–6; schooling, 22, 100–3; Maynooth student, 103–5; photograph, 101–2; portrait 16; historian, 21, 114–16; archaeologist and antiquary, 117–25; archivist, 133–7; folklorist, 142–5, 152–3; his overall objectives, 110, 111–12, 166; publications, 54–5, 70, 78, 112–14, 154–5, 161, 162, 165, 166; letters from bishops to, 161–3, 170–2; pastoral work in Navan, 50–1; testimonial from Navan Young Men's Society, 161; advancement in clerical career, 127; visits to Liverpool, 69–70, 72–7, 106–9, 112, 163–7; political views, 63–84, 90–9, 111–12, 124, 164–5, 166; views on Irish society and economy, 82–3, 90–9, 161; romantic and conservative views, 117–19, 123–5; relationships with clerical colleagues, 126–32; personality, 127–8, 177–8; loyalty to his school, 129–30; attachment to Slane friends, 131; premonition of death, 178; last illness and death, 154–6, 177–8; funeral, 155–6, 178; anniversary Mass, 179; gold watch, 161; walking-stick, 159; *Sagart Aroon*, 164, 166, 177
Cogan, Charles, of Shalvanstown, 69, 176.
Cogan, Francis, 54, 69, 100, 103, 176
Cogan, John, C.C., Delvin, 176
Cogan, Michael, 100
Cogan, Patrick, 176
Cogan, Thomas, jun., 69

Cogan, Thomas, sen., 69, 100, 176
Colgan, Fr John, historian, 35
Collège des Irlandais, Paris: see *Irish College*.
Collège des Lombards, Paris: see *Irish College*.
College Hill, Mth, 172–3
Commissioners of the Peace, 66
Compostela, Spain, 16
Conaty, Nicholas, bishop of Kilmore, 171–2
Congalach mac Máelmithig, Uí Néill highking, 113
Connell, James, P.P., Dunboyne, 57
Constantinople, 25
Conyngham, Elizabeth, marchioness, 38, 39
Conyngham, family of, 36, 44, 183
Conyngham, Henry Burton, third baron and first marquis, 38, 39, 52, 98, 183
Conyngham, William Burton, 37, 38, 39, 44, 183
Conyngham Road, Dublin, 38
Cookstown, Mth, 148
Corbally, Matthew, 102
Corbally, M.E., Member of Parliament, 73–5, 167–70
Corbalton Hall, Mth, 74
Cormac mac Airt, legendary king, 33, 58
Cormac's House, Tara, 56, 68
Costelloe, Richard, of Killglyn, 128.
Counter Reformation, 21, 34, 39
Coyne, Joseph, priest of St. Finian's, Navan, 128
Crackenstown, Mth, 137
Cromwell, Oliver, leader of parliamentary forces in English Civil War, 18, 35, 36, 94, 107
Croppies (Men of '98), 28, 56, 58–60, 80, 82, 91
Cruisetown, Mth, 134
Cúchulainn, Ulster epic hero, 112
Cullen, Paul, archbishop of Dublin, 71, 114
Cully, Offaly, 144
Culmullen, Mth, 120
Curraha, Mth, 57, 60, 150
Cusack, family of, 26, 34, 121
Cusack, James, bishop of Meath, 141
Cusack, Sir Thomas, Lord Chancellor of Ireland, 33

da Como, Fra Emanule, 34
Dangan Castle, Mth, 93
Davis, Thomas, poet, writer and
   politician, 62
de Lacy, Hugo, Anglo-Norman lord,
   27
de Profundis, 118, 146
Delvin: see *Nugent*.
Delvin, Wmth, 85, 176
Derby, Lord, (Edward Smith Stanley),
   British Prime Minister, 170
de Ros, Lord, 73–4, 167–8
Derry, John, bishop of Clonfert, 171
Derrypatrick, Mth, 172
Destiny, Stone of: see *Lia Fail*.
Dind Shenchas, 32
disease: blindness, 142; cholera, 45, 49,
   50, 65, 146, 157; pneumonia from
   wettings, 147; typhoid, 130
disestablishment of Church of Ireland,
   71, 157
dog shows, 168
Dominican Friary, Donore, 146
Dominican Friary, Drogheda, 18
Dominicans, 107, 144, 146, 148
Donaghmore, Mth, 22
Donaghpatrick, Mth, 141–2
Donatus, bishop of Fiesole, 116
Donnymore, Mth, 57
Donore, Mth, 96, 103, 146, 148
Dormstown Castle, Mth, 142
Dorset, duke of (Lionel Sackville), 91
Douai, France, 35
Dowth, Mth, 32, 41, 53, 54
Doyle, Luke, priest from Ballymore,
   130
Drogheda, Louth-Mth, 18, 36, 40, 48,
   50, 54, 75, 100, 107, 131, 173
Drogheda Argus, newspaper, 50, 51, 54,
   73, 107
Drumconrath (Drumconragh), Mth,
   27, 147, 153
Dublin, 36, 38, 48, 75, 82, 106, 114,
   157, 174, 179; All Hallows College,
   103; archbishops of, 35, 71, 114,
   138–9; exhibitions, 16, 27, 45, 71,
   121, 180
Duff, J., priest of St Finian's, Navan,
   101, 179.
Duffy, Charles Gavan, 62
Duffy, Edward, C.C., Ballinacargy,
   148–9

Duffy, John, P.P., Castletown-
   Geoghegan, 142–3
Duffy's *Catholic Magazine*, 115
Dugdale's *Monasticon*, 95
Dulane, Mth, 23
Duleek, Mth, 57, 113, 114, 129, 141,
   156, 158
Dunan, Patrick, priest at Dowth, 41
Dunboyne, Lord, 136
Dunboyne, Mth, 57, 105, 154, 176
Duncan, Fr, Meath priest, 75, 175
Dundalk, Louth, 171
Dungarvan, Waterford, 103
Dunsany Castle, Mth, 172
Dunshaughlin, Mth, 60, 78, 79
Durrow, Offaly, 96, 99, 147, 153
Dysart, Wmth, 141

Edgeworth, Henry Essex, de Firmont,
   Abbé, confessor to Louis XVI, 136
Edmund Street, Liverpool, 108
Education, 53, 63, 86, 102, 120
Eglish, Offaly, 142
elections (general), 64–5, 75
Elizabeth I, 94, 121, 143
emigration, 45–6, 82, 84, 108, 147–8,
   165, 181
Emmet centennial, 81
Endowed School Commission, 103
England, 147–8
Eniskeen (Enniskeen, Kingscourt),
   Cavan and Mth, 128, 141
Enlightenment, 20, 39
Ennis, Richard, P.P., Donore, 146
Erry Hills, Offaly, 141
Everard, family of, 138
evictions 45–7, 49, 53, 64, 65, 67, 68,
   69, 71–7, 163, 167–70, 172–5, 180–1

Fagan, William, P.P., Kilbride, 120.
famine, 24, 45, 62, 65, 68, 69, 72, 76,
   91, 109, 157
Farbill, Wmth, 47
Farrelly, Luke, C.C., Rathkenny, 128
Fenians, 52, 54, 70, 71, 80–4, 90, 157
Fennor, Mth, 113
Ferns, Wexford, 138
Ferrall, Patrick, P.P., Beauparc, 75
Ferrall, Patrick, P.P., Donnymore and
   Kilbride, 57
Fiesole, Italy, 116
Fingal, Earl of (Plunket), 55, 60
Finglas, Dublin, 179

Fitzherbert, Maria Anne, wife of George IV of England, 136
Fitzwilliam, Lord Lieutenant, 89
Fleming, Christopher, sixteenth-century lord of Slane, 29
Fleming, Christopher, twenty-second baron of Slane, 36, 44–5
Fleming, Patrick, O.F.M., of Louvain, 34, 35, 44, 119
Fleming, Randall (Ragnall), twenty-first baron of Slane, 44
Fleming, Thomas, O.F.M, archbishop of Dublin, 34
Fleming, Thomas, P.P., Drumconrath, 147
Flemings, family of, 36, 37, 39, 102
folklore, 21, 78, 98, 142–5, 152–3
Fontenoy, Belgium, 150, 152
fonts, medieval 16–7, 45, 120, 123
Fore, Wmth, 72, 121, 130, 141
Four Masters (O'Clerys), 118, 140, 179
France, 36, 53, 91, 131, 149–52
Franciscan College, Hill of Slane, 29
Franciscan Convent, Multyfarnham, 143, 144
Franciscan Friary, Hill of Slane, 29, 175
Franciscans, 31, 32, 34, 35, 143, 144, 179
Frankford (Ballyboy), Offaly, 125, 129, 144, 150
French language, 103
French Revolution, 57, 60

Gaelic League, 154
Gaelic lords, 36
Gaffney, Matthew, bishop of Meath, 135
Galtrim, 88
Galway, 62
game laws, 67–8, 83, 123
Gargan, D., P.P., Nobber, 146
Gargan, Edward, P.P., Castlepollard, 148
Gaughran, Laurence, bishop of Meath, 136
Gavin, Thomas, C.C., St. Mary's, Drogheda, 131
Geoghegan: see also Mageoghegan.
Geoghegan, Eugene (Owen), bishop of Meath, 144–5, 153
Geoghegan, Patrick, P.P., Tullamore, 147

George II, 169
George IV, 36, 38–9
Geraldines, 44
German language, 103
Gernonstown, Mth, 97
Gibney, Patrick, P.P., Castletown-Kilpatrick, 128
Gibraltar, Spain, 100
Gladstone, William Ewart, British Prime Minister, 157, 173–5
Glasnevin, Dublin, 28, 81, 156
Glennenerrim, Mth, 141
Gormanstown, Mth, 111
Goss, Alexander, bishop of Liverpool, 171
Gosselin, M., historian, 104
Gosson, Richard, C.C., Mountnugent, 147
Gough, P.P., Curraha, 150–1
Grange, The, Mth, 172
Graziers of Meath, 65, 74, 75, 77, 122, 181
Guardian newspaper, 54

Hackett, John, P.P., Longwood, 150
Hall, Mr and Mrs, travel-writers, 46, 48
Halligan, Fr, priest in charge of Kilbride, 57
Hand, John, founder of All Hallows, 103
Hanoverians, 36
Harcourt Place, Dublin, 38
Hare Island (Inis Aingin), Lough Ree, Wmth, 110
Harp that once through Tara's Halls, 59
Hayestown, Mth, 146, 147
Healy, Patrick, P.P., Castlejordan, 120
Hennessy, William, Irish scholar, 140
Henry II, 94
Henry VIII, 121
Heronstown, (Lobinstown), Mth, 176
Higginstown, Mth, 176.
high crosses, 20, 70, 99, 113, 118, 156
Hitchcock, Thomas, O.P., of Donore, 148
Hoey, John, P.P., Castlejordan, 145
Hogan, priest of Clongowes, 126
Home Rule (Independence Party), 52, 62, 63, 64, 71, 75, 78, 82
Hope, Luke, C.C., Skryne, 178
Horan E., C.C., Navan, 178
houses, 68, 73–4, in Navan, 181–2; in Offaly, 182–3

Hussey, family of (Barons of Galtrim), 88

Immaculate Conception, College of, Prague, 35
Inchcleraun, Longford, 108
Inchmore, Wmth, 121
Independence Party (Party of Independent Opposition), see *Home Rule*
Industrial Revolution, 20
Infirmary Hill, Navan 48
Inis Aingin: see *Hare Island.*
Iniskeen: see *Eniskeen.*
Innismot, Mth, 147
Irish Brigade (France), 35, 150, 152
Irish Brigade (64th Royal Lancashire Volunteers), 164
Irish College, Paris (Collège des Irlandais, Collège des Lombards), 89, 97, 104–5, 150–1
Irish House of Commons, 53
Irish identity, 21–2
Irish language, 23–4, 40–4, 46, 136
Irish nationalism, 26–30, 61–5, 74, 112, 124, 154
Irish peasant tradition, 40–4, 69, 78
Irish State Papers, 140
Irish Tenant League, 70; see also *Tenant Right.*
Italy, 92, 116, 162, 179

Jacobites, 36
James I, 94
James II, 91
Jesuits, 130, 143
Johnson, Esther (Stella), 93
Johnson Samuel, English writer, 115
Johnston, Francis, architect, 37
Johnston, Graham, landlord's agent, 73–4, 167–8
Johnstown, Mth, 16, 45, 105, 121, 178

Kearney, Fr John, Trim chaplain, 86
Keena, Mr, landlord, 75, 173–5
Kells (Ceanannas Mór), Mth, 40, 49, 65, 70, 75, 78, 86, 88, 96, 97, 99, 115, 136, 158, 173
Kelly, J., priest of St Finian's, Navan, 101.
Kelly, Matthew, Maynooth historian, 104–5, 126, 133, 151
Kelly, Patrick, P.P., Kilskyre, 63, 151–2

Kellystown, Mth, 43
Kempston, Rev., rector of Mullagh, 173
Keogan, C., C.C., Trim, 178
Keonan, Patrick, P.P., Curraha, 57
Kieran, M., archbishop of Armagh, 171
Kilbeg, Mth, 27
Kilbeggan, Wmth, 63
Kilberry, Mth, 142
Kilbixy, Wmth, 128; see also *Ballynacargy* and *Sonna.*
Kilbride, Mth, 57, 120
Kilbride, Offaly, 147
Kilbride Pace, Wmth, 123
Kilcairn: see *Kilcarne.*
Kilcarne, (Kilcarn, Kilcairn), Mth, 16, 45, 121, 160, 172
Kilcarty, Mth, 172
Kilcloon, Mth, 128
Kilcormick, Offaly, 125
Kildare, 60
Kilkenny, 104; Confederation of, 35
Killagh, Mth, 144
Killeen, Mth, 142, 172
Killegland, Mth, 28
Killglyn, Mth, 128
Killucan, Wmth, 130
Killybegs, Donegal, 53
Kilmainhamwood, Mth, 27
Kilmessan, Mth, 75, 172
Kilrush, Clare, 68, 76, 77
Kilskyre, Mth, 27, 63, 78, 151, 178
Kiltale, Mth, 75, 172
King John's Castle, Trim, 86
King's County: see *Offaly.*
Kingscourt, Cavan, 128, 141, 150
Kinnegad, Wmth, 130, 139
Knowth, Mth, 32, 113

Lady Well, Slane, 31, 58
Ladyrath, Mth, 69, 176
land: struggle for rights to, 24, 74, 165; reclamation of waste, 74, 182. Land clearances: see *evictions.*
Land Act, 157, 173–4
landlords, 63, 65, 67, 71, 72–7, 74, 90, 168, 174; see also *evictions* and *violence.*
Lanigan, John, historian, 104–5, 179
Laracor, Mth, 93
Laytown, Mth, 50, 107, 109, 163
Lentaigne, Mr, Inspector-General of

Prisons, 121
Lenten pastorals, 49–50, 63, 64
Leonard, George, P.P., Oldcastle, 146, 148
Lewis, see Louis
Lia Fáil (Stone of Destiny), 59, 61, 92
Limerick, 38; Treaty of, 94
Lismullen, Mth, 33, 121
Liverpool, 46, 50, 84, 94, 106–9, 112, 150, 163–7, 171, 178
Lloyd, Tower of, Mth, 88
Loan Fund, 130
Lobinstown, Mth: see Heronstown.
Lodge's Peerage, 37
Lóegaire, Irish highking, 31
Logan, Robert, bishop of Meath, 96, 151–2, 158
London, 46, 76, 114
Londonderry regiment, 52
Longfield scheme, 174
Longford, 62, 89, 108
Longwood, Mth, 148, 150
lords lieutenant of Ireland, 89, 91
Lough Lene, Wmth, 72, 141
Lough Ree, Roscommon-Longford-Wmth, 108, 110
Loughan, Mth, 27
Loughrea, Galway, 103
Louis XIV, 97
Louis XVIII, 136, 151
Louth, 42, 103
Louvain, Belgium, 35
Lowe, Barry, priest hunter, 142
Lucas, Frederick, 71, 113–14, 146, 166
Lynally, Offaly, 95
Lynch, John, Irish scholar and historian, 104
Lynch, T., P.P., Painstown, 178

McAlroy, Andrew, C.C., Navan, 148
McAlroy, Matthew, P.P., Tullamore, 127, 138–9
McAuley, Awly, administrator, Castletown-Geoghegan, 150
Mac Bráduigh, Fiachna, Irish poet, 42
MacBrady: see Mac Bráduigh.
MacCabe, Cathaoir, Irish poet and harper, 42
MacCarthy, Maynooth historian, 104, 126
McCormick, M., administrator, Mullingar, 149
McCormick, William, priest of St.

Finian's, Navan, 101, 131, 178
MacCuarta, Séamus Dall, Irish poet, 42–4, 90
MacCullen, Richard, P.P., Kells, 136.
McDermot, George, P.P., Oldcastle, 149
McDermot, Patrick, P.P. Castletown-Kilpatrick, 96, 150, 152
MacEgan, Stephen, O.P., bishop of Clonmacnoise and (later) Meath, 107
McEneroe, Fr, archdeacon of Sydney, 103
McEvoy, Edward, Member of Parliament, 73–5, 167–70
McEvoy, N., administrator, Kells, 86
MacGettigan, Daniel, archbishop of Armagh, 103
MacHale, John, archbishop of Tuam, 40, 71, 131, 161–3, 170–1
MacSolly, John, Irish scribe, 42
Macken, Richard, Slane priest, 131
Macken, Sr Mary Gertrude, of Slane, 131
Magdalen Steeple, Drogheda, 18, 48
Mageoghegan, Abbé, historian, 35, 151
Mageoghegan, Anthony, bishop of Clonmacnoise, 35, 126
Mageoghegan, Conal, annalist, 35
magistrates, 67
Malines (Mechelen), Belgium, 165
Mansion House conference, 175
Marie Antoinette, French queen, 150
Markystown, Mth, 142
Martin, James, of Oldcastle, 41
Martin, speaker at Mullagh meeting, 175
Marysville, California, 103
Mass, Penal Day, 41, 85, 141; Stations, 147; see also sacraments.
Mass Hollow, Oldcastle, 141
Masterson, John, P.P., Rathmolyon, 150
Mathew, Theobald, priest and temperance crusader, 156
Mayne, Wmth, 128
Maynooth, Kildare, 42, 45, 94, 100, 103–5, 119, 126, 133, 134, 148, 151
Mazzini, Giuseppe, Italian revolutionary and writer, 168
Meade, Francis, priest of St Finian's, 101, 129–30
Meade, Thomas, priest from Ardee, 130

Meath, 27, 33, 57, 65–8, 75–7, 99, 146, 162, 172–5, 180–2
Meath diocese, 26–7, 107, 110; archive of, 133–9; maps of, 185–90; map of parishes, 186
Meath People, newspaper, 49, 51, 109, 111
Meath Tenant Right Society, 71; see also *Tenant Right*.
Meaux, France, 150
Meedin, Wmth, 124
Meighan, Richard, P.P., Moynalvy, 97
Mellifont, Louth, 33
Mide, kingdom of, 27, 154
Millbrook, Mth, 41
Minster, Thanet, Kent, 39
Molloy, Constantine, 60
Monasterboice, Lth, 20
Monasteries, dissolution of, 25, 93, 121
Monknewtown, Mth, 42, 119
Mont Ste Geneviève, Paris, 97
Mooney, Donat, O.F.M., 144
Moore, Bartholmew, C.C., Multyfarnham, 130
Moore, George Henry, parliamentarian and Tenant Right leader, 71, 75
Moore, James, priest of St Finian's, Navan, 101, 130, 178, 179
Moorechurch, Mth, 123
Morgallion, Mth, 66
Morgan, Christopher, C.C., Skryne, 128–9, 130
Mound of the Hostages, Tara, 56
Mount Charles, Lord, 98; see also *Conyngham*.
Mountainpole, Mth, 88
Mountjoy Square, Dublin, 179
Mountnugent, Cavan, 147, 176
Moyagher, Mth, 147
Moycashel, Wmth, 35
Moylough, Mth, 106
Moymurthy, Mth, 123
Moynalty, Mth, 27, 42, 43
Moynalvy, Mth, 75, 97
Muiredach, tenth-century abbot of Monasterboice, 20
Mullagh, Cavan, 42
Mullagh, Hill of, Wmth, 141
Mullagh, south Meath, 75–8, 96, 172–5
Mullen, family of, 69
Mullen, John, Navan J.P., 111, 161, 179
Mullen, Michael., P.P., Kilbixy, 128, 148–9

Mullen, R., priest of Sonna, 64
Mulligan, Philip, P.P., Slane, 97
Mulligan's, of the Big Bush, Mth, 173
Mullingar, Wmth, 62, 96, 127, 131, 138, 139, 149, 157, 158
Multyfarnham, Wmth, 130, 143, 144
Muratori, Lodovico Antonio, Italian historian, 162
Murphy, John, of Boulavogue, priest and Wexford leader in 1798 rebellion, 150
Murphy, Mrs, of The Grange, 172
museums, 134

Napier, Joseph, Attorney-General for Ireland (1852–3), 170
National Association of Ireland, 71
Navan, (An Uaimh), Mth: 16, 40, 50, 75, 100–1, 106, 122, 138, 148, 157, 158–9, 172, 173, 178–9; map of, 193; bishop's house in, 157–8; building of church in, 102, 148; burial of Bishop Plunket in, 158; evictions in, 72–4, 167–70; Halls' account of, 181–2; workhouse in, 19, 49; rioters in, 136; saintly priest near, 147; slums in 19, 48–51, 72–4, 181–2; cemeteries 22; cholera in, 146; population, 109–110; CYMS, 110–11, 161, 163; Engineering Works, 158; Cogan's friends in, 128–30; see also *St Finian's College* and *St Patrick's Classical School*
Neill, monumental mason, 179–80
Netterville, John sixth viscount, 41, 53
Nevers, France, 150
New York, 148
Newgrange, Mth, 32
Newtown, Trim, 87
Newtown, Wmth, 142
Nicholls, Dr R.D., Navan, 179
Nicholls, Dr, vicar general of Meath, 75, 175
Nobber, Mth, 27, 42, 100, 130, 134, 146, 176
Nugent, family of, 35
Nugent, Christopher, baron of Delvin, 121
Nulty, Thomas, bishop of Meath, 45, 62, 67, 68, 71, 120, 127, 136, 138, 155, 179

Ó Dálaigh, Peadar Dubh, Irish poet, 88

O'Beirne, Thomas Lewis, Church of
Ireland bishop of Meath, 89, 96,
122
O'Brien, Paul, priest and Irish scholar,
42–3
O'Brien, William, Irish poet, 42
O'Brien, William, P.P., Ballymore, 148
O'Carolan, Turlough, musician and
poet, 42
O'Clerys: see *Four Masters.*
O'Connell, Daniel, the Liberator, 28,
30, 52, 56, 58–9, 61–3, 74, 80, 91,
92, 113, 154, 156–7, 164
O'Connell, Eugene, U.S. bishop, 103
O'Conor, Charles, of Belanagare,
antiquary, 37
O'Curry, Eugene, Irish scholar, 22,
111, 115–16, 126, 140
O'Daly: see *Ó Dálaigh.*
O'Donnell, Briget, famine victim, 76.
O'Donoghue, Daniel, P.P.,
Rathmolyon, 150
O'Donovan, John, historian and Irish
scholar, 22, 46, 118, 140
O'Donovan Rossa, Fenian leader, 81
O'Growney, Eoghain, Irish scholar,
154
O'Hanlon, Fr John, historian and
hagiographer, 29, 157, 179
O'Higgins, Joseph, president of St
Finian's, Navan, 101, 156, 178
O'Neill, dynasty of, 44
O'Neill, Gen. John, Irish-American
Fenian leader, 54
O'Neill, James, of Crackenstown, 137
O'Neill, John, Navan, 179
O'Neill, Patrick, Navan, 111, 161
O'Neill, Peter, Navan, 161
O'Rafferty, James, P.P., Tullamore,
138, 139
O'Reilly, Edward, Irish scholar, 43
O'Reilly, Eugene, president of St
Finian's and P.P., Navan, 72–3,
102, 129, 159
O'Reilly, Hugh, Irish priest in Paris,
151
O'Reilly, John Boyle, Irish-American
poet, writer and Fenian activist, 50,
53–4, 60, 61, 78–81, 84, 107, 111,
155
O'Reilly, Myles, P.P., Kilskyre, 78
O'Reilly, Peter, P.P., Kingscourt, 63,
150

O'Reilly, priest of Drumconrath, 147
O'Reilly, Thomas, priest from
Hayestown, 146, 147
O'Renehan: see *Renehan.*
O'Sullivan, Philip, Irish historian, 104
Offaly (formerly King's County), 33,
68, 95, 96, 99, 105, 106, 107, 121,
125, 127, 128, 129, 140, 141, 142,
144, 150, 151, 180, 182–3
Old English, 33, 34, 57
Oldbridge, Mth, 90, 91
Oldcastle, Mth, 41, 68, 103, 141, 146,
148, 149, 152
Omeath, Louth, 42
oral tradition, 141–2
Orangemen, 60, 88, 142–3
Orthodoxy (Greek), 25
Ossory, 36, 138

Painstown, Mth, 178
Pale, the, 27, 34–5, 39, 40, 55, 94, 121,
143, 157
Papal States, 73, 168
Paris, France, 41, 89, 97, 104, 105,
129, 149, 151, 152
Parliament, members of, 73–5, 114,
167–70
Parma, Italy, 150
parsons (Church of Ireland): see
Protestants.
Pavia, Italy, 105
Peace Preservation Act, 80
Pearse, Emily, 180
Pearse, James, monumental sculptor,
frontispiece, 156, 179–80
Pearse, Patrick, leader of Easter Rising,
22, 81–2, 112, 156, 180
Pearse, William, 180
Penal Days, chapels, 41; laws, 90, 92,
117; Mass, 41; see also *Popery
Code.*
Phoenix Park, Dublin, 38
photography, 134
pilgrimage, 31, 32, 120, 146, 147, 172
Pius VI, pope, 150
Pius IX, pope, 92, 109, 114, 165
plague (Black Death), 24
Platten, Mth, 100
Plunket (Plunkett), family of, 26, 34
Plunket, Michael, P.P., Ratoath, 28
Plunket, Oliver, saint and archbishop
of Armagh, 28, 119, 142, 147

Plunket, Patrick, bishop of Meath
(died 1679), 137, 142
Plunket, Patrick, bishop of Meath
(died 1827), 55–9, 64, 89, 97, 100–
2, 118, 127, 135, 136, 138, 150,
151, 153, 155, 157, 158, 159
Pococke, Richard, Church of Ireland
bishop of Meath, 36, 122
Poland, James, administrator, Navan,
158
Poor Law, 73
Popery Code, 26, 36
population, 45–6, 48–9, 68, 69, 75–6,
109–10
Portland, duke of, viceroy, 89
Portloman, Wmth, 79
Portugal, 38
potatoes, 65, 68
Power, Nicholas, president of St
Finian's, 102
Prague, Czechoslovakia, 35
Presbyterians, 60
Preston, Lancashire, 107
priest hunters, 78, 85, 88, 142
priests: career advancement, 120, 155;
continental training of, 149–52;
graves of, 117–19; horses of, 143,
153; hardships of, 144–7; Penal
Day, 117–19, 151; *sagart aroon*, 119,
152, 155, 164, 166, 177; travels of,
148–52; see also *burials, churches,
folklore, sacraments.*
proselytisers, 85–6
Protestants: bishops, 36, 89, 94, 96,
116, 122; parsons, 96, 144, 173;
gentry, 150, 152; favourably
described by Cogan, 23, 79, 94, 95–
6, 98–9; supportive of Cogan, 75,
166, 173; attended Cogan's funeral,
156, 178; unfavourably described by
Cogan, 78, 98–9, 122; see also
ascendancy, burials, churches and
tithes.
Puritans, 147

Quakers, 114

Rahan, Offaly, 105
Rankin, Martin, of Liverpool, 108, 165
Rathconrath, Wmth, 145
Rathcore, Mth, 140
Rathkenny, Mth, 46, 66, 88, 128, 176
Rathmolyon, Mth, 129, 150

Ratoath, Mth, 57, 137
Rebellion of 1798, 21, 52, 55–60, 70,
91, 96, 97, 100, 142, 147, 150
Reeves, William, historian, 94
Reformation, 20, 118, 121, 141
Reilly, Phillip, P.P., Monknewtown,
119
Renehan, Laurence, Maynooth
historian, 126; *Collections* of, 104–5
Repeal movement, 30, 62, 63, 74, 80,
90, 113, 164
Republicans, Irish, 91
Ribbonmen, secret society, 55, 64, 65,
66, 70, 80, 153
roads, building of, 123
Robertstown, Mth, 146
Rochfort Bridge, Wmth, 124
Rome, 105, 127, 150, 155, 161
Rooney, John, priest of All Hallows,
and C.C., Frankford, 128–9
Roscommon, 37, 103
Rosemount, Wmth, 148
Rosnaree, Mth, 42, 96
Rothery, William, of Navan, 179.
round towers, 22, 29, 171
Rousseau's Dream, 59
Royal Irish Academy, 37, 38
Rushwee, Mth, 66

Sackville: see *Dorset, duke of.*
sacraments, Confession, 97, 147;
Confirmation, 153; Eucharist, 97–8,
152, 177, 179; Extreme Unction,
142; Holy Orders, 147, 158; see
also *Mass.*
Sagart Aroon: see *priests.*
Saints, Communion of, 28, 92
Salamanca, Spain, 105, 150
Sandymount, Navan, 48
Saul, Peter, of Drumconrath, 153
Schomberg, Reinard, duke of, 91
secret societies, 55, 64, 111, 145, 153;
see also *Captain Rock, Carders,
Ribbonmen, White Boys* and
Whitefeet.
Seville, Spain, 150
Shalvanstown, Mth, 69
Shannon Harbour, Offaly, 182
Shannon river, 118
Sharp, Edmund, monumental mason,
180
Sheridan, James, O.S.B., of Moylough
and Liverpool, 106

Sillary, Anne, mother of Anthony Cogan, 23, 89, 159, 176
singing, 161, 167
Sisters of Mercy, Navan, 50–1; Drogheda, 131
Skryne, Mth, 33, 47, 74, 80, 129, 178
Slane, Mth: 31–46, 58, 65, 66, 69, 94, 95, 97, 100, 105, 107, 113, 128, 130–1, 137, 155, 156, 157, 176–80; maps of area, 191–2
Slane Castle, Mth, 31, 32, 37, 38, 58
Slane, Hill of, Mth, 29, 31, 33, 47, 100, 175
Slane, Lower, barony of, 66
Smyth, Mr, speaker at Mullagh meeting, 175
Sonderborg, Denmark, 83, 168
Sonna, Wmth, 64, 130; see also *Ballynacargy* and *Kilbixy*.
Sorbonne, Paris, 151
SS Michael and John, Dublin, 179
St Andrew, 160
St Anthony's College, Louvain, 35
St Columbanus, 35
St Columkille, 99, 115
St Erc, 31, 32
St Erc's Hermitage, Slane, Mth, 31, 58
St Finian's College, Mullingar, 102, 158
St Finian's College, Navan, 100–3, 111, 128–30, 149, 156, 158–9, 178, 179
St Finian's Day, 102
St Francis Xavier, 97
St Ignatius Loyola, 97
St Isidore's College, Rome, 34
St James, of Compostela, 16
St Jarlath's, Tuam, 162
St John, 16
St John's Well, Mth, 172
St Kieran, 107; St. Kieran's Well, 49
St Laurence's Gate, Drogheda, 18
St Mary's Abbey, Drogheda, 18
St Mary's Abbey, Trim, 87
St Mary's, Liverpool, 106, 163–4
St Patrick, 31, 112, 177
St Patrick's Classical School, Navan, 158
St Patrick's Day, 145
St Patrick's, Liverpool, 178
St Peter, 16, 123
St Peter's, Rome, 161
St Sulpice Seminary, Paris, 41

St Sulpice Seminary, Toulouse, 150
Stackallen, Mth, 33, 42, 120
Staholmock, (Staholmoy), Mth, 42
Stamullen, Mth, 57, 123
Stations (Masses), 147
Stella: see *Johnson, Esther.*
Stepney, George, of Durrow, 96
Stokestown, Mth, 176
Stradone, Cavan, 42
Suibhne, Clonmacnoise scholar, 107
Summerhill, Mth, 75, 93, 173
Swainstown, Mth, 172
Swift, Dean Jonathan, 70, 93
Syddan (Sydden or Lobinstown), Mth, 27
Synge, John Millington, dramatist, 22.

Tablet newspaper, 17, 50, 86, 112–14
Táin Bó Cuailgne, Early Irish epic, 112
Tallaght, Dublin, *Martyrology* of, 47
Tara, Hill of, Mth, 28, 31, 33; battle of 55–6, 58–61, 91, 121
Temperance, 110, 156
Tenant Compensation Bill, 74
Tenant League, 75, 146
Tenant Right, 63, 69, 71, 113, 150, 156, 157
Tenant Right League, 62, 71
Thanet, Kent, England, 39
Thierry, Jacques-Nicolas-Augustin, French historian, 115
Thurles, Tipperary, 103
Timmons, Terence, P.P., Duleek, 129
Tithes, 65, 66, 85
Toar, Wmth, 142–3.
Tobertinan, Mth, 75
Tormey, Michael, teacher in St Finian's, Navan, and C.C., Rathmolyon, 75, 129, 175
Toulouse, France, 150
towns, 47–51
Trevet, Mth, 140
Trim, Mth, 25, 40, 75, 86, 87, 93, 148, 172, 173, 178
Trimgate Street, Navan, 108
Trimlestons (Trimblestons, family of Barnewall), 41
Troy, John Thomas, archbishop of Dublin, 138–9
Tuam, Galway, 40, 131, 138, 162, 170
Tubber, Offaly, 130, 144, 148, 176
Tullamore, Offaly, 60, 127, 138, 140, 147, 153

Turin, Wmth, 85
Turks, 25, 85
Tuscany, Italy, 116
Tyrellspass, Wmth, 128
Tyrill, Mary Claire, of Stokestown, 176

Uí Néill dynasty, 27, 113
Ulster, 60
Union, Act of, 30, 38, 39, 52, 53, 58, 169
United Irishmen, 21, 52
United States of America, 46, 47, 51, 53, 54, 68, 103, 147–8, 148, 150, 155–6
Ussher, James, Church of Ireland, archbishop of Armagh, 94, 116

Vallency, Charles, antiquary, 37
Vatican, archives, 140; First Council, 127, 155
Vianney, Jean-Baptiste-Marie, saint and curé of Ars, 146
violence, agrarian, 26, 64, 65–7, 68, 80; faction fights, 145; political uprisings, 57, 76–7, 84; sectarian, 60–1, 65–6, 88, 98; stoning, 146; in anecdotes, 78–80; in Navan, 136

Walsh, Denis, P.P., Rosnaree and Donore, 96, 146, 160
Walsh, Paul, priest and historian, 154
Walterstown, Mth, 178
Ware, Sir James, 94
Warrenstown, Mth, 172
watches, 153, 161

Wattenbach, Wilhelm, historian, 115
Webb, Mr, Dunshaughlin Protestant, 79, 96
Wellesley see *Wellington*
Wellington, duke of (Arthur Wellesley), 93
wells, holy, 118, 120, 172
Western Australia, 54
Westmeath, 27, 33, 47, 63, 64, 68, 77, 79, 85, 96, 99, 106, 121, 127, 128, 129, 130, 142, 143, 144–5, 148–9, 150, 151
Westmeath Act, 80
Westmeath Committee, 80
Westminster, 53, 82
Wexford, 150
Wexfordmen, 21, 59
White Boys, secret society, 145
Whitefeet, secret society, 66
Wild Geese, 54, 105
Wilde, Sir William, 22, 29, 41, 48, 123
Wilkinstown, Mth, 176
William III, 90, 91
Windsor, Berkshire, 39
Wisconsin, U.S.A., 148
Wolf Tone, Theobald, leader of United Irishmen, 21, 28
workhouses, 19, 49, 72, 76, 86
Wyatt, James, architect, 37

Yellow Furze, Mth, 178
Yellow Steeple, Trim, 87
yeomanry, 55, 59, 60
Young Irelanders, 62, 71